TH   THE **NHS**

THE FUTURE OF THE NHS

Edited by Dr Michelle Tempest

© The Authors and XPL Publishing, 2006

ISBN (paper): 1 85811 369 5

ISBN (cased): 1 85811 370 9

Printed in the United Kingdom

An e-book licence for this title can be purchased through our website www.xplpublishing.com or that of our partners www.myilibrary.com

For my beloved parents and sister

CONTENTS

WHY IS THE NHS IMPORTANT: SOME TESTIMONIALS

The NHS testimonials start this book stating many reasons why the NHS is so important and therefore the necessity to plan for the future of the NHS:

Whatever the criticisms that are levelled against it at home, I find when I travel abroad that the NHS is greatly respected right around the world, both for the standard of its care and for the ideals it embodies.

John Simpson, BBC World Affairs Editor

The creation of the NHS in 1948 was the second major victory for Britain, after the defeat of Nazism. This war-torn nation resurfaced with a humanitarian vision of free health care for all, and as an institution the NHS remains a stunning testimony to human altruism and the principles of a caring, civilized society. Today, the NHS is in dire need of better health care itself, and future governments owe it to our precious creation not just to preserve it but to inject it with all the resources it needs to flourish, grow, and blossom. If we look after it, it looks after us. It should be at the top of our list of priorities in the Chancellor's annual budget, so that we take pride not just in the idea of the NHS, but in its delivery too. Britain has a wealth of medical research expertise to draw on among its scientists, much of it at the forefront internationally, and giving the NHS exciting opportunities to translate such knowledge into first-class clinical care should be any government's perpetual new year's resolution.

Professor Simon Baron-Cohen, Director of autism research and author

The NHS would not have been invented if the calculator had come first. Thank goodness it didn't.

Jeremy Vine, BBC Radio 2 Current Affairs

It's not the Monument, the great, oft blundering, creaking, micro-managed, macro-distained state within a state, which defines the NHS. It's not the political, wheeler-dealing, panic revolutionizing hierarchy of out of depth managers: on a ward one minute, promoted catastrophically the next, leaking budgets and morale and sound innovation through fingers palsied by unanchored responsibilities. It's the people, dammit. The courageous, the kind, the knowledgeable, the patient, the hard working, the dedicated, the unrewarded. They're the NHS. They're it's future. They're the hope. Because people *rise*.

Paul Meloy, Charge Nurse

A national health service is the litmus test of any decent society. The question is not whether we should have one, but how good we can make it.

John le Carré, author of espionage novels

The NHS is home to some of the world's finest medicine. The United Kingdom punches above its weight in science and innovation. The challenge now is to spread the best that the NHS offers to all.

Our Service aims to provide comprehensive healthcare to all in society and in that respect, it is unique in the western world. Our ability in Britain to address health issues in the round, from preventative medicine through to acute care, affords us a chance to tackle the health inequalities that remain so pronounced and pervasive.

Sir Liam Donaldson, Chief Medical Officer

An NHS providing a universal health service free at the point of use is worth fighting for. Despite unprecedented levels of investment in the past few years we have a situation where a significant number of hospital trusts and primary care trusts cannot balance their books. We have just two years left before additional investment levels return to more normal levels. As a doctor who has devoted most of his working life to the NHS I don?t want us to lose it. The public, the professions and the politicians must have an open debate to thrash out what it takes to save the NHS.

Mr James Johnson, consultant surgeon and chairman of the British Medical Association

The NHS is not only a great Health Service, it is also the embodiment of an attitude towards one's fellow man. The fact that we have it amounts to a communal declaration that this society does care about its citizens and their welfare.

Professor Alexander McCall Smith, Medical law professor
and author of No.1 Ladies' Detective Agency series

The NHS is a great British institution with roots that stretch deep into the modern British psyche. In almost 60 years, it's become part of the fabric of the nation, and those roots have helped it weather storms of relentless reform and droughts of arid uncertainty. Money, however, is only part of the equation. Valuing the vocation of caring, defending the dignity of the sick and improving the patient experience—these are just as important. "I'm a patient, trust me, listen to me, care for and about me". If every NHS health professional could say that that is what they did, what a wonderful testimony to the NHS that would be.

Kevin Shinkwin, a grateful recipient of life-saving neurosurgery
and care on the NHS

I have always been a big supporter of the NHS and its future must be planned for.

Lawrie McMenemy, Britain's longest serving football coach

PREFACE

The health of the people is really the foundation upon which all their happiness and all their powers as a state depend.

Benjamin Disraeli

This book was first conceived towards the end of 2005 after hearing an NHS patient describe the staff as the "quiet heroes of the country". It is only through working together with the same common goal of improving health that a team can succeed. This sparked the idea of planning for the future of the National Health Service. 2006 is an important year for the NHS, as it marks 60 years since the implementation of the National Health Service Act 1946. Therefore, it is an ideal time to start planning for the future of the service and to ensure 60th birthday celebrations are not a sign of retirement. I decided to ask people at the helm of multidisciplinary teams, intimately involved in the service, what goals they envisaged for the NHS. It was hoped that by gathering together some of the most eminent and respected health care professionals, policy makers and opinion formers, this book could go some way to pooling their collective wisdom into one volume and help start what might be the great health debate in this country.

Throughout the preparation of this book I have been determined to make it as balanced and as open a debate as possible, by inviting people from across geographical, professional and political boundaries and this diversity is hopefully reflected in those who took part in the challenge. There are few more momentous and controversial questions facing society than the NHS and the book aims to give a lucid introduction to the central issues.

The chapters do not necessarily reflect the policy of the Institutions or medical Royal Colleges, but instead are ideas, suggested by individual authors. The information stated is as understood by the authors on the 31 January 2006.

Dr Michelle Tempest

ACKNOWLEDGEMENTS

There are some things for which words are never enough and this page is an example of where there could never be enough expression of my gratitude. First, I would like to thank all the influential contributors who so kindly offered their valuable time to write chapters making this venture possible. I know that without their words of wisdom the book would never had been more than just a concept, and for that I remain eternally grateful. I would also like to thank each one of them for making working with them a very pleasant and enjoyable experience. Through their kindness and benevolence I hope that this book succeeds in pushing forward the boundaries of the NHS. I would also like to extend this thanks to their families, friends and work colleagues, who offered them support.

Second, I would like to continue my thanks to the following people:

To those who loved and supported me: My parents, Heidi, Tim and Ivana, who are all a constant source of love, inspiration, and encouragement; alongside bringing light into my life.

To those who believed in me: Andrew Griffin (xpl publishing), Derek Draper and Simon Mort.

To those who had to listen about the book: Emil Bernal, Dr Michael Lord, Professor John Keown and family, Dr Tina Malhotra, Dr Jan Rosenzweig, Dr Victor Chua, Dr Priya Patel.

For the book cover design: Heidi Tempest and Jane Adams

For technical support: Garry Wright (www.3001.co.uk)

For PR support: Geoff Potter (Stonehenge public relations)

To those I work with: Dr O'Flynn, Dr Rubenstein and the CRHTT: Sarah Ager, Graham Clements, Anne Gregory, Diane Homewood, Sue Hood, Tuija Juusti-Butler, Caroline Lumb, John Mallet, Louise McCarthy, Paul Meloy, Tina Penistone, Manuel Regueira, Jeanette Sandy, Anne Smith, Yan Spooner and Paul Warden

To those I have worked with: Dr Girling, Dr Shapleske, Dr Winton, Dr Walsh, Dr Vithayathil, Dr Ramana and Dr McKenna.

There are so many other people to thank, and I can not possibly name them all here, but to try and include a few: Dr Richard Dempster, Paul Mellor, Dr Ron Agble, Mark Attwood, Adam Scott, Jonathon Djanogly, David Ruffley, Amanda Cooper, Jo Holland, Olwen Leeland, Mary Flinders and the countless secretaries who were so kind during the process of the book development. Thanks to all who helped me convert my enthusiasm about this venture into a reality.

AUTHORS

Dr Michelle Tempest MA LLM MB BChir

She is a community psychiatrist for the Crisis Resolution and Home Treatment Team. She is qualified in medicine and law and teaches at Cambridge University.

Right Hon Patricia Hewitt MP (Labour) Health Secretary

She was appointed Secretary of State for Health in May 2005 and has been a Member of Parliament since 1997. In 1993 she wrote "About Time", a book focusing on changes in work and family life. She was Deputy Chair of the Commission for Social Justice and was a member of the Social Security Select Committee before taking up her Ministerial post.

Andrew Lansley CBE MP (Conservative) Shadow Health Secretary

He has been the Member of Parliament for South Cambridgeshire since May 1997. He is the Shadow Secretary of State for Health and a Vice-President of the Local Government Association. From 1999 to 2001 he was the Shadow Minister for the Cabinet Office and was responsible for policy co-ordination in the Conservative Party.

Professor Steve Webb MP (Liberal Democrat) Shadow Health Secretary

He is the Member of Parliament for Northavon and is the Liberal Democrats' Spokesman on Health. From 1999–2005 he was the Spokesman on Work & Pensions.

Dr Robert Winter MD FRCP

Consultant Physician and Medical Director of Cambridge University Hospitals' NHS Foundation Trust.

Professor Peter Friend MA MB BChir MD FRCS

He is the Professor of Transplantation at the University of Oxford, Director of the Oxford Transplant Centre, and a Consultant Surgeon specialising in Transplant and Hepatobiliary surgery at the Oxford Radcliffe NHS Trust.

Dr Mayur Lakhani MRCP FRCGP

Chairman of Council, Royal College of General Practitioners, Visiting Professor in the Department of Health Sciences, University of Leicester School of Medicine

Mr Jim Wardope MB ChB FRCSEng FRCSEd FFAEM

President of the Faculty of Accident and Emergency Medicine and Consultant at the Northern General Hospital, Sheffield.

Dr Alastair McGowan MB ChB FRCPEd FCEM

He is the Immediate Past President of the Faculty of Accident and Emergency Medicine and Consultant at St James's University Hospital, Yorkshire.

Professor Peter Crome MD PhD FRCP FFPM

He is the Professor of Geriatric Medicine and Deputy Head of Keele University Medical School as well as President-Elect, British Geriatrics Society. He is a Consultant Geriatrician with a special interest in the evaluation of health services for older people and the treatment of common disorders of later life, including stroke and dementia.

Professor Alan Craft MD FMed.Sci FRCPCH

He is a Professor of Child Health and a Consultant Paediatrician. He is National President of Royal College of Paediatrics and Child Health and Chairman of Academy of Medical Royal Colleges. He is also the Head of Child Health at the University of Newcastle. He has published over 250 original papers, review articles and chapters in major journals and books over the last 25 years. He is a regularly invited speaker at major national and international meetings.

Dr Simon Lenton FRCPCH MFPH

He is Vice President at the Royal College of Paediatrics and Child Health. He works in Bath as a Consultant paediatrician with a special interest in community child health.

Professor Jim Thornton MD FRCOG

He is a Professor at the Academic Division of Obstetrics & Gynaecology and Child Health, City Hospital, Nottingham.

Dr Peter Simpson MD FRCA

He is President of the Royal College of Anaesthetists with special interests in training, examinations, assessment and accreditation of doctors and anaesthetists. He is President of the European Society of Anaesthesiology.

Dr Nick Astbury FRCOphth FRCS FRCP

He is President of the Royal College of Ophthalmologists and is a Consultant Ophthalmic Surgeon at the Norfolk and Norwich University Hospital NHS Trust.

Dr David Stone FRCP

He is a Consultant Cardiologist and Director of Education at Papworth and Associate Dean at the Faculty of Clinical Medicine. He is the co-Chair of the Ethnicity Online project and has major research interest in cardiac imaging.

Professor Karol Sikora MA MBBChir PhD FRCR FRCP FFPM

He is Dean of Britain's first independent Medical School at the Universities of Brunel and Buckingham. He is an editor of the standard UK postgraduate textbook Treatment of Cancer which this year goes to its 5th edition. He was Professor of Cancer Medicine and honorary Consultant Oncologist at Imperial College School of Medicine, Hammersmith Hospital, London where he was Clinical Director of Cancer Services for 12 years. He was seconded as Chief of the WHO Cancer Programme in 1997.

Mr Peter Butler MD, FRCSI, FRCS, FRCS(Plast)

He is a Consultant Plastic Surgeon and Honorary Senior Lecturer at the Royal Free and University College Hospitals, London and a

Consultant in Plastic Surgery at the Massachusetts General Hospital, Boston, USA. He is a council member of the British Association of Plastic Surgeons (BAPS). He has published over one hundred articles in the field of plastic surgery.

Professor Peter Tyrer FMedSci

He is Professor of Community Psychiatry, Imperial College, London in the Department of Neurosciences and Mental Health Medicine.

Professor Rod Griffiths CBE MB BSc FFPH FRCP

He was the regional director of public health for the West Midlands Regional Health Authority until his retirement in May 2004 and is currently the President of the Faculty of Public Health. He was awarded the CBE in 2000.

Mr Derek Draper MA Clinical Psychology

He is a former political adviser and was the author of "Blair's 100 Days" (Faber). He is a psychotherapist in private practice in Marylebone, London and during his training worked as the development director of a community counselling centre in northern California. He is a member of the British Association for Counselling and Psychotherapy (MBACP). He writes monthly columns in the magazines "Psychologies" and "Therapy Today".

Sylvia Denton, FRCN, CBE, OBE, MSc, RN, RHV

President of the Royal College of Nursing. She has recently retired from her post as lead nurse/Senior Clinical Nurse Specialist in breast care. Sylvia was awarded the CBE in the New Years Honours List in 2006 for services to health care.

Jane Naish MSc, MA, RN

She is a policy adviser at the RCN. She has a background in nursing, sociology and health policy.

Dr Mosaraf Ali MBBS PhD

After qualifying as a doctor he continued his studies into complementary medicine. With continuous help and encouragement from Prince Charles he established a clinic where both complementary and conventional treatments are integrated. He opened the Integrated

Medical Centre in London with a team of fifteen doctors and therapists.

Claire Rayner OBE

She is president of The Patients Association and is the UK's best known agony aunt. She has a long and successful career as a journalist, broadcaster and writer, but began her working life as a nurse at the Royal Northern Hospital in London.

Professor Shelley Heard MBBS MSc PhD FRCPath

She trained as a medical microbiologist. She has been a chief executive of an acute trust and for the last 10 years has been a postgraduate dean for medicine in London. She is also currently the National Clinical Advisor for the Modernising Medical Careers (MMC) programme.

Professor Elisabeth Paice MA FRCP

She is Director of Postgraduate Medical and Dental Education for London. She developed the Hospital at Night concept and has published on stress in doctors; doctors in difficulty; workplace bullying; flexible training; and other aspects of medical careers.

Professor David E Neal FMedSci, FRCS

He is Professor of Surgical Oncology at the University of Cambridge & Member of PMETB. He has published over 300 articles, chapters and books and has raised over £20 million for his research programme. He is an elected member of the Council of the Royal College of Surgeons of England and a past Chairman of the SAC in Urology.

Professor Mark Walport FMedSci, FRCP

He is the Director of the Wellcome Trust and Chair of UKCRC & MMC Academic Careers Sub-committee.

Professor Ewan Ferlie BA MSc PhD

He is Director of the Centre for Public Services Organisations and Head of the School of Management, Royal Holloway University of London.

Dr Chess Denman MBBS MRCPsych

She is a Consultant Psychiatrist in psychotherapy at Addenbrookes hospital where she runs the Complex Cases service which specialises in the treatment of personality disordered patients. Dr Denman is the secretary of the Royal College Faculty of Psychotherapy, a member of the Society of Analytical Psychology and a founder member of the Association of Cognitive Analytic Therapists.

Mr Daniel Barnett, LLB

He is a leading Barrister in employment law and author of three employment law textbooks, including co-author of the Law Society Handbook on Employment Law. He has advised and defended a number of NHS trusts in unfair dismissal and discrimination claims. He frequently comments in national and specialist press on employment law matters.

Dr Colin Payton FRCP MFOM

He is a Consultant Occupational Physician and Clinical Director of Occupational Health and Safety at the Royal United Hospital, Bath.

Dr Joan Trowell FRCP

She is a University Lecturer in Medicine and a Consultant Physician at the Oxford Radcliffe Trust. She is a member of the General Medical Council and until recently she was chairman of the GMC's Fitness to Practise Committee.

Mr Paul Buckley

He is the Director of Strategy and Planning, General Medical Council.

Mr Tim Kevan MA

He is a Barrister at 1 Temple Gardens with expertise in personal injury (including clinical negligence), sports, consumer and general common law. He is the author of nine legal textbooks and edits three legal newsletters (www.pibriefupdate.com, www.lawbriefupdate.com and www.medicolegalbriefupdate.com).

Dr Gerard Panting MA MRCGP DMJ

He is the Director of Policy, Medical Protection Society.

Mr Tony Harrison MA

He is a Fellow in Health Policy at the King's Fund. He has published extensively on the future of hospital care, the private finance initiative, health research policy and waiting list management.

Professor Alan Maynard BA BPhil HonDSc FAMS Hon MFPHM

He is the Professor of Health Economics and Director of York Health Policy Group at York University. He has worked as a consultant for the WHO, the World Bank, the European Union and the UK's Government Department for International Development. He is widely published in many books, specialist journals and the mainstream media. Since 1997 he has been Chairman of the York NHS Trust.

Mr Daniel Hannan MA MEP

He is a leader writer for The Daily Telegraph, author of 6 books and MEP for South East England.

Dr Eamonn Butler MA PhD

He is Director of the Adam Smith Institute, an influential think-tank which for more than twenty years has designed and promoted practical policies to promote choice and competition in the delivery of essential services. He frequently contributes articles to national magazines and newspapers on subjects such as health policy, economic management, taxation and public spending, transport, pensions, and e-government.

Professor Nick Bosanquet

He is a Professor of Health Policy at Imperial College, London and a health economist who first carried out research on NHS funding in the 1980's for the York Reports sponsored by the British Medical Association, the Royal College of Nursing and the Institute for Health Services Management. He has been Special Adviser on public expenditure to the Commons Health Committee since 2000. He is a non-Executive Director of a Primary Care Trust in London.

Mr Andrew Haldenby

He is the Director of Reform, an independent, non-party think tank whose mission is to set out a better way to deliver public services and economic prosperity.

Dr Jessica Allen PhD Bsoc Sci

Jessica Allen is Senior Research Fellow and Head of Health and Social Care at the Institute for Public Policy Research. At IPPR, she is currently working on a project exploring public expectations and a sustainable health system. Prior to joining IPPR, she worked at the Kings Fund and at Unicef. She holds a PhD from the University of London and has lectured at the University of Greenwich and LSE.

Ms Jennifer Rankin MA

Jennifer Rankin is a Research Fellow in Health and Social Care at the Institute for Public Policy Research. At IPPR, she is currently working on a project exploring public expectations and a sustainable health system.

CHAPTER 1

INTRODUCTION

Dr Michelle Tempest

"It is health that is real wealth and not pieces of gold and silver."
Mohandas Gandhi

This book considers the questions surrounding the most important
pillar of modern society, the National Health Service (NHS). The
NHS was forged in the furnace of the Second World War, with memories of the 1930s depression still very strong. The founding principles
of the NHS reflected above all a sense of idealism and nobility of
purpose, originating in William Beveridge's Report of 1942 and
finally implemented in 1948. The NHS was founded upon the principles that healthcare must be freely available to all from cradle to
grave and that provision must be based on need rather than ability
to pay. So radical was the idea that its architect, the Health Minister
Aneurin Bevan described it as "the biggest single experiment in social
service the world has ever seen undertaken." Interestingly, many of
the principles established for the NHS arose out of Bevan's own
involvement in the Tredegar Workmen's Medical Aid Society some
twenty years earlier.

Whilst many may see it as clichéd or old-fashioned to be harking back
to those early days, it is nevertheless important to realise that the
circumstances of its formation has left a very important legacy. Those
noble aims and ideals were quickly translated within the NHS into a
strong ethos of public service that, when coupled with the already
existing philanthropic instincts of the medical profession, created
what is frequently described as a beacon to the rest of the world.
Whatever problems beset the NHS its founding spirit lives on and
remains at the very heart of the system.

However, despite the unimpeachable intentions of those who work within the service there have been difficulties that were perhaps inevitable when developing a system of such magnitude. Indeed, the difficulties faced by the NHS today were foreseen even in those early years, Bevan himself predicted in 1945 that "administration is going to be the chief headache for years to come."

Spiralling costs in the 1950s led to the introduction of the NHS's first charges: for prescriptions and dental services. This reflected another issue which remains just as important to date: what level of health care can be provided for free and to whom? Medical practitioners have always had to deal with balancing the desire for perfection, with the need to be realistic and get the best possible results with the resources available. Medical advances and an ageing population have only served to heighten this inherent tension within the service.

The 1960s saw a growth in the NHS with the emergence of a better distribution of GPs and the growth of health centres. However, this too reflected another element in the NHS debate: the so-called ratchet effect, where whatever monies are ploughed into the NHS, they can rarely be taken back.

The 1970s and 1980s were primarily concerned with another important issue for the NHS: how can such an enormous organisation be managed effectively? Regional Health Authorities were introduced in 1974 and general management took over from consensus management following the Griffiths Report 1983 which, incidentally, recommended that clinicians be involved in the management processes.

The development of the NHS in the 1990s reflected the wider social and political change that had taken place in the 1980s: the rise in market competition for the provision of services generally. This development seemed at odds to some, with the concept of a state-funded NHS. However, politicians found a way through this potential conflict by the introduction of internal markets, where services remained free but room was made available for competition and private provision.

All of these developments reflect the inherent tensions within the system: providing free health care, whilst avoiding burdening the economy to such an extent that it collapses; keeping the pride a single system can develop, whilst avoiding stifling it with inefficiency and bureaucracy.

WHAT NEXT?

Whilst there have been numerous developments and reviews, there has never as yet been a root and branch study of the system looking at it from first principles. In the 1970s the then Prime Minister Lord Callaghan, instituted a great debate on education reform, where the aim was to encourage the entire country to talk about what would be best for the future education of the nation's children. Perhaps it is now time to repeat this exercise in relation to our national health service, in a year that marks sixty years since the implementation of the National Health Service Act 1946. The combination of this important anniversary and the NHS's domination of the front pages each week, means it has never been a more appropriate time to undertake such a review and to start such a debate.

As with any experiment, eventually the results have to be collated and the effects assessed before any conclusions can be drawn. However, the NHS has always belonged to the people and not just the professionals and it is hoped that this book will help to spark such a debate across the country, not just within the common rooms of universities or the wood-panelled walls of Whitehall.

The British people are right to be proud of the service the NHS provides. We live in a world of increasing health awareness, however, each time we discuss the NHS it seems to be in terms of debts, dirt, or decay. Patients rarely seem to be the centre of attention; rather headlines focus on doom and gloom. Perhaps it is because of the very fact that NHS is synonymous with sickness, we have learned to accept reports of ill health within the body of the service itself. However, what would happen if we turned that on its head? If we decided that because of the fact that it deals with illness it must be strong and successful? If rather than looking to point the finger, apportion blame, use it as a political pawn or find scapegoats, we instead wanted to see a new and optimistic NHS?

It is a rare privilege to be able to discuss a topic that is literally a matter of life and death. The NHS has countless tales of heroism and serves millions of patients, however, who looks after the health of the NHS?

In psychiatric language it could be said that the NHS is stuck in a cycle of addiction, needing quick fixes fast, and spending almost any sum of money to get them. Perhaps it is time that this is reviewed and that the NHS is sent for its own form of specialised rehabilitation. Modern media may encourage policy-makers to flirt with the dangerous game of short-term fame with no long-term gain. However, the NHS is too important to be sucked into this strategy and we must act now to stop the NHS from hitting the self-destruct button. The NHS deals with real life, real people and real problems and it is hoped that longer term planning will be a basis for a future healthier NHS.

So, where do we start with this process, to acquire long-term strategies for successful rehabilitation? In medicine, when a patient presents, the doctor starts by taking a history and then examining the systems. This book also takes this approach and I would like to thank the contributors who are some of the most involved, knowledgeable, busy and important people from many walks of the NHS for giving their valuable time to contribute to this NHS consultation.

The early chapters in the book express the views of leading members from all three main political parties, Labour, Conservative and Liberal Democrats, to offer constructive comments about what options they see for the future vision of the NHS. The book continues with chapters from top NHS professionals, experts at the forefront of their specialty, who collectively bring centuries of experience. Their wealth of knowledge is unrivalled, admired and invaluable; they are the leading authorities across a broad range of hospital specialties. These chapters discuss how they see the future of their area of expertise, not to apportion blame, but to have a vision, aiming towards improvement. The chapters then proceed to discuss how the NHS is managed, trained, regulated and funded. After explaining how the current funding system works the book progresses onto thinking of alternative and innovative methods of tackling the complex financial issues. The book seeks to bring a multidisciplinary, eminent expert team together, with a wide range of perspectives, to set out views clearly and understandably; to enable the general reader (whether lay person or professional) to comprehend better the cardinal questions involved in this NHS debate.

The NHS is a massive organisation; in fact, it is the fifth largest employer in the world, employing over 1.33 million people. When you consider the number of employees in global terms, this equals around three times the population of Malta or Barbados. After adding in the number of patients being treated at any one time, it brings the total NHS population to be around the size of an African country, such as Botswana or The Gambia. Thinking of the NHS as a country of this magnitude brings home the difficulties involved in how to manage an organisation with a vast number of patients, an unstable economy, an ageing infrastructure and one that does not produce saleable goods. However, this is offset by the fact that unlike any other country on earth, the NHS has one single and extraordinary asset – its population is driven and united by an overwhelming desire to do good. Upon these foundations are hard working, dedicated employees who are the cornerstone to the service. As a result the NHS succeeds in saving lives, curing illnesses, caring for the sick and troubled, with a world class display of humanity which continues twenty-four hours a day, seven days a week.

The aim of this book is to be constructive, not destructive, and to highlight the fact that we must all work together to plan for the future NHS. After all, irrespective of size, shape, colour, class, culture or religion, inside our organs are the same. It is imperative that every person is involved in the debate. It is not just for the 'experts' in the disciplines concerned, but for everyone – doctors, nurses and patients, lawyers and clients, legislators and voters, young and old – because the debate crosses every age group and every social divide. Every person must contribute to the debate, not least, because how we answer the questions raised about the NHS, will ineluctably have a profound effect on the very nature of society as we know it. The book collates views surrounding the NHS debate, to allow the reader to be informed rather than ignorant, rational rather than emotional, and to evaluate competing and various ideas.

The Future of the NHS enables the reader to take the first step into the most exciting debate of our times. The profound questions facing the NHS could not be more momentous, and in this crucial year for the NHS this book is relevant, timely and necessary to encourage the people to join the great debate. For those who wish to contribute to the debate via the internet online then please log onto **www.thefutureofthenhs.com**.

SECTION I
POLITICAL

CHAPTER 2

THE LABOUR VISION FOR THE NHS

Rt. Hon. Patricia Hewitt MP,
Secretary of State for Health

Ask people what makes them proud to be British and most will say the NHS. But if the NHS is to meet the needs of the British people, and to reward them for the investment they are making in it, then the NHS must continue to change in ways that bring direct benefits to patients and users. In this chapter I want to explain the nature of that change, and to describe what a reformed NHS will look like.

We are at a crucial moment in the history of public services in this country: a fork in the road, with two clear paths signposted ahead. After thirty years in public life, with my passion for social justice and equality undimmed, I know both the path I want to take, and the steps necessary to get us there.

We start with our values – the values of a health service funded by all of us, available to each of us, free at the point of treatment, with care based on our need and not our ability to pay.

These values are non-negotiable. They make the NHS unique. The changes we are making are not simply consistent with our traditional values: they are the best way of securing our values in a rapidly changing world.

Our goals spring from these values. We want to secure the best possible health – for every individual and every community, so as to reduce and eventually eradicate health inequalities.

THE IMPROVEMENTS LABOUR HAS MADE

We've come a long way since Labour was elected in 1997.

The NHS always sat uneasily alongside the sweeping reforms of the 1980s. It is a tribute to its founding values, of equal access, free for everyone at the point of need, that the NHS survived the 1980s. It is a tribute to its staff that in the 1980s the flame of the NHS, never went out.

But waiting lists went up. Buildings were left unrepaired. Salaries stagnated. Patient care suffered. At the end of the 1980s, one in ten NHS hospital patients were waiting more than two years for treatment.

By the 1990s, many commentators were openly discussing the end of the NHS. It is not sustainable, they said. A tax-funded health service belongs to the past. We need private insurance, they said. But they were wrong.

In January 2006, waiting lists fell to their lowest level since records began. More than 19 out of 20 people get seen, treated, admitted or discharged within four hours at A&E. We are refurbishing and building more hospitals than ever before. Between 1979 and 1997, 10 hospital schemes over £50 million in cash terms were approved and proceeded to construction.

We are improving long-neglected services like mental health, with more effective ways of managing severe mental illness in the community alongside better in-patient care. We are treating more people than ever before – and, most important of all, we are saving more lives than ever before with 43,000 lives saved from cancer in the last seven years and almost 60,000 lives saved since 1997 from coronary heart disease.

We're achieving these results because of our staff – more of them than ever before with 190,000 more frontline staff than 1999, and, I'm proud to say, better paid than ever before. This can be attributed to the investment – funding doubled already to £70 billion in the last financial year, and increasing to over £90 billion by the end of 2008.

So if investment and reform are working, why do we need more change?

First, because there is still so much more to do.

Second, because of the extraordinary changes taking place in health-care, all over the world.

And third, because of the need to get better value for taxpayers' money.

First, let's look at what still needs to be done. From the start of January 2006 no-one will be waiting more than six months for their hospital operation. A huge improvement when we remember that, not so many years ago, over thirty thousand people – many of them elderly and in great pain – had been waiting a year or more for something as simple, but as life-transforming, as a hip replacement.

It doesn't happen in France or Germany, and it shouldn't happen in the UK. That is why, by the end of 2008, when NHS funding will have reached nearly 10 per cent of total national wealth – around the European average – we have promised that no-one will wait more than 18 weeks from GP referral to hospital treatment.

It is a huge challenge, but one that we can meet – provided we continue to match investment with reform. Even this achievement, essential though it is, won't be enough to meet people's rising expectations. People expect more choice and more control over their health and their healthcare.

Our patients and users are also better educated and better informed than ever before. Newspapers, magazines, radio and television are all responding to people's thirst for health and medical information. The internet makes everything – from clinical trials to personal experience and everything in between – potentially available to everybody. There are more self-help groups in our country than there are GP practices.

There are other, profound changes in our society. More of us are living far longer. More babies with serious disabilities are living through childhood and into adulthood. There is more geographical mobility, more ethnic and religious diversity, more people are living by themselves, and changing work and family patterns.

We need to put far more emphasis on prevention rather than on cure. The UK spends less of its health budget on prevention than almost any other developed country. We now have an opportunity, with our reforms, to shift the whole emphasis of the NHS from acute care to prevention, to health and social care in the community.

At the same time, we need to do far more to reduce the glaring health inequalities in our country. Consider the fact that, for every three parents from the best-off professional classes who lose a baby, five parents from the worst-off community will suffer a similar tragedy.

It is over thirty years since Julian Tudor Hart coined the phrase 'the inverse care law' to describe the fact that those in greatest need often get the poorest services from the NHS. Today, even after the improvements I have outlined, we must do more to tackle the problem.

The pioneering work Richard Titmuss, Brian Abel-Smith and others showed that the NHS all too often supplied 'poor services to poor people.'

As Brian Abel-Smith wryly commented

> 'If socialists believed forty years ago that all that was needed to equalise health status between social classes was to remove the money barriers to access to health care, they were seriously mistaken.'

Despite the commitment of the NHS to equal access, the poorest people are still at the greatest risk of falling ill. Even with the well documented links between poverty, social exclusion and ill health they still tend to get the poorest services. The poorer the neighbourhood, the scarcer the GPs, the less frequent the preventative consultations – and the lower the public satisfaction. The least well-off are nearly one-third more likely to need a hip replacement than the best-off – but they are one-fifth less likely actually to get it.

Over the next two years, we will not only invest £135 billion in the NHS, but we will allocate it far more fairly than in the past. In 2002, when we updated the resources allocation formula, we found that the worst-off areas were over 20 per cent below their target funding level. By the end of 2007/8, no area will be more than 3.5 per cent below target. The communities with the greatest needs will be getting, on average, around £1,700 per head, compared with around £1,200 in the healthiest neighbourhoods. Because that investment comes with a more transparent financial system than ever before, we have a unique opportunity to ensure that the funding in the most disadvantaged areas makes a real difference to those with the greatest needs, by ensuring that they get the greatest help.

The second reason why we must keep on with change and reform is the global transformation in healthcare that is taking place.

In a world where people travel far more, a world of the Internet, people's expectations of health services are no longer shaped simply by their own experience and that of their family and friends. They compare the NHS with what they see on holiday, or working, studying or living abroad. They know, immediately, that a new drug – not yet approved for NHS use – is available in France or Germany or, at least for those with insurance, the United States.

But healthcare is also being transformed in India and China. Indian entrepreneurs – already so dominant in e-commerce – are now setting out to create world-class health services. A recent McKinsey study predicts that, by 2012, India will earn over £2 billion in medical tourism. But the internet combined with cheap air travel is creating a global market in healthcare for people who are willing to travel for their treatment. Just as national economic policy has been profoundly affected by globalisation, so national health policy will be affected by developments abroad.

And the third argument for change is the simple fact that, with these new expectations and new drug treatments, the pressures on NHS spending are relentless. But if we are to match people's rising expectations, finance new drugs and new treatments, and deal with deep-seated inequities within our system, then we have to get every penny of value from every pound we invest.

THE FOUR STRANDS OF REFORM

At the heart of our vision is a patient-led health and social care system which:

- supports your health and well-being, instead of waiting until you are sick;
- offers you personal and comprehensive care, not just one-size-fits-all solutions or fragmented and frustrating services;

- offers you a choice of first-rate services, without waiting, in clean and modern surroundings;
- offers healthcare rooted in the NHS's fundamental founding value: free at the point of use, based on need, not ability to pay.

For the last five years, Government has relied heavily upon national targets and a system of command and control. But heavy performance management demoralises staff and risks distorting priorities. An NHS that is performance managed by Whitehall is inclined to face inwards towards the Department of Health, not outwards towards its patients and users. Although it has been essential in getting improvements in the short term, it is not a long-term solution to public service reform.

Instead, we need to embed the reforms and change the culture as well as the system. The best practice in almost every aspect of care that can be found somewhere in the NHS, needs to become the norm everywhere. So we need to ensure that, throughout the NHS, there are the right incentives for continuous improvement, innovation and better value for money – and we need to use the remaining years of very fast financial growth to create that new system.

There are four elements to our reforms which work together to create the self-improving NHS we seek:

a) More choice and a much stronger voice for patients;
b) More diverse providers, with more freedom to innovate and challenge poor performance;
c) Money following the patients, rewarding the best and most efficient and giving the others a real incentive to improve;
d) A framework of regulation and decision-making that guarantees quality, fairness, equity and value for money.

(A) MORE CHOICE AND A STRONGER VOICE FOR PATIENTS

If we want to create a self-improving health service that designs its services around patients, rather than making patients fit in around the service, then we need more choice and a stronger voice for patients and users.

At the start of 2006, every patient needing a hospital referral has the right to a choice of at least four – and that range will build up until, by the end of 2008, every NHS patient will be able to choose, for elective treatments, from any hospital, anywhere in England that can provide care to NHS quality and NHS price.

As patients get more choice, hospitals get more incentives to improve. If better hospital food really matters to people – and we know it does – then hospitals will be judged accordingly. The same is true about cleanliness and infection rates, access to toilets and bathrooms, telephones and television, the helpfulness of staff, and the sense, above all, that – each patient is being treated as a valued individual, with dignity and respect.

When it comes to elective treatments, such as hip replacements and cataracts, maternity services, primary healthcare and the management of long-term conditions and the care of the elderly, then the more we can offer people a real say in how their services are designed and delivered, the better.

We expect every healthcare organisation to engage with patients and the public so that their needs and experiences shape the way services are designed and delivered – especially Primary Care Trusts (PCTs) who have the job of analysing and understanding local health needs; they are all responsible for planning, designing and securing services to meet those needs; and, crucially, shifting the emphasis from treatment to prevention and public health.

Alongside strong PCTs, we need GPs with more responsibility, more accountability for the public money they are spending – but also more freedom to get the services that their patients need. Hence our commitment to extend Practice Based Commissioning to all primary care practices by the end of 2006.

By ensuring, that every GP has an indicative budget from their PCT, and proper information about how their own referral patterns compare with other local GPs, we will give every practice a strong incentive – working with other GPs and the PCT itself – to improve support for people with long-term conditions, reduce emergency admissions and pull services out of acute hospitals and into the community, where they are most convenient for patients and better value for money.

GPs who manage their budgets well will have more freedom to innovate and invest. GPs who don't will be held to account by their PCT.

As funding for PCTs becomes fairer, we will also over time move GPs from budgets based on historic activity to budgets based on fair shares. This will help to tackle the injustice that all too often has seen the communities with the greatest health needs receive the worst health services.

(B) MORE DIVERSE PROVIDERS

We want to unleash the huge potential for innovation within the NHS, as well as outside it. I have come across countless examples of NHS staff who want to change the way they work to improve patient care but are too often frustrated by the way 'the system' works.

Three years ago, the creation of Foundation Trusts was hugely controversial. Today, I would be amazed if anybody seriously wanted to abolish them. There are now 32 foundation trusts, serving a quarter of the population, with a turnover of over £6 billion. Nearly half a million people are members of foundation trusts – more members than the mainstream political parties.

The involvement of the independent sector – private and not-for-profit – has been more controversial still. In the overall scale of the NHS, the independent sector is small beer – even with the whole of the second wave of independent sector procurement. It only makes up about 10 per cent of electives and accounts for around 1 per cent of the total NHS budget. But a small part of the NHS budget is enough to attract new providers, who will bring more innovation and more competition to other independent sector as well as NHS organisations. Relatively small changes can have a big impact on the system as a whole.

In cataracts, for instance, independent sector providers have brought extra capacity, innovation, particularly mobile surgical units, and high levels of productivity. This has helped to bring down waiting lists in this area to a maximum of three months by complementing the significant increases in procedures carried out by the NHS.

What we have done on hip replacements and other elective treatment, we will now do on diagnostics. One of the only ways we will achieve our 18 week pathway – 18 weeks, maximum, from GP referral to start of hospital treatment – will be to achieve an unprecedented increase in diagnostic capacity, both in the NHS itself and in the independent sector. We simply won't abolish waiting lists otherwise. So from November 2005, patients waiting more than 20 weeks for CT and MRI scans have been offered the choice of an alternative provider with spare capacity so their maximum wait will be 26 weeks. From April 2006, that will be extended to all imaging scans with the alternative offered at 16 weeks if patients do not have a date within 20. And we are already out to tender for £1 billion worth of additional diagnostic procedures of additional scans from the independent sector, which will help to double the number of MRI scans available to NHS patients.

More capacity is essential. But so is more innovation, along with more challenge – more competition – for inefficient and under-performing providers. And that will come from different NHS hospitals, from Foundation Hospitals, with their greater freedoms, and via the independent sector.

Foundation Trusts were created as a new form of public organisation. The social enterprises that are now growing in many other sectors of the economy offer another model of public organisation that is starting to spread, particularly within community health and social care.

Already, within Primary Care Trusts, there are many different models of service provision. Many PCTs are taking the lead in creating new community hospitals, walk-in-centres open 7 days a week and improved inner-city primary healthcare practices. As we ask PCTs to strengthen their role as commissioners, they will be able to continue providing services as well. But there will also be room for new providers. For instance, in six areas where there aren't enough GP services and where PCTs, with our support, are inviting any interested party to come forward with their proposals. This might include GPs who want to expand, nurse practitioners who want to lead a service, the not-for-profit sector or private firms. As with the new walk-in centres in commuter centres, the only test will be who can offer the best services to patients, with the best value for money, all of it free at the point of need.

In the new NHS, there will be an element of competition – on quality, effectiveness and responsiveness to patients' needs. As that drives the less good hospitals to improve – or sees their services replaced by better providers – it will be good for patients. Because competition and diversity of provision must develop on a level playing field, every organisation caring for NHS patients will have to meet minimum standards of safety, quality and conduct, enshrined in the national contract.

We also want hospitals to collaborate – where appropriate, with each other, and with local GPs and PCTs. So the requirement to share information and work jointly to create integrated services will also be set out in the national contract. It's worth remembering that the most successful global organisations are, often simultaneously, competitors, collaborators, suppliers and customers of each other.

(C) MONEY FOLLOWS THE PATIENTS

The third element of our reforms ensures that, as patients and users choose, money will follow. Already, we are trialling payment by results, for elective and emergency admissions in foundation trusts, and for elective admissions in other NHS hospitals. From April 2006 a single national tariff will cover planned, emergency and outpatient care in hospitals. Payment by Results is essential to make patient choice work.

For the first time in nearly 60 years, Payment by Results means that every hospital will understand how much it is spending to provide a particular treatment – and every hospital will have an incentive to become more efficient. That is particularly important, given the deficits we now face in the NHS. Last year, overall, these amounted to less than half a per cent of the total NHS budget. Three-quarters of NHS organisations are in balance or surplus, with most of the deficit concentrated in about 40 organisations, which is just 7 per cent of the total number.

Historically, hospitals were given an annual block grant, based not on the work they did, but on what they got last year. Efficient hospitals who did more, did not necessarily get more money. Inefficient hospitals did not necessarily get less. There was no real incentive to improve. The old system was neither fair or efficient.

Because the system is now far more open and transparent than we have had it before, it is revealing underlying deficits that in the past were often concealed, and because payment by results gives every hospital a real incentive to improve its clinical effectiveness and its cost efficiency, the new system will help to solve the problem of the deficits, and, even more importantly, to raise productivity across the NHS.

We still have much to do to improve the design and operation of Payment By Results (PBR). That is why we are proceeding carefully with PBR, testing it this year and moderating its impact over the next two years. And that is why we are working with NHS clinicians and leading thinkers to ensure that PBR and the tariff system delivers efficiency and excellence as we move forward.

Each element of our reforms brings benefits. But together, as patients exercise more choice, as different hospitals challenge each other to provide the best quality, and as payment by results exposes differences in practice and therefore in cost, so every clinician, manager and organisation will have an inbuilt incentive to compare themselves with the best. They will be encouraged to innovate and improve, to give patients the best possible care – and taxpayers the best possible value for money.

(D) A NEW REGULATORY FRAMEWORK

The fourth and final element in our reforms is a framework of regulation and decision-making that guarantees safety and quality, ensures proper stewardship of public funds and reflects our commitment to equity. It also needs to ensure good information is available for patients, carers and staff to support choices in healthcare.

We are now reviewing how we regulate and inspect health and social care services; how we protect essential services – including A&E – that might otherwise be jeopardised by weaknesses or changes in other services such as orthopaedics and trauma; how we deal with organisations in financial trouble; and how we reduce the bureaucracy of inspection and regulation while improving safety and quality for patients and the public.

CONCLUSION

By the end of 2008, this Labour government will effectively have abolished NHS hospital waiting lists. Patients and users will have more choice and control over their services. In place of the old monopoly, we will have a far greater variety of hospitals, GPs and other services – public, private and not-for-profit, all part of the NHS family – with more freedom to innovate and more incentive to respond to people's needs. Poor services will be taken over or replaced by better providers. Strong Primary Care Trusts – the local NHS – will work with GPs, patients and users to get the best from acute hospitals and to reshape services in the community.

We will view the National Health Service not just as hospital buildings, but as a network of services, helping us to stay healthy, as well as treating us when we are ill.

As we finally put right the historic under-funding of the NHS, the NHS will combine its founding values – equal access to care based on clinical need, not ability to pay – with a modern commitment to personal service, continuous improvement and better value for money.

Now is the best – indeed, the only – opportunity we will have in my lifetime to secure a health service that is true to its founding values, but fit for modern demands.

Based on a lecture delivered at the London School of Economics, December 2005.

CHAPTER 3

THE CONSERVATIVE VISION FOR THE NHS

Andrew Lansley CBE MP,
Shadow Secretary of State for Health

The National Health Service is a unique institution. Nowhere else in the world is such a huge proportion of national healthcare resources devoted to a single centrally-organised and directed system. With such a centralised service, one should at least expect to see a service in which there is certainty about mission and strategy.

Yet the critical characteristics of uniformity and consistency are not part of the NHS. Beneath the veneer of the NHS logo and brand, it is a service in which disparities and contradictions abound. That is a measure of the extent to which the NHS is not living up to its potential. These contradictions mean the NHS has all the complexities and bureaucracy of a huge organisation without the benefits of scale and consistency being delivered in practice.

The examples are legion. While they say that resources are be redirected towards primary care, the key Government target for the next two years is to be the time taken to first in-patient treatment in hospital. Time to treatment is targeted, but time to subsequent treatment is not even measured. While call-to-needle times are measured and targeted, only in a few places is primary angioplasty being actively pursued. In some places, stroke patients aren't even admitted to a specialist stroke unit, while in others they are scanned immediately and assessed for thrombolysis. New Cancer drugs can be prescribed in some places, but not in others. While a national bowel cancer screening programme will roll out in the coming months, thousands of men don't get the ultrasounds scans which would spot abdominal aortic aneurysms.

Resources provided to PCTs in the most deprived areas are double those provided in the healthiest part of the country, yet in the latter areas deficits are high and services are being out back. In a hospital servicing contrasting areas, patients are being discharged with community services in place in the more deprived area, and not available in the more prosperous one.

These are not divergences resulting from devolution or decentralisation; they are the inconsistencies of an organisation which lacks cohesion and consistency of purpose.

This lack of clarity is a principal reason why simply asking the question: "what is the future of the NHS?" will give so many different answers.

A political consensus in support of the values and principles of the NHS is important but no guarantee of the future of the NHS. The public's support for the NHS, and hence its future, may depend upon the service's ability to respond to rising expectations. In a service which consumes the same proportion of national income as the healthcare sector in France (as could be the case by 2011) public support could normally require that the service delivers comparable levels of health outcomes. Yet the disparities between health outcomes in France and in Britain remain intractably wide. Will public support ebb? Perhaps not. High levels of relative spending on the NHS in Scotland and Wales have not borne fruit in better health outcomes, nor even in lower waiting lists for treatment, yet public support for the NHS is undiminished in those countries. Four year-old referrals in Northern Ireland are being transferred to English hospitals. Yet one doesn't hear rumblings in Northern Ireland against the NHS.

It is entirely possible, therefore, that the NHS will retain public support and political allegiance regardless of its relative success. But the opportunity cost of consuming ten per cent of national resources without achieving positive productivity gains and health outcomes would be enormous.

That is why, if we are serious about the future of the NHS, we must offer to the service not just allegiance and support, but the clarity of purpose and incentives for positive improvement which are essential to the delivery of a far more successful health service.

The mission of the Government must be clear: to deliver progressively improving health outcomes with the improvement of the poorest occurring fastest. The mission of the National Health Service would be to deliver a high-quality comprehensive health service for all, based on need not ability to pay, and capable of maximising health-related quality of life.

The distinction between the two is that the NHS should treat the patient; while government should treat society. Public health objectives must be the government's responsibility to attain, utilising the influence and actions of government, whilst the NHS supports the Government in their public health objective and provides the health services, whether on a population-wide basis or individual basis, which the needs of its population and patients require.

Therefore, the first element in securing the future of the NHS is to deliver improved public health and is in large part extraneous to the NHS itself. If we can engage the public successfully, and government effectively, in improving public health outcomes, we can ensure that demands for health care do not make the task of the NHS unsustainable and we will enable the NHS to meet its objectives in a context of progressively improving health outcomes. It is a desperate fact of life for many leading clinicians when they deliver first-class medicine whilst the population they serve is not only suffering from poor physical and material circumstances, frustrating their efforts, but are also inflicting increasing harm on themselves through poor diet, lack of exercise, alcohol and drug use, smoking, poor sexual health and family breakdown.

Achieving success in public health requires a partnership between the Government, public and the NHS.

We cannot, and must not, regard the NHS as carrying the burden of combating ill health alone. The cliché that the NHS must become a health service, not an illness service, is true, to the extent that emphasis on primary and secondary prevention can and should be effectively delivered through the NHS, via GPs, health visitors and school nurses. More effective awareness campaigns, as promised in the Cancer Plan but not yet delivered, would clearly assist in earlier diagnosis and improved survival rates. However, the burden of reducing the prevalence of cancer is more than simply the product of health advice or intervention; it depends critically on social action.

So, we need to be clear about the distinction between the Public Health Service, within and beyond the NHS, and the role of the NHS itself. This is perhaps illustrated by the mechanisms of resource allocation. The greater health needs of some areas should be reflected in greater allocation of resources, but we need to be clear how far this is required in order to provide primary and secondary prevention services, on the one hand, and to respond to increased morbidity on the other. Simply distorting the quantum of NHS resources in the hope that it will lead to better health, without evidence-based interventions, will only serve to distort and undermine the consistency of NHS services to individual patients.

The second element on securing the future of the NHS is to return the service to its staff. If the public trust the NHS, it is the doctors, nurses, midwives, paramedics and professionals who they put their faith in. If they entrust themselves to the professional staff, the least we can do is ensure that the professional judgement and expertise of NHS staff is given the fullest possible opportunity to deliver. Of course, this means abolishing targets which run directly contrary to the clinical judgements of doctors and nurses. It may also mean tempering the choice of patients with the intermediary decisions of GPs or nurses, in determining the right course of action to facilitate the best care for patients. Patient choice is rarely exercised in isolation, even in the current private sector context; it is within a framework of clinical advice and best practice. Likewise for the NHS, a patient-centred service is not a demand-led free-for-all. It is a professionally-led service which responds to the needs and decisions of patients, reflected in individual patient choice and the collective patient voice. Nor is it a professional free-for-all; professional leadership also means clinically-proven and evidence-based approaches, in which professionals measure themselves against exacting clinical standards, including performance management, to ensure the best value-for-money for their patients from the resources devoted to their service.

It is within this nexus of professional autonomy and responsiveness to patient choice and voice that the future character of a National Health Service needs to be forged. One approach could be to make it wholly devolved. Local services, run by locality commissioning groups, agreeing local priorities with local clinical teams. It is a conceivable scenario, but it is a *national* health service only to the extent that it is funded collectively through the consolidated fund. Do we expect more? I think we do expect more, not only in the sense that the resulting inequalities of access for patients would be unsustainable in a centrally-funded service, but we also expect better, in the sense that we are looking for the benefits of evidence-based decision-making and the dissemination of best practice, and even of specified national entitlements to care, to be determined through a nationally-based expert clinical and patient consensus.

This points to a central future role for the National Institute for Health and Clinical Excellence (NICE) in the future of the NHS. Notwithstanding debates over the methodology of NICE, we need there to be a mechanism for reaching conclusions on the relative clinical effectiveness and the cost-effectiveness of treatments and clinical practice. This will enable consistent standards of service to be offered through the NHS, and for national entitlements to care to be established, with transparent decisions being made about the resource implications and boundaries of NHS provision.

'National', therefore, in the context of the NHS would represent the development of nationally specified entitlements to care and nationally-determined guidance on the relative effectiveness of practice and treatments, as well as national funding, even if in many respects the priorities for service development and performance are set locally or professionally. NICE appraisals and guidelines would therefore become a central resource in supporting priority-setting and demand management locally and nationally.

Standardisation across the NHS would derive not so much from political or managerial requirements as from clinical needs for reliability and quality.

Divergence in the services would not be ironed out. They would, however, be more transparently the result of decisions made by local commissioners (including GP budget-holders) and the choices of patients.

Despite the role to be played by nationally-determined standards, this need not impose excessive uniformity of provision, still less does it require a monopoly of supply. So, the third element needed to secure the future of the NHS is to deliver greater efficiency through a plurality of providers in circumstances of effective competition.

Professional ethics and a duty to co-operate in the interests of patients is not in the least incompatible with the achievement of competition in supply to the NHS. And it must be understood that only through competition can the potential for delivering productivity gains, and reaching the capacity needed to ensure the achievement of choice and quality, be fulfilled.

This does mean that new and independent healthcare providers should be free to supply NHS services. It also means that NHS providers should be given the institutional freedoms necessary to enable them to compete on equal terms. A reformed regulatory framework should apply across the healthcare sector, with independent statutory regulation (divided between 'Monitor' as economic regulator and the Healthcare Commission, as quality and value-for-money inspectorate) to ensure that competition is real, or competitive pressures are applied, on the one hand, while an independent body ensures that quality and standards are not compromised in response to these pressures. Competition in the provision of NHS services will necessitate the development of payment-by-results and the national tariff, even if there is progressive use of benchmark pricing and price competition to enhance efficiency incentives. In the current context of NHS changes, this would have the benefit of defining not only the direction of reforms, but also the destination, i.e., the regulation of all healthcare providers, within which the needs of the NHS can be met through the purchasing decisions of the NHS commissioning bodies, and via a framework of licensed healthcare providers who, through the terms of their licences, have obligations to supply to the NHS.

It is through these commissioning bodies, be they GP budget-holders, clinical networks or Primary Care Trusts, that the fourth and final element in securing the future of the NHS must be delivered. That is, to reconcile finite resources with apparently insatiable demand. While, at the national level, Ministers would decide whether NHS entitlements to care (derived by NICE) would be funded through allocations to NHS commissioners, this would only set limited specific boundaries to NHS services. In the great majority of cases, when and to what extent to satisfy – or manage – demand will fall to NHS commissioners. Past experience with total purchasing pilots for GP fundholding has illustrated some of the potential for promoting efficiency and managing demand more effectively in the community. If we are to escape from rationing by waiting lists or bureaucratic obstruction, then the only way forward must be for gains in efficiency to be complemented by innovative demand management by clinicians and nurses working closely with patients. I am sure the introduction of real GP budget-holding – real budgets, a real capacity to utilise savings, and the ability to negotiate and hold contracts – is essential to effective demand management.

We simply don't know what increases in capacity can be realised by giving greater freedoms to the NHS and by realising the incentives of competition and choice. If they are as great as has occurred in other countries when monopoly systems have been overturned, the fact that increases in NHS financial resources will moderate after 2008 will not necessarily mean financial collapse or service reductions. On the contrary, even the cost consequences of employing highly-skilled staff in a high-tech environment can be offset by highly innovative and enterprising responses to competition. Nor does competition deliver a zero-sum game of winners and losers: competition is a tide which lifts every boat.

So – to summarise. The future of the NHS will not be secured by political rhetoric. It must be secured by a clear and consistent strategic approach, focused on delivering the mission of the NHS. There are, I believe, four elements to this strategy: a Government and NHS which acts to deliver improved public health outcomes; an NHS which is professionally-led and patient-centred and in which the professionals – doctors, nurses and managers – are trusted to deliver, free from day-to-day political interference; a plurality of providers in a competitive environment; and a devolved responsibility for GPs and NHS commissioners to promote innovative and effective management of demand for NHS services.

None of this demands major institutional upheaval. It does demand the carrying-through of reforms implicit in the rhetoric of patient-choice and contestability. If this fills NHS staff with a sense of foreboding, I hope they will resist it and seek out the opportunities for professional autonomy and decision-making available in a more enterprising NHS, free from day-to-day political interference and within an independent statutory framework.

The fact is, of course, that none of this can be achieved without the skill, care and leadership given by the staff of the NHS themselves. Managers free to manage; doctors able to offer clinical and professional leadership; nurses able to focus on the needs and care of patients; and all the staff of the NHS able to realise the potential of their service.

No-one can realistically imagine a future NHS without funding pressures and divergences in practice and outcomes. Yet we can look forward to an NHS which not only is funded in line with European norms but, more to the point, meets and exceeds European average health outcomes; an NHS in which patient needs and choices and the decisions of professionals dictate service design and delivery; an NHS in which differences are the result of legitimate decisions not arbitrary postcode lotteries; and an NHS in which patients put themselves in the hands of empowered professionals not in the embrace of an unaccountable bureaucracy.

CHAPTER 4

THE LIBERAL DEMOCRAT VISION FOR THE NHS

Professor Steve Webb MP,
Liberal Democrat Shadow
Secretary of State for Health

The current debate about the future of the NHS is unhelpfully polarised. An observer would be forgiven for concluding that there are only two possible positions. The first is that a sleepy and inefficient NHS needs shaking up by the rigours of market discipline and competition. The alternative position is that there is nothing much wrong with the NHS that can't be solved by pouring in yet more money and leaving a largely unreformed NHS to get on with it. The reality is that neither of these extreme positions stand up to rigorous scrutiny.

THE MARKET-DRIVEN APPROACH

The Government's market-led approach certainly has the merit of simplicity. It argues that competitive markets usually deliver lower prices, higher quality and greater innovation than markets where one or two providers have become dominant. If this works for supermarkets, the argument runs, it should also work in public services.

According to this theory, the problem with the NHS is that it is a monopoly which has little incentive to improve efficiency because most patients (or "customers") cannot register their disapproval by going to another provider.

The solution to this problem has been to create a pseudo-market in public health care where quality is rewarded and, equally importantly, failure is penalised. The main elements to this market are "patient choice", where the patient can choose from a list of providers, "payment by results", where each procedure attracts a particular tariff, regardless of the actual costs of provision, and "contestability", where market entry is encouraged by subsidies and guarantees to new entrants.

However, as an economist by training and background, I am concerned that the Government seems oblivious to the limitations of this market-driven approach.

The first problem arises with the clash of ideologies. The public service ethos of working towards the public good requires inequalities in the system to be reduced. Yet markets have a tendency to reinforce them. The concept of a "fair" outcome is alien to market economics. Economics undergraduates are taught that the only thing that matters is efficiency. Any resultant inequalities can be left to be dealt with by some other means, for example through the tax and benefits system. When patients are turned into consumers who shop around for the best deal, there will certainly be winners. The well-educated, articulate and mobile will increasingly dominate the best healthcare provision, just as they do the best education. But the vulnerable and marginalised will end up with the cast-offs.

The second problem is that entry and exit from the health market is far from the costless and smooth transition envisaged in the text books. A local hospital that cannot compete with a shiny new private unit will steadily lose patients and income and may eventually find that whole departments have to close. Before long, the hospital and its staff become trapped in a downward spiral of falling morale, redundancies and the threat of closure. We are already seeing the effects of this as hospitals tighten their belts and freeze recruitment or postpone non-urgent operations.

This painful process is an inevitable consequence of a market-driven approach to running the NHS. We should not be surprised that we see today simultaneously record sums being spent on the NHS and yet a majority of NHS Trusts running a deficit and planning cuts. Market mechanisms depend on the creation of winners and losers, and the losers are being told more ruthlessly than ever before that no-one is going to bale them out.

Of course, what is developing in the NHS at present is not a free market at all. New providers have been offered favourable prices to undertake NHS work – more than their "competitors" in the NHS would be paid – and are offered guaranteed volumes of work. This has led to the bizarre situation of NHS scanners lying idle whilst a more expensive privately-provided scanner operating from a trailer in the hospital car park is fully occupied.

The market also undermines the sharing of good practice within the NHS. If I am an NHS manager and know that my job depends on being more efficient than rival hospitals, the last thing I will want to do is share good practice with others. One of the curses of the NHS has been variability in standards within the health service. Turning the NHS into a series of competing units is likely to reinforce those divisions.

In short, therefore, the simplistic market-led model of NHS reform is riddled with problems which will become steadily more acute as the reform process rolls out.

THE "DO NOTHING" APPROACH

Those who reject the market approach have been accused of simply concluding that nothing needs to be done to reform the system, and that the Government should simply throw more and more money at the NHS until all the problems are solved. This is a simplistic view point.

The UK is set to spend as much of its national income on healthcare as many comparable European nations by 2008. We therefore have a duty to look ever more closely at how that money is spent. The current picture is one of local hospital closures, increasing health inequalities, and the neglect of certain illnesses and treatments in favour of those that grab more headlines. This suggests that existing mechanisms for ensuring the delivery of efficient healthcare are inadequate.

There must – to borrow a phrase – be a third way.

THE LIBERAL DEMOCRAT APPROACH

In my conversations with health professionals and patients around the country, a collective groan goes up at the thought of yet more upheaval and change in the NHS. Primary Care Trusts were barely given time to bed down in their roles before they were issued with a mid-summer letter from the NHS Chief Executive ordering them to restructure themselves. The professionals are increasingly weary, and the patients are increasingly confused.

However, if we believe that the current reforms are going in the wrong direction, the brakes must be applied sooner rather than later. I am a believer in evolution rather than revolution, and this applies particularly to the health service. What the NHS needs is keyhole surgery, but what it is currently getting is amputation with a rusty hacksaw.

Surveys show that patients do not primarily want a choice of five different hospitals, some far away from home, and about which they may know very little. The choice that people want is that of a good, responsive, local hospital – familiar and close to home. People also want some say over the future of their local hospital; they are usually deeply interested in plans for expansion or closure.

The Liberal Democrats believe that the key to reinventing the NHS, whilst remaining true to its founding principles, lies in a rediscovery of the notion of accountability. Within the present structure of the NHS, the power of those who pay for it to shape what it does is extraordinarily weak and indirect.

But what if accountability and activity in the NHS were to be radically decentralised so that local people actually knew what was going on in their local NHS and could help to shape its strategic direction? What if we directly elected people on the basis of their priorities for local health services and who were accountable if they failed to deliver? And what if local health bosses were in turn answerable to those people?

This approach could radically reshape the way in which the NHS operated. Instead of being a top-down organisation, still at the mercy of ministerial whim (or mid-summer letters from NHS chiefs), the pattern of local health services would be determined locally and accountable locally. Local NHSs could still work together where it made sense – for example to deliver specialist services which were only viable for larger population groups – but their primary focus would be on local health needs.

The precedent for this model already exists in Denmark, whose publicly-funded NHS is one of the most popular with its citizens in the whole of Europe. Its key feature is that despite a population only one tenth the size of England, the Danish healthcare system is itself run as fifteen smaller local units, each serving a population of typically a third of a million people. It will shortly be moving to units of one million people – but is still a far cry from the unit of 50 million people covered by the English NHS. The Danish system delivers efficient healthcare, with a public service ethos, accountable to local people.

In addition to local accountability, we need to see co-operation, not competition, operating within the health service. Some parts of the NHS are under-performing because of a failure to share best practice, both clinically and managerially. The practices of the top performers should be spread throughout the NHS.

There also needs to be a systematic and intelligent monitoring system so that poor performance is picked up early. We must identify units whose relative performance is declining and take steps to put things right early, rather than allow "market mechanisms" to drive them under. An approach based on co-operation and local accountability is far more likely to raise standards and morale than the ill-judged market-driven approach that we face today.

One further very important change that needs to happen is an end to the arbitrary and artificial distinctions between what counts as "health" and what counts as "social care". This problem is seen at its worst in care for elderly people in England, where "nursing" care is available free on the basis of need but where "social care" is free only on a means-tested basis and tens of thousands of people still have to sell their homes each year to pay for care. One consequence of this problem can be that elderly people are physically moved from one establishment to another at a very vulnerable time in their lives, simply because their needs are now classed as "health" needs rather than "care" needs.

The key to overcoming this problem is to merge budgets between health and social care. There are already individual local examples of this, but the approach needs to be rolled out nationally.

One great advantage of such an approach is that where a health intervention will cost the health service money but will save a greater amount on social service spending, it starts to become attractive.

Where the cost-effectiveness of interventions are being assessed locally, a holistic approach would be taken and the taxpayer and the patient would be the beneficiaries. Pooling of budgets would also get rid of unnecessary bureaucracy as there would no longer be any need to categorise whether a particular intervention was "health" or "social care".

A HEALTH SERVICE NOT A SICKNESS SERVICE

Structural improvements to the NHS are important, but I would also like to see a cultural shift in the perception of the NHS. We need to move away from the view of the NHS as a sickness service, simply dealing with the consequences of ill health – and start building its role as a genuine health service – tackling the causes of preventable disease and death. Prevention, as they say, is better than cure.

Causes of ill health such as poverty, poor diet, lack of exercise, poor housing and smoking contribute to the declining health of the population, and in turn place greater pressure on the NHS. The 2002 Wanless Report, "Securing Our Future Health: Taking a Long-Term View", set a very high price on neglecting the public health agenda. It suggested that by 2022, doing nothing in this area will add £30 billion to the cost of healthcare.

The Government has paid lip service to public health, whilst concentrating on building NHS capacity to treat an ever-growing number of sick people. Recent legislation coming to Parliament was going to include a "Health Improvement and Protection Bill." By the time the Bill reached the House of Commons, the words "Improvement and Protection" had been dropped; this was presumably an admission that the Bill would do little to contribute to either. In addition, the Cabinet initially agreed to an odd compromise on proposals to ban smoking in public places. They decided, amid much controversy – including opposition from the Health Secretary herself – to ban smoking in pubs that served food, but not in those that didn't. Ministers admitted this had nothing to do with the health of the population, and everything to do with trying not to upset the industry. The Government's later decision to grant its own backbenchers a free vote on the smoking ban was an admission that its policy was incoherent, but the whole episode illustrates the low priority being given to public health measures.

This is not a responsible approach to protecting the health of the population. The NHS has an important role to play in enabling people to take control over their own health, and in supporting people to make healthy choices. This should involve an approach that crosses traditional departmental boundaries of "health", "education", "transport" etc. In this, local agencies are often better equipped to work together than unwieldy government departments, and there is scope for a whole range of initiatives.

For example, the local NHS can be instrumental in helping to develop "health literacy" programmes in schools, including teaching children about a healthy diet. Local councils can ensure that their transport policies encourage people to walk or cycle rather than taking the car everywhere. Social support networks in the community can help to look after the elderly, and people with disabilities or mental illnesses. The media can target sexual health messages at teenagers and other key groups, whilst the Government can ensure improved access to sexual health and GUM clinics, and services for people with HIV/AIDS. Health inequalities between rich and poor areas are growing, and local authorities can be instrumental in targeting support at poorer sections of the community, and improving the quality of social housing.

For people who are living with long-term conditions and illnesses, such as diabetes, asthma, arthritis and depression, there should be a duty on the local NHS to support patients and their families in managing their illness – through self-care programmes, and enabling them to become experts in the details of their condition and the treatments and therapies available.

These initiatives fall outside the traditional remit of the traditional NHS – and there are many more issues which could be included here – but a "joined-up" approach across departments and agencies could play a vital part in preventative healthcare, which in turn would ease some of the strain on the primary care sector – GPs, dentists and hospitals alike.

CONCLUSION

The future of the NHS must not be reduced to a choice between market mania or a nostalgic yearning for a mythical golden era. While retaining the principle of a national health service, we need much more "human-sized" healthcare provision with openness about what is going on. We need more emphasis on preventative healthcare, which cuts across traditional agency boundaries and supports and encourages people to live healthier lives.

It is time to reinvent the NHS in a way that delivers top quality care in an efficient and accountable way. To do anything less would be the real betrayal of the National Health Service.

SECTION II
PRACTICE AREAS

CHAPTER 5
THE FUTURE OF MEDICINE

Dr Robert Winter

My professional life as a consultant in the NHS has been divided into two phases: first a rewarding and enjoyable and challenging 10 years spent as a physician working in a busy acute general hospital and now as a consultant and medical director of a large university teaching hospital. In both I have witnessed the remarkable professionalism and commitment that underpins the NHS but I have also seen how it is possible to improve services and I have developed an understanding of the some of the issues around this. This brief perspective, therefore, reflects my own experience working both as a 'hands on' consultant physician and also as a medical director. In looking forward I will attempt to consider what the future might hold for tomorrow's physician – qualifying in 2006 and aiming to spend her professional life first training in, and then working for the NHS – the specialist, clinical investigator and teacher of 2020.

It is important to reflect that now, perhaps more than at any time in the past 30 years for any consensus emerging amongst both the public and the major political parties as to what the core set of values in the NHS should be. Amongst these, an underlying commitment to being free at the point of delivery, a desire for universality of provision (avoidance of a two-tiered system based on ability to pay) and greater choice (whatever that may mean) is shared. The 2020 vision for the future – and the challenge for all working in the NHS – must be to take these and other ideas as they emerge and to crystallise them into a first class service that better reflects customers wishes. This should meet broader expectations of dignity, autonomy, confidentiality, prompt attention, quality of basic amenities, access to social support and choice of care providers. This will present many challenges and, if successful, will involve radical change and reconfiguration.

The huge achievements of the NHS should not be overlooked. Judged by many top-line criteria, the NHS has helped to deliver major improvements in health: life expectancy has increased by three years for every decade since 1948; cure and long-term survival in many previously fatal common malignancies is now the norm; access to, and individual faith in, high technology medicine is greater than ever before. The past few years, in particular, have seen major new investment coupled with much shorter waiting times, greatly improved emergency medical care and a coordinated approach to cancer and heart disease – through clinical networks and National Service Frameworks – with a higher proportion of patients referred for potentially curative or definitive treatments.

The NHS has also provided a unique platform for training and research and has been a catalyst for innovative biotechnology and pharmaceutical collaborations and enterprise – leading to new discovery, better treatments and wealth creation. The World Health Organisation (WHO) World Health Report 2000 ranked the UK ahead of the Germany, Sweden and the United States in terms of performance – a method of comparing how efficiently countries translate expenditures into health systems outcomes. Put simply, the NHS provided better health outcomes at a lower unit cost than the alternatives of social insurance or private insurance.

Paradoxically, although the scope of modern medicine is immeasurably greater than it was, the optimism generated by its advances seems to have evaporated. In short, 'medicine is doing better, but feeling worse'. Although individual satisfaction with treatment is often high, expressed dissatisfaction with healthcare systems is global – 70–80% of all adults in United Kingdom, Australia, Canada, New Zealand and in the United States consider that their health system needs either fundamental change or to be rebuilt completely according to The Commonwealth Fund 2001 International Health Policy Survey. No country has been successful in confronting the spiralling costs of high technology healthcare, although the NHS has arguably done this better than most other health systems.

Information (but not knowledge) about health and disease, once the exclusive preserve of doctors, is now available to everyone who has access to Google or PubMed or NHS Direct. Much of the mystique of medicine has evaporated and doctors have had to change how they see themselves. Medical professionalism and good medical care in the new millennium is being redefined in terms of a partnership between the doctor and the (expert) patient working in the context of managed health systems. Already, the vital compact that exists between doctor, patient and the state, and the environment in which doctors train and work has changed – and is poised to change further.

What, then, are the high impact, high certainties in the future NHS? Firstly – inevitably – there will be new diseases. An example of this is seen in infectious disease – the impact of HIV, human prion diseases, SARS and avian flu could not possibly have been predicted. These will be tackled with research tools the power of which would once have been considered inconceivable: within a few weeks of the SARS outbreak the responsible corona virus was identified and fully sequenced (compared with the years for the same to be achieved with HIV).

Second, there will be new discoveries – in 1980 the British National Formulary listed two anti-viral drugs – idoxuridine and amantidine – there are now 36, with effective treatments for HIV, hepatitis B and C and herpes virus infections – at a price. The last 15 years has witnessed the sequencing of the human genome, a description of human genetic variation, the development of high-throughput and accurate sequencing and genotyping technologies. During this time we have also seen the unfolding of the antibody story and the emerging scientific field of proteomics – the analysis of proteins expressed within cells. These are all complex areas that have already begun to influence clinical practice, but the potential rewards are greater still. By comparing the genes and proteins in normal and diseased cells, novel treatments of scientific and commercial importance can be discovered. The concept that differences between individuals in the effects of a treatment is due in part to a person's specific genetic make up is being reflected in the discipline of pharmacogenomics – the interaction between a pharmacological agent and a person's genome. In the future drug treatment is likely to be in part tailored to a person's genes and to the genetic profile of the individual tumour or individual infective agent – ushering in an era of personalized medicine, the aim of which will be to produce biological therapies or vaccine approaches at specific genetic and immunologic targets. The disease that will have the most significant and immediate impact by the "post-genome" research is, of course, cancer but there will be a much wider applicability across most medical specialities. Molecular/DNA based diagnostics and chip technology will be developed in bulk for routine clinical use. Imagine yourself as a physician or patient in 2020 where information about prognosis and the responses to different treatments can be predicted with accuracy at the outset, allowing integration of diagnosis with therapy. This is to ignore the potential of other high impact, low certainty new discoveries such as stem cells and nanotechnology that promise so much but have yet to deliver meaningful clinical benefits. The impact of these new discoveries on clinical practice in the future NHS and the associated cost and ethical issues will be profound.

High quality research, both basic and translational, will continue to be a key driver for improved outcomes across all specialties. The future of research is thus of fundamental importance to every physician and to every patient in the future NHS – notwithstanding the major contribution that research based industries make to a knowledge and technology-based economy. The NHS will need to position itself to attract and generate as well as to benefit from research. Investment in the clinical academic career pathway in the NHS will need to be strengthened so that the best young doctors and brilliant clinician scientists continue to be attracted. The current proposals in the Walport report, on careers in academic medicine and research, and the development of a new National Health Research Strategy, 'Best Research for Best Health', both promise to strengthen research within the NHS and are a timely reaffirmation of the importance of academic medicine and research to the future NHS.

Thirdly, the pattern of disease is also set to change. Research of the last few years has confirmed that poor health is very often the result of interplay between genetic susceptibility and lifestyle factors. One rather depressing near certainty is the fact that in future the NHS will continue to manage more disease that correlates with a high risk activity lifestyles – whether individually or collectively. Obesity is just one important example of the way in which lifestyle can profoundly alter the pattern of disease. In 1980, at around the time that I qualified as a doctor, 8% of women and 6% of men were obese – defined as having a body mass index (BMI) of greater that 30. The projected figures for 2010 are 27% women and 25% men. Assuming that current trends will continue unabated this will lead to a 54% increase in diabetes, a 28% increase in hypertension, a 18% increase in heart attack and a 5% increase in stroke. These are frightening statistics – not just in terms of the human cost but also in terms of the burden that this will place on resources in the future NHS. With 30% of people under the age of thirty being significantly overweight or obese the cost of this cohort as they present with the complications of diabetes, excess cancers, cardiovascular and cerebrovascular diseases will be unprecedented. Alcohol misuse and other drug abuse are areas where lifestyle related disease is also set to increase. Between 1987 and 2001 the UK saw an increase in cirrhosis mortality in men by over two-thirds according to WHO data and the UK now has the steepest rise in Western Europe. In its report 'Alcohol – can the NHS afford it?' the Royal College of Physicians presented evidence that up to 12% of total hospital expenditure could be accounted for by alcohol misuse. Another disease related to lifestyle, Chlamydia, a common genital infection of young, sexually active people has increased steadily since the mid-1990s and rose by 8.6% between 2003 and 2004 – with a rise of 6% in females and 12% in males. In the UK in 2004, the highest rates of Chlamydia were found among 16–19 year old females and 20–24 year old males. The complications are distressing and expensive, including infertility, ectopic pregnancy and chronic pelvic pain. There can be little doubt that the physician of 2020 will be seeing proportionally more lifestyle diseases – probably approaching epidemic proportions. The extent of the epidemic will be largely determined by the success of public health and other measures to influence high risk behaviour. A paradox is that those most likely to engage in behaviour that is associated with poor health are the group least likely to be accessed by advice campaigns. Against the general background of increases in lifestyle diseases can be set the one success story which gives hope. A combination of influences including a forty year campaign led by the Royal College of Physicians and more recently Action on Smoking and Health (ASH) and the British Lung Foundation has bought about a real public understanding of the catastrophic health consequences of smoking. This, in tandem with tax increases and legislation, has led to sustained decreases in the percentage of smokers – particularly in men where the proportion has fallen from more than half to less than a third, with a direct impact on the rates of heart attack and lung cancer in the community.

When life expectancy increases in a population it is usually accompanied by an increase in the number of years in poor health. For example, average male life expectancy in 1981 was 71 years of which 64 years were in good health; by 2001 this increased to 76 years and 67 years respectively. Thus, on average, in 2001 there were nine years of poor health at the end of life rather than seven in 1981. This trend, very familiar to health economists, is likely to place a severe burden on resources and the approach to long term conditions and care of the elderly will need to change to reflect this. The NHS of 2020 will need to have well-developed 'Expert Patient' programmes where patients with diabetes, asthma, arthritis, hypertension and other long term conditions learn to develop self-management programmes that may avoid hospital attendance and reduce visits to the GP surgery and improve outcomes. Improvements in treatment have meant that many cancers and HIV need to be viewed as long term conditions. Again, the use of computer based decision support, and advice by e-mail or by text will be needed to reduce cost and give a much more convenient and more systematic service.

Information technology enabled service improvements with an integrated paperless system of medical records will occur as the NHS 'Connecting for Health' project matures and gains in clinical engagement and ownership – despite initial difficulties. Shared e-medical records between 'primary' and 'secondary' care (terms that should have outlived their usefulness by 2020) and electronic prescribing – where checks and safeguards are built-in – together with clinical decision support will all improve patient safety. Almost certainly ever more powerful new digital imaging technologies will continue to transform diagnostic approaches and will be supported by rapid access picture archiving and storage. Taken all together, I believe that this will lead to a demand for a new approach to the way in which information is structured and delivered, so that its value is maximized as it is networked to the physician's computer in the clinic.

'Everything can be measured, and anything that can be measured can be managed' – the future NHS will need to continue to develop learning about how to use key performance indicators intelligently to produce change and service improvement. To anyone who can remember the generally dysfunctional state of the typical Accident and Emergency department 15 years ago the notion that 98% patients would be seen and treated in less than four hours would seem faintly Orwellian. Despite their many critics the successful use of targets has been one of the most powerful factors in a massive improvement in emergency care. The read-across to other areas is that simple, proven, management techniques using well-chosen key performance indicators can produce benefit – well illustrated by the Myocardial Infarction National Audit Programme (MINAP) with 'door to needle time' for clot-busting thrombolysis, giving NHS patients with heart attacks amongst the best results internationally. The important caveat is that these key performance indicators must be clinically relevant, clinically owned and, wherever possible, clinically led. The best medical care in the NHS has and will always be delivered by well-led and well-motivated clinical teams. Unsurprisingly, well-led teams have higher patient (and staff) satisfaction, better clinical outcomes and low staff turnover – a virtuous cycle. Further development of the clinical multidisciplinary team – whose minimum viable size will depend on specialty – represents the best approach to the many challenges that changes in staffing and in the patterns of work will present in the future NHS. Perhaps the most significant problem operationally in the NHS at the moment is the fragmentation of continuity of care, an overlooked aspect of quality, and the effect that this has on training and on the provision of high quality patient care. The European Working Time Directive, the move to shift working, provision for flexible training and a greater proportion of doctors taking career breaks to obtain balance between their work and their own family life are all factors that have posed a threat to the continuity of patient care. The well-led clinical team provides the best means of delivering high quality consultant-provided care in hospital, with appropriate training, support and clinical governance structures to maximize continuity and quality. In the future large hospital the principle of early triage will need to be developed, where patients are seen first by the relevant specialist team. This will be a powerful driver to the further development of larger multi-disciplinary teams.

There has been much discussion about the optimum size of hospitals, a better integration of primary and secondary care in polyclinics or community hospitals, and about the minimum viable size of each individual service required to provide safe, high quality 24/7 emergency care. As part of this debate the management of long-term conditions and the care of the elderly, including decisions around better, out-of-hospital care at the end-of-life will need to be developed in the future NHS. In parallel, a new healthcare market is emerging that will fundamentally alter the way in which healthcare is delivered – a new market that promises to change patient into customer. How will the new entrepreneur-led and clinician-led players in this new market engage with emergency care, long-term conditions, and the interface between health and social services? Or will their main role be in low risk elective surgery – and what will be their contribution to training and research? A detailed consideration of the organisational changes that this will entail is the subject of other contributions. However, it is clear that a culture of continuous revolution with multiple, rushed re-organisations can be wasteful and de-motivating – and can lead to a stop-go cycle with the unintended bipolar consequences of analysis paralysis alternating with achiever fever. Over the last 15 years the NHS has become increasingly politicised – for some time clinical decisions about an individual patient's treatment have been a legitimate currency for political debate and point scoring at the highest level. Perhaps what is now needed is a new, wiser and more integrated approach with a longer cycle of planning – it has been suggested that the successful experience of other important public sector organisations, for example the Bank of England, where a group of experienced individuals have been given freedom to act within strictly defined parameters, could have relevance to the organisation of the future NHS.

So is the future of the NHS a scenario where the elderly are living longer yet in less good health towards the end of life, the young with more ill-health related to lifestyle and all demanding access to high cost, high technology drugs and resources because they are there? Will societal values be characterised by a moral commitment to universal access to care (but not prepared to pay for it), dissatisfaction with the health system yet satisfaction with their own health care, a belief in high technology medicine and a lack of self-blame for the system's problems. This scenario is undesirable and unsustainable. Or will the future NHS see a developing scenario of greater reliance on self-care, with the focus on keeping people well and responding to demands for a more holistic approach to health, where individuals take more responsibility for healthy diet and lifestyle. This possibility is wholly compatible with high quality, science and evidence-based medical care that will be transformed by personalised medicine and by exciting new treatments and technologies. Perhaps the challenge for the future NHS will be to develop this synthesis – a more holistic, integrated approach with an emphasis on keeping people well and a service that better reflects high, but reframed, consumer expectations. This will provide a more balanced and therefore a more hopeful future – the basis of a new kind of modern NHS. If this can be achieved we may be on the cusp of a new enlightenment.

CHAPTER 6
THE FUTURE OF SURGERY

Professor Peter J Friend

The medical world is heavily influenced by tradition, much of which predates the National Health Service, and no area within medicine is more traditional than that of surgery. Medical students have always spent a disproportionate amount of time learning surgery in relation to the level of surgical knowledge that is required by most practising doctors, or the number who become surgeons (although most medical schools have now gone some way to redress this). This preponderance of surgical influence in the formative lives of prospective doctors has always been justified by the view that exposure to surgical practice provides both an education in medical method and experience in looking after seriously ill patients – and that these skills are generic. Whether or not it can be justified, the fact is that surgery has always had a strong identity within the medical world – reinforced by the presence of the Royal College of Surgeons, representing all surgical specialists and responsible for supervising their professional training.

However, the medical world, both in the UK and around the world, is at a time of radical change – traditional professional boundaries and, by implication, identities are under review. It is right, therefore, to consider in what way the practice of surgery should fit into a modern medical hierarchy.

THE CHANGING FACE OF SPECIALISATION

The development of highly technical modern medicine has led to the development of new specialties and sub-specialisation of many of the older specialties. Many patients require the integrated services of several specialists – this is seen most clearly in the recent guidelines for the organisation of cancer services in the UK, in which all cases are discussed by the 'multi-disciplinary team' – comprising medical specialists, chemotherapy specialists, radiotherapy specialists, radiologists and pathologists, as well as surgeons. Thus the surgeon – who used to direct the progress of a patient often single-handedly – is now part of a 'committee' that determines how the patient should be treated. The surgeon is usually the 'lead clinician' of the team.

It is this multi-disciplinary team that is the key to the way the health service of tomorrow will look. Specialists will work together in groups based on the diseases that they treat – so gastrointestinal surgeons will work with medical gastroenterologists and specialists in the radiology and pathology of the gastrointestinal system. Clinical teams will be increasingly system-based, cutting across traditional professional boundaries.

THE IDENTITY OF SURGERY AS A SPECIALTY

These changes lead to a number of important questions. Will the Department of Surgery no longer be a feature in the hospital of tomorrow? Will hospitals simply have operating departments to provide facilities and anaesthetic services for surgery carried out by surgeons employed in other departments? Is there any reason to retain an organisational structure that groups together individuals with widely diverse technical skills (which are largely non-interchangeable), treating patients with widely diverse conditions? Surely surgery, as a specialty will be broken down into its component parts and subsumed into the new, multidisciplinary disease-specific specialties?

There are several reasons to believe that this vision will not translate into reality and that surgery as a specialty will survive intact.

First, the issue of training: current surgical training requires a broad experience of surgery before specialisation. This is important not only because it makes for more adaptable and rounded surgeons (skills picked up in one area are invaluable in another) but also because it allows surgeons to select their chosen subspecialty on the basis of real experience.

Second, research and development: a broad view of surgical practice is important for the intellectual and technical development of surgery – cross-fertilisation between surgical specialties is vital to the lateral thinking that underpins any technical innovation. There are real concerns that the role of the surgeon might become denigrated to that of a technician – an individual highly skilled in a very limited repertoire of operative procedures, but with case selection and postoperative management of the patient carried out by other, non-surgical, doctors. Thus such radical restructuring of the system would effectively remove surgically-orientated doctors from any direct involvement in overall patient care. Indeed, at this stage, it would be possible to argue that the surgical technician would not need a medical school education. But for the operating surgeon to be a real contributor to research and innovation, he/she needs to have considerable understanding of the disease process and the broad scope of medical treatment.

Third, provision of an adaptable and responsive service: there are many instances where a surgeon must have a broad range of knowledge and skill. Emergency surgery is unpredictable and over-specialisation is potentially dangerous, particularly in small hospitals where sub-specialists cannot be available in all areas at all times. It has often been noted that the price that is paid for increasing expertise by day (as a result of sub-specialisation) is decreasing expertise by night (as specialists wrestle with problems outside their own immediate area of experience). Even in planned surgery, however, the ability to 'think outside the box' can be vital – particularly in complex or unusual cases or those in which unexpected findings occur. Breadth of training and experience are crucial under these circumstances.

Finally, following such a path goes against the grain – surgery is a generic skill. Young doctors decide first to become surgeons and later which sub-specialty to develop – and most surgeons, even after many years of specialisation, see themselves as surgeon first, specialist later. Surgeons share a vital interest in the operating theatres – for a surgeon this is the centre of the hospital with a unique culture. The fact that surgeons have more in common with each other than with other specialists is partly self-fulfilling – surgeons spend long years of training and specialist exams together; this shared experience is bonding. There is great strength in the 'camaraderie' of effective surgical departments and this is a benefit that should not be discarded lightly.

SURGERY AS A TECHNOLOGY-DRIVEN SPECIALTY

The range and scope of surgery has changed almost beyond recognition over the last forty years. Although some of the change has been due to widespread implementation of best practice – providing a uniform level of service where once it was patchy – most of the change has come as a result of technology-driven advances. These advances have been both in surgical technique and supporting developments in non-surgical areas.

Most improvements in medical practice come at a high financial price – the new technique is better for the patients but more expensive for the Health Service. However, occasionally both the patient and the Finance Department can benefit from the same advance. A good example of this is the development of laparoscopy, otherwise known as minimal access surgery or key- hole surgery.

For many years laparoscopy was the preserve of gynaecologists who became skilled in introducing a telescope into the abdominal cavity in order to make a diagnosis and carry out simple procedures – for example sterilisation by applying metal clips to the fallopian tubes. The view obtained was simply not adequate for more complex surgical procedures until high quality video technology became available in the 1980's. It became clear that, by inserting three or more instruments through separate tubes (ports) placed in the abdominal wall and inflating the abdominal cavity with carbon dioxide, it was possible to carry out much more complex procedures. This was popularised in the 1990's with the rapid spread of laparoscopic removal of the gall bladder. Previously this was a common operation that necessitated a 15–20 cm cut through the muscles of the abdominal wall and five days in hospital (or more). With the benefit of laparoscopy the patient could be discharged home the morning after surgery or even on the day of surgery – purely because there was no longer a long and painful muscle incision. This was of great benefit not only to patients who no longer feared a painful convalescence, but also to hospitals, which could provide the same service with fewer beds and less cost.

The success of laparoscopic gall bladder surgery was followed by intensive efforts to apply the same principles to other operations. Surgeons worked with the manufacturers of laparoscopic instruments to produce more and more sophisticated devices which could be deployed through a 10 or 12 mm port in the abdominal wall. As well as removing the gall bladder, it is now possible to remove the colon, the spleen, the kidney and the stomach in this way. However, the cost-benefit seen in gall bladder surgery has, to an extent, not been repeated – the cost of the complex (and usually single-use) equipment has partly negated the cost-saving of shorter hospital stays. Also, the effect of making the operation (for the patient) simpler and less painful has been to increase the demand – patients who once would have lived with painful gall stones are now referred for surgery.

This illustrates an important principle – surgical innovation generally leads to an increase in demand and overall cost. Surgical advance is expensive – as in so many areas of medicine, the pace of technological advance may not be matched by the ability of even a prosperous economy to pay for it. The next generation of minimally invasive surgery will involve robotic procedures. Whereas laparoscopic surgery involves operating from outside the body using long instruments under video-imaging, robotic surgery involves carrying out the entire operation from within the abdominal cavity using robotic arms controlled remotely by the surgeon. Such devices already exist and are in use in a small number of medical centres, but are hugely expensive to buy and operate. The cost of carrying out large-volume surgery in this way would require a major shift of resources – substantial benefits will need to be shown before this could become a reality.

Reassuringly, there are some areas in which newer therapies are not only better for patients but also less costly. A well-known example of this is kidney transplantation. Transplantation is a treatment for kidney failure which is an alternative to dialysis. Not only has it been shown to provide a much better quality of life compared to dialysis (patients feel well and live normal lives), but life expectancy is approximately double that of patients on dialysis. Although the immediate cost of a kidney transplant is substantial, the maintenance costs are much lower than continued dialysis and the long-term costs are much less.

For the most part, however, surgical advance is a sure way to increase the cost of treatment. Increasingly, cost pressures are subject to scrutiny and it is important to demonstrate overall benefit if a new surgical technique is to be implemented – this is very similar to the need to demonstrate that a new drug is better than previous drugs before it can be introduced widely. Improved efficacy in surgical techniques is, however, notoriously difficult to prove.

ASSESSMENT OF SURGICAL TECHNOLOGY

If a pharmaceutical manufacturer wishes to introduce a new drug, clinical trials have to be carried out in which some patients are given the new drug and others the best existing drug. A number of objective measures (for example blood pressure in the case of a new treatment for hypertension) are used in order to compare (consenting) patients in the two groups. It is usually possible to conceal, from both the patient and the doctor, which patient is in each group – in this way the results can then be analysed statistically without risk of bias.

If the trial involves a new operation, the situation is more compli- cated. First, it is impossible (often) to conceal from the patient or the doctor whether the new or the old operation has been done. Second, a critical factor in the outcome is the skill of the surgeon – and the surgeon is likely to prefer one procedure to the other (usually the new one). Third, the outcome measures can be very subjective (for example postoperative pain in the case of a new key-hole operation). Even the length of hospital stay can be influenced by the expectations of both patient and doctor. Also, patients are reluctant to take part in a trial of a new operation in which they might be 'randomised' – and have no control over which operation they have. Finally, surgeons gener- ally prefer to treat all their patients with a new technique when it becomes available and can be reluctant to submit patients to the old technique even in the interests of a clinical trial.

It is for these reasons that the majority of new surgical techniques have been introduced without the sort of rigorously controlled clinical trials that have been routine in the pharmaceutical industry for many years. This is likely to become a more prominent issue in the future – it will be a challenge to evaluate new technology effectively to ensure safety for patients and cost-effectiveness for the health care provider.

SURGERY AND ALLIED TECHNOLOGIES

Although in each surgical specialty there are technical frontiers, in many cases the benefit surgical treatment is limited by non-surgical factors. For example, the relatively disappointing outcome following surgery for many cancers is because the disease has often spread outside the original site before diagnosis. Major advances in cancer surgery are therefore likely to be in combination with other types of treatment – including new chemotherapy drugs, the use of gene therapy or the use of anti-tumour vaccines.

In the field of transplantation, technical issues are no longer the major cause of failure – control of the immune response to a foreign (transplanted) organ remains the largest challenge. It is likely that, in the medium term, it will be possible to induce 'immunological tolerance' – whereby the patient's immune system is reprogrammed to treat the transplanted organ as self rather than foreign. This will require a solution from basic immunology applied to a surgical problem.

Anaesthesia is one of the key factors in the development of modern surgery and the ability to operate safely for long periods on seriously ill patients is fundamental to current practice. Despite extraordinary advances, very little is known about the way in which anaesthetic drugs work. We should anticipate continued advance in the ability of anaesthetists to support more and more complex operations, whilst allowing rapid recovery immediately afterwards.

Advances in radiology have been the most spectacular of any in recent decades. As a result of a variety of imaging technology (CT scanning, nuclear magnetic resonance, ultrasound, radioisotope scanning), the degree of information available to the surgeon is vastly greater. This enables better case selection and complex operations to be planned in a way that was never possible. It is clear that this is a trend that will continue.

SURGERY AND CHANGING TECHNOLOGY

Radiology will impact on the future of surgery in many ways – many procedures that once required open surgery will be carried out under radiological guidance. Already many cardiovascular operations have been supplanted by radiological techniques – these include many patients who once would have undergone coronary artery bypass surgery and now undergo placement of a 'stent' to open the narrowed artery – avoiding the need for an operation. This same technique is also being used in other arteries – the practice of cardiac and vascular surgery is already changing as a result.

This has important implications and illustrates the need for surgery to adapt and for its practitioners to be adaptable. Conditions that were once common indications for surgery, may be eradicated, or treated successfully without surgery – such as duodenal ulcers which are now mostly treated by drugs. These changes can occur quickly, and surgeons should be capable and prepared to learn new skills and, above all, embrace change rather than resist it. This reinforces the need for broad-based surgical training – so that surgeons are capable of responding to a changing environment.

SURGERY AND TRAINING

The training of surgeons, previously the sole responsibility of the Royal Colleges of Surgeons, is now under the overall jurisdiction of the newly founded Postgraduate Medical Education and Training Board. It is likely, however, that the Royal Colleges will continue to run postgraduate training, with responsibility for the challenging task of ensuring that the supply of trained surgeons is tailored to the need and with the correct mix of specialty training. Demand for specialists is notoriously difficult to predict – it is influenced by many factors including healthcare funding, new technology and political initiatives. Added to this, the impact of the European Working Time Directive (which will impose a maximum of 48 hours work per week) will have a serious impact on the lives of both trainees and trained surgeons. Current (interim) legislation has produced a major reduction in the clinical exposure of junior doctors and the way in which surgeons are trained is changing as a result. The traditional system of apprentice-ship is becoming replaced with a more active training process to enable a surgeon to achieve competence with less than half the clinical contact time of his/her predecessor.

SURGERY AND REGULATION

Surgeons can look forward to a future in which their performance is more closely scrutinised than ever before. In recent years a number of highly public cases have illustrated the risks in allowing surgeons to practice for many years without a formal means of monitoring the results of their surgery. This is a principle that applies to all doctors, but the results of surgical underperformance are much the most obvious and easiest to define. Already hospitals are subjected to 'league table' comparisons of many parameters and the patient death rates of individual cardiac surgeons are available.

Although transparency is clearly a good principle, the use of a simplistic measure of outcome could damage the service and cause unnecessary anxiety to many patients. For example, it is only useful to compare death rates after surgery if the risk factors have been taken into account. Crude death rates can be extremely misleading – one hospital or one surgeon may be the best in the country but if the most difficult and highest risk cases are referred, then the mortality may still be above the national average. If crude mortality becomes the marker by which surgeons are judged, then there will be a natural tendency to refuse to take on high-risk or complex cases. This would be very much to the disadvantage of patients.

Clearly, the public needs to be assured that all surgeons are subjected to regular appraisal of their ability, but a much more sophisticated method needs to be devised than that currently being proposed.

SURGERY AND SAFETY

Hospitals are remarkably dangerous places and patients face a range of hazards too numerous to list. The challenge within the specific area of surgery is to carry out a relatively complex process, which involves a sequence actions delivered by many different health-care staff, without error. There are many points in the patient pathway at which error potentially causes serious harm. Some of these have been addressed effectively; for example, errors of patient identification are relatively few – it is very unlikely that the wrong patient will get as far as the operating theatre before the error is detected. Other risk points are much less well protected.

Increasing awareness of the frequency and consequences (including financial cost) of hospital error has stimulated current interest in the area of hospital safety. The medical world in general and surgery in particular can learn a great deal about safety procedures from the airline industry, which has been strikingly successful in reducing the risks to very large numbers of passengers in what is intrinsically a hazardous environment.

SURGERY IN PRIMARY, SECONDARY AND TERTIARY CARE

As surgery becomes part of a complex multidisciplinary team, there is increasing need for a logical, stratified approach for the delivery of surgical services to the population. Whereas once, most hospitals did most types of operation, there is now a move to centralisation of more major surgery. This ensures that patients undergoing rare or complex operations will be looked after by a team that is familiar with all aspects of the treatment. It is now recognised that good results need more than just an excellent surgeon and that all members of the team must deliver effectively.

The health service of the future will provide surgery at three levels. Very minor procedures will be dealt with at the primary care level (by general practitioners). Other minor procedures (e.g. hernia repairs), intermediate procedures (e.g. gall bladder surgery) and commonly occurring major procedures (e.g. colon cancer) will be treated at both district general and tertiary referral hospitals. Some of this work will also be carried out in the independent treatment centres, recently established. Complex and/or rare procedures will be centralised in tertiary referral hospitals.

This level of central planning is already having an effect on cancer surgery – for example, any hospital that offers a service for pancreatic cancer surgery now has to demonstrate that the catchment population of that service is more than two million. Also, regulations are being introduced to ensure that all patients are treated according to national guidelines and that the quality of the outcome is audited properly. These are all changes to ensure that patients anywhere in the country can expect to receive an appropriate and consistent standard of care.

CONCLUSIONS

The surgical service of the future will be a much more closely managed organisation than at present. Surgeons will operate in larger teams surrounded by specialist colleagues in allied areas. Many procedures will be multidisciplinary (perhaps combining a surgeon and a radiologist), and long-term care will involve non-surgical specialists. Innovation will be controlled and new technology will be subjected to rigorous evaluation before widespread implementation. The repertoire of the individual surgeon will be less than before and his/her individual performance will be monitored carefully. In many respects running a surgical programme in the future will resemble running an airline – with more planning, more safety checks and regular revalidation of all team members. If properly implemented, this will provide a better, safer service for patients and a more cost-effective service for the provider.

CHAPTER 7

THE FUTURE OF GENERAL PRACTICE AND PRIMARY CARE

Dr Mayur Lakhani

This article does not necessarily reflect the policy of the Council of the Royal College of General Practitioners.

INTRODUCTION

What will the NHS look like in the future? There is no doubt, as this book shows, that the health service will continue to be the subject of concerted policy development, debate and change. This will affect all our futures: public, patients and doctors. Developing an efficient, effective and responsive health care is a world wide pre-occupation of governments and think tanks. The stakes are high: this should not be seen as some sort of academic debate about how best to configure a health service – this is a serious issue about the health and well being of patients. A serious issue that deserves a serious discussion. One finding is clear in most analyses: a system that has a primary care orientation is favoured [1].

Good general practice must continue to be an essential component of the future NHS, as it is now. But I see a greater role for general practice. Whilst great strides have been made in the quality of general practice, the full potential of general practice, in improving health and well being of patients, has not been realised. This requires a step change in thinking by recognising the potential of primary care to tackle strategic issues such as health inequalities, quality and patient safety.

DEFINITION OF GENERAL PRACTICE AND PRIMARY CARE

Primary care has been defined as: "the first level contact with people taking action to improve health in a community." In a system with a gatekeeper, all initial (non-emergency) consultations with doctors, nurses or other health staff are termed primary. Care as opposed to secondary health care or referral services.[2] International comparisons of healthcare systems show beyond doubt the success of the primary care in the United Kingdom[1]

Within the NHS general practice is a central component of primary care. General practice is defined as: "an academic and scientific discipline, with its own educational content, research base and clinical activity, orientated to primary care and built on fundamental principles."[3]

FACTS AND FIGURES ABOUT GENERAL PRACTICE

The Audit Commission in 2002 found that general practice is a well-used and valued public service. Eight out of ten people visit their general practitioner (GP) every year and 99 per cent of the population are registered with a GP.[4]

The average number of GP consultations per person per year (UK) (in 2003) is shown below:

– 3 visits per year for men
– 5 visits per year for women
– 4 visits per person per year

Average Practice List Size 2004, in the UK is 5,995 patients. There are 10,465 practices in the UK and 62,733, 945 patients are registered with a GP.[5]

In 2004, the number of GPs (UK) was 41,397. The number of practice nurses was 12,927. In 2003, the number of GP Consultations (UK) was a staggering 259,000,000. The average medical practitioner makes 6,958 consultations a year.[6]

WHAT IS SPECIAL ABOUT GENERAL PRACTICE?

In the UK, general practice has several distinctive features.

- A registered list system (GPs responsible for defined groups of patient in a geographical community)
- Life long medical record (mainly electronic now)
- Holistic and Team based care (nurses, receptionists, new roles such as health care assistants and physicians assistants)
- Comprehensive care – (most problems being dealt with in primary care with short term referral as needed)
- Gate keeping (GPs refer to consultants)
- First contact care (patient seeking help for undifferentiated problems)
- Care for a well defined population (which allows preventative treatment such as immunisation and screening)
- Trusting doctor-patient relationship focussed on personal care
- Confidentiality

The essence of general practice is the doctor-patient relationship. This has been captured succinctly by Ian McWhinney:[7]

- Unconditional and open-ended commitment to one's patients
- Defined in the relationship with a person as opposed to a condition/disease
- Relationship is prior to content
- Commitment to patients before we know what their illness will be

The issue of the relationship between a doctor and patient is all important. Patients value continuity and interpersonal care. This value may become more necessary as complexity in health care increases. Patients do not like having to constantly repeat information to different health care professionals. In the future, I am clear that the lynchpin of an effective and efficient NHS will be relationship based care, with primary health care teams responsible for a defined and registered group of patients. The primary care system of the future will encourage relational continuity and performance measures of it[8] – this is important because optimum person focussed care may take between 2 to 5 years of a doctor – patient relationship to build.

A key aspect is the care of older people – particularly those with multiple medical conditions – referred to co-morbidity. Here good primary care can make all the difference. The unique skills of a GP are dealing with uncertainty and managing co-morbidity – the simultaneous presence of apparently unrelated conditions. Deprived communities have a greater incidence of co-morbidity problems. With an aging population the burden of co-morbidity is likely to increase. The future GP role in the management of co-morbidity will be to operate at a high biomedical level focussing on diagnosis, prescribing, and co-ordination of care including mediation between specialists. The care of children also forms an important aspect of general practice.

WHY DO PEOPLE SEE THEIR GPS?

It is easy to produce a list of the top twenty reasons or so why patients consult a GP. However it is important to remember that in many instances the patient does not have a clear cut reason for consulting. The task of the doctors is to uncover the reason(s) for the consultation so that the therapeutic endeavours can be focussed. Often the patient may be unaware of the real reasons for consulting as this depends on a complex series of factors. The tasks of the consultation[9] can be summarised as:

- Discover the reason for presentation,
- Offer ongoing care e.g. chronic disease management
- Promote healthy living
- Modify health seeking advice.

The Royal College of General Practitioners promotes patient centred consultations in the training of GP registrars and recommends that GPs become adept in the consultation process. This is routinely assessed in the examination of the Membership of the Royal College of General Practitioners (MRCGP). This gives an opportunity to practice evidence based medicine in patient centred consultations involving shared decision making.

WHAT ARE THE CURRENT PROBLEMS?

Whilst there is no doubt that general practice is valued and trusted by the public, achieving consistently 70–80% satisfaction rating, there are increasing concerns about the accessibility and responsiveness of GP practices. It is a common concern – inability to book appointments in advance and also not being able to access GPs out of hours. The new contract for GPs introduced in 2004 brought in a quality and outcomes framework that reward achievement for delivering evidencing based targets in a variety of chronic diseases and rewarding patient experience. In the same contract GPs were allowed to opt out of twenty four responsibility for care, with PCTs running the out of hours services. It is considered by some members of the public, and some GPs, that this development has been damaging for general practice – the routine service being available only from 8:30 to 18:30. However, in some areas GPs are actively involved in leading urgent care systems and play a pivotal role in provision (Agnelo Fernandez-personal communication).

The problems faced by general practitioners include fragmentation of care, the need for improved support and communication between primary and secondary care, and a desire for longer consultation times.

These issues were major factors in the UK government bringing forward proposals for making general practice more responsive in a White Paper published in January 2006.

THE WHITE PAPER ON CARE IN THE COMMUNITY

The Department of Health published a health and social care white paper called *Our Care, Our Health, Our Say*.[10] This is a significant document that is aimed at reshaping the NHS by transferring services from hospitals to the community. It also aims to: empower patients; integrate health and social care provision; focus on prevention and health promotion; emphasise co-ordinated and streamlined services and to bring about the development of general practitioner services. This direction change has been widely welcomed although there are concerns about the implementation of the proposals, capacity issues – with an estimated shortage of 10000 GPs and the risk of fragmentation with multiple providers.

HOW SHOULD PRIMARY CARE BE ORGANISED IN THE FUTURE?

The potential is there for improvements – we put forward a model predicting the shape of primary care in 2015.[11] In this model (*Figure 1*) we suggest the idea of community networks. Practice teams

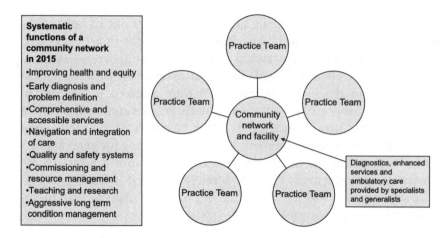

Figure 1: Community Networks: A model of organisation of primary care in the future and the key functions

will work in networks that will be actively managed organisations with strong systems of leadership and governance. The functions of the networks will be to ensure quality of care, support clinical behavioural change, monitor resource use, and commission care. The networks will enable enhanced access to health care particularly out of hours or for unscheduled care. In this model GPs may also have patients in hospital with specialists and generalists working closer together within clinical care pathways. We put forward the idea that acute hospitals are for seriously ill patients or for specialised procedures. Many out-patients clinics that currently take place in hospitals can be safely moved to the community if done in a supported and managed way. Examples include dermatology, and musculoskeletal disorders. Of course proper x-ray facilities and clinic facilities are needed. Many patients need to go to hospital now that could be managed more appropriately in the community – take the example of someone with a shoulder problem who needs an injection – this can be given by a trained physiotherapist or a GP, many of whom do this already. The model is based on values such as relationship based care and GPs would be central to patient care particularly to navigate and co-ordinate care.

This is important, as at one stage life was simple – there were GP practices and hospitals – basically two tiers. Now the NHS is much more complex with many interfaces and patients having several points of entry and provision of care: interfaces include GP practice, nurse triage, out-of-hours co-op, walk in centres, A&E, NHS direct,

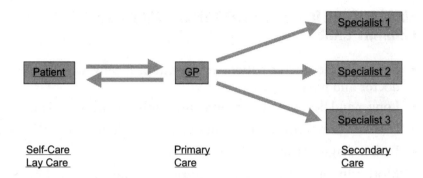

Self-Care   Primary   Secondary
Lay Care   Care   Care

Figure 2:   Primary Care Orientation – the preferred model * adapted
with acknowledgements to Professor Chris Van Wheel

alternative primary care providers, GPs with specialist interests,
intermediate care and hospital care.

Gate keeping – or navigation of the patient journey which is a modern
description of the gate keeping function is vital in the NHS and is
depicted in Figure 2.

PLATINUM LEVEL OF QUALITY IN GENERAL PRACTICE

There will be exceptional levels of quality and safety of care in general
practices working at a 'platinum level' (i.e. beyond the gold standard),
focussed on a patient's perspective.

EDUCATION, TEACHING AND TRAINING

Let us not forget the major role that GP practices play in preparing
tomorrow's doctors. Up to one third of GP practice are involved in
teaching undergraduate medical student and this number is likely to
rise. But much more than that we have to look at training nurses and
therapists and other grades. 90% of the work of the NHS is done in
the NHS. I would prefer practices to formally link up to a medical
school and university in their area to foster teaching training and
research. This is especially important as in order to give more time to
patients in the consultation, we need more general practitioners.

SOME FUTURE DEVELOPMENTS THAT I WOULD LIKE TO SEE IN PRIMARY CARE

- Maintain the doctor-patient relationship, ideally with a named doctor and nurse
- Longer and flexible consultation times with patients say 15 minutes
- Focus on prevention, health and well being including mental health
- Earlier diagnosis and problem solving
- More support for patients in information, decision making and following treatments
- Strong systems for quality (Platinum level quality)
- Integrated primary health care teams – at the moment sometimes care is provided by the employer is and not the best skills of the person
- Better communication between hospitals and GP practices
- More tests and procedures, and services in primary care
- Better care and access particularly for urgent problems
- Strong general practice services in deprived areas
- Sexual health services to be provided in GP services
- Patients should always have: a choice of seeing a GP, choice of seeing a named GP and choice of registering with preferred practice.[12]
- The GP as the navigator (as opposed to the gatekeeper)
- Improving management of co-morbidity which is found more in deprived communities.

SOME FUTURE DEVELOPMENTS THAT WOULD BE OF CONCERN TO ME

- If the NHS charged people to see a GP (this would disadvantage poor people)
- If the NHS allowed patients unfettered, direct access to specialists (this has a risk of reducing efficiency, cause fragmentation and reduce overall quality)
- If registration with a practice was compromised (a key principle of family medicine that allows for planning care for well defined

populations), allowing access to care from any facility without registration

- If patients were categorised into their diseases and conditions that providers would then compete for
- If hospitals started providing primary care
- If there was too much specialisation in general practice – first and foremost the role of a GP is to see undifferentiated presentations.

CONCLUSION

Good GPs will be essential to ensure an efficient and effective health care service. Generalists are important in a health service.

The key functions of primary care are diagnosis and problem definition, supporting and enabling patients, ensuring quality and safety of care, health promotion, gate-keeping and navigation to other services, co-ordination of care particularly for patients with co-morbidity, reducing health inequalities and engaging with communities. It is my strong opinion that the essence of general practice, based on relationships and a longitudinal commitment to whole person medicine, is not only an enduring feature of the philosophy of primary care but also central to a healthy and functioning society that values caring and humanity. Although the future is uncertain, we can be sure that people will still get sick, or think they may be sick, and then they will value care from a doctor they know, and who knows them.

REFERENCES

1. Starfield B. The Effectiveness of Primary Healthcare. In Lakhani M (Ed.), *A Celebration of General Practice* (pp. 19–36). Oxford: Radcliffe Medical Press Ltd, 2003.
2. European Observatory on Health Systems and Policies webpage. Glossary Entry for Primary Health Care. www.euro.who.int/ observatory/Glossary/TopPage?phrase = primary + health + care
3. World Organisation of Family Doctors. *The European Definition of General Practice/Family Medicine* Europe: WONCA, 2002. www.euract.org/html/pap04102.shtml
4. Source; *A Focus on General Practice in England* Audit Commission, 2002.

5. *Statistics for General Medical Practitioners in England: 1994–2004.* London: DoH; 2004.
6. 17th edition (2005–2006) of the *Compendium of Health Statistics* published by the Office of Health Economics).
7. McWhinney, IR. The essence of general practice. In Lakhani M (ed). *A Celebration of General Practice.* Abingdon: Radcliffe Medical Press; 2003. p1–18.
8. Continuity of Care. Paper SDO/13b/2001. http://www.sdo.lshtm.ac.uk/continuityofcare.htm SDO/13b/2001
9. Stott NC, Davis RH. J R Coll Gen Pract. 1979 Apr; 29 (201):201–5. The exceptional potential in each primary care consultation.
10. White Paper. *Our Health, Our Care, Our Say,* is available at www.dh.gov.uk.
11. Lakhani M, Baker M. Visions of primary care in 2015. Good general practitioners will continue to be essential *BMJ* 2006;332:41–43 (7 January).
12. Baker R. The Clinical Observer: on the up or over the hill? *Br J Gen Pract* 2005; 55: 468–71.

CHAPTER 8
EMERGENCY MEDICINE: PAST, PRESENT AND FUTURE

Mr Jim Wardrope and Dr Alastair McGowan

INTRODUCTION

Emergency medicine will be one of the cornerstones of the future National Health Service. The specialty recently changed its name from Accident and Emergency Medicine but still "casualty" is often used, a trend kept alive by the popular BBC television programme. Since its creation 30 years ago, emergency medicine has been at the forefront of change and innovation in the delivery of care. The pace of change has accelerated over the past 5 years. New investment and new ways of working have lead to one of the successes in improving access and timeliness of care for patients. Yet the future holds many challenges and uncertainties.

THE SCOPE OF THE EMERGENCY MEDICINE

Emergency Medicine is at the sharp end of NHS care. In England, over 13 *million* patients will visit an Emergency Department this year, equivalent to almost one quarter of the population. Emergency Medicine manages a huge spectrum of illness. 5%–10% of patients will have a potentially life threatening problem, often requiring treatment in the resuscitation room. 30–40% will have significant illness or injury needing admission to hospital or investigation to exclude serious illness. Approximately 50% of the work is so called "minor injury or illness" but from the patient perspective, they need a timely and effective service. Some of these "minor problems" can cause significant disability and even mortality if not properly assessed. Our work requires knowledge of all the major braches of medicine.

25% of our patients are children. 20–30% will require admission to a hospital bed. Emergency Medicine departments have major responsibilities in the response to major disasters. Some departments are very active in out of hospital care. The Emergency Department is one of the most popular areas for clinical training for doctors from many specialties.

However Emergency Medicine can only ever be part of the Emergency Care System. This includes primary care, community care services, the ambulance service, NHS Direct and the other hospital specialities.

A BRIEF HISTORY

The management of the sudden illness and injury is as old as medicine. It is only relatively recently that a specific specialty was formed whose expertise lay in the assessment and early treatment of the acutely ill. Before the 1960s, most "casualty" departments were staffed by junior doctors with little of no supervision or training. Two very influential reports the Platt[1] report and the Bruce[2] report highlighted the need for training, expertise and leadership. "Accident and Emergency Departments" were created and consultants appointed in A&E Medicine in 1975. The specialty has grown from those first 25 appointments to over 700 consultants in England in 2005. At the same time, the specialty has flourished in the USA, Canada and Australasia.[3]

In the late 1990s the NHS plan highlighted A&E as a priority area for modernisation and growth. In 2001 Reforming Emergency Care[4] set out the goals for modernisation of the service. The specialty has changed a great deal in the past five years with unprecedented growth in investment and staffing.

THE CURRENT SITUATION

In England there are about 200 Emergency departments. These range in size from departments who might see less than 100 patients per day to those that might see 300–400 patients per day (120,000 new patients per year). According to government statistics 98% of patients are treated and discharged or admitted within 4 hours of arrival.[3] This represents a transformational change in the timeliness of treatment for patients. In spite of a 10% increase in total attendances and a 20%

increase in the numbers of these patients who are ill enough to require hospital admission, patients were seen, treated and left the department much more quickly (*Tables 1 and 2*).

Period	Number of attendances	% not admitted/discharged within 4 hours
Q2 2002/03	3,096,000	23%
Q2 2005/6	3,403,000	2%

Table 1 Number of attendances to major emergency departments and % of patients not seen treated and admitted/discharged within 4 hours of arrival.[5]

Period	Number of admissions	% not admitted within 4 hours
Q2 2001/02	539,000	13%
Q2 2005/6	701,000	1%

Table 2 Number of admissions to hospital through the emergency department and time delay from decision to admit to leaving the ED.[5]

This change has been brought about by a number of different mechanisms:

- Increased investment: £100 million pounds was spent on modernising the often out of date "casualty" departments.
- Markedly increased revenue and staffing for emergency departments.
- 100% increase in consultants in recent years.
- 50% increase in Specialist registrars over the past 3 years.
- The widespread use of nurses to see and treat certain types of patients such as minor injuries.
- More senior doctors supervising clinical care.

In addition working practices have changed. Staff are targeted at different "streams" of patients so that the patients with less serious problems do not have to wait while the more serious are managed.

Emergency medicine remains at the forefront of training in acute care. Research in the specialty is growing but is still very under resourced compared to other specialties.

In summary, Emergency Medicine in 2006 is a vibrant, exciting and growing area of patient care. Given the right conditions there is no reason why this should not continue.

THE CHALLENGES FOR THE FUTURE

The trends of the past and projections for the future allow us to map the main challenges. The numbers of patients attending have grown very significantly from 3,096.000 in the period 2002-2003, to 3,403,000 in 2005-2006 (*see Table 1* above). Not only have the numbers grown but a larger proportion of patients requiring hospital admission are now seen and assessed in the Emergency Department (*see Table 2* above).

HOW HAS THIS HAPPENED?

There has been a great public health success in improving life expectancy and in the treatment of many common diseases. There are many more, older and very elderly people living at home. Older patients are vulnerable to episodes of ill health. Modern society with its geographical and social mobility results in increasing numbers of the elderly living on their own with no readily available family support. A minor fall or minor illness may tip the balance in their ability to live at home.

The success in the management of patients with heart disease and chest disease has increased the numbers of patients living with these problems. These very common diseases are subject to periodic exacerbations that require hospital investigation or treatment.

Primary care has always provided a great deal of the front line emergency care and much of this work is still carried out by family doctors. However there have been major changes to the delivery of primary care, firstly the move away from an individual practice based care of emergencies to "co ops" or deputising service care of emergencies, often with significant amounts of telephone triage. This coupled to recent changes in the GP contract, have lead to a perception of problems of access to primary care for urgent consultations. The recent White Paper[6] seeks to address this problem and to improve access.

Challenges for the future

- Increasing numbers of patients
- Increasing numbers of patients with complex medical problems
- Increasing demand for better quality of care
- More elderly patients living at the margins of safety in the community
- Problems in staffing specialist services in smaller hospitals
- Increasing need to supervise doctors in training
- Shift in the care of emergency problems from primary care
- Need to increase the evidence base in emergency care
- Reduced growth in NHS finances

Changes in hours of work for junior doctors have caused problems in staffing in some specialties in smaller hospitals. This had lead to a tension between the need to preserve local services and the need to provide full specialist services.

Changes in junior doctor training and public expectations have created demands for more direct care by trained doctors.

Over the past 4 years the NHS has seen real growth in resources. The outlook for the next 5 years is less certain. There will not be the same growth. There is evidence that demands are even now outstripping capacity and resources. The current level of success in emergency care is fragile. Hospitals are still operating at or near maximum capacity. Success has only been achieved by a number of extra-ordinary measures to improve throughput. Extra staff have been employed, especially to cover busy periods such as weekends, nights and Bank holidays. To remove the management focus from emergency care would result in a swift return to the days of queues of trolleys on hospital corridors and long waits for minor injury care.

THE FUTURE OF EMERGENCY MEDICINE

Emergency Medicine will lie at the core of the future emergency care system. This will require continuing adaptation to meet the changing needs of patients and services that serve them.[7]

FORMING AND LEADING EMERGENCY CARE NETWORKS

Emergency Medicine is the specialty best placed to advise and lead the emergency care networks of the future. Emergency care should be viewed as a continuum of care from the community through intermediate care to secondary and tertiary care. Over the last 7 years, a number of initiatives have been started to try and reduce the demand on Emergency Departments. While these services deal with large numbers of patients, they have not stopped the increase in demand on Emergency Departments. This may be partly due to a lack of cohesion and common goals.

The concept of the emergency care network is to provide leadership and direction to provide the most appropriate level of care for the acutely ill or injured patient. Patients would like this care to be delivered as near to their homes. Good primary care and local minor injury/illness units can fulfil this role. This is one of the main recommendations of the White Paper, "Our health, our care, our say. A new direction for commissioning services".[6] However the most severely ill and injured will require a level of facilities and expertise that cannot be provided in every locality. Neurosurgery, interventional cardiology, cardiothoracic surgery, plastic surgery are examples of "tertiary services" that require expensive facilities and concentration of expertise to achieve the best outcomes. Patients have always had to travel to access these services. In the future even the secondary level services of general surgery, orthopaedics, paediatrics, ear nose and throat surgery and ophthalmology may not have a 24 hour presence in some district general hospitals. The challenge for emergency care networks will be to provide the systems of care to allow the assessment, early management and appropriate transfer for patients whose needs cannot be met by local services.

There are great opportunities for Emergency Medicine to lead the creation of co-ordinated systems of out of hours primary care, intermediate care, the ambulance service and community resources.

INCREASING THE NUMBERS OF TRAINED EMERGENCY PHYSICIANS: MORE SENIOR DOCTOR PRESENCE IN EMERGENCY DEPARTMENTS

The volume of complex cases arriving in the Emergency Departments requires greater availability of experienced doctors. In the past an emergency department might have only two or three consultants who could provide leadership and would provide an on call service and attend to the needs of the most seriously ill patients. At present many departments employ between 4 to 8 consultants. They often provide clinical presence in the evenings and for part of the weekend. The College of Emergency Medicine recommends that senior doctors should be present in the Emergency Department (ED) 24 hours per day. At present, there are not enough trained doctors to achieve this goal. Numbers of doctors in training for Emergency Medicine have increased by 50% over the past few years and further expansion is recommended by the College and the Department of Health Workforce Planning Team. By 2015 we hope to have enough trained doctors to provide consultant presence in the ED for 18 hours per day, 365 days per year.

WORKING WITH AND ADVISING NURSES, EMERGENCY CARE PRACTITIONERS AND MEDICAL CARE PRACTITIONERS

One of the key elements of the NHS Plan and Reforming Emergency Care[7] was that other professional staff should be encouraged to expand their training and expertise to asses and treat patients who would traditionally be seen by doctors. Emergency Medicine has been spearheaded the adoption of such roles. Emergency Nurse Practitioners (ENP) care for large numbers of patients with minor injury, up to 20% of the caseload in some cities. Other nurses have gained expertise in the management of chest pain or of suspected deep vein thrombosis. There are a few nurse consultants. Such roles will expand in the future. Just as Emergency physicians were involved in the planning, education and advising ENP services, we would see a future key role in assisting the development of Emergency/Medical Care Practitioners.

One element of these developments must be the setting of standards of competence and setting up systems to ensure competence. Emergency Medicine has been at the forefront of developing robust competency based examinations and we feel we have much to offer in helping other professional groups.

WORKING WITH OTHER MEDICAL SPECIALTIES, ESPECIALLY PRIMARY CARE, ACUTE MEDICINE AND ANAESTHESIA/CRITICAL CARE

Throughout this article we have stressed the need for all parts of the emergency care system to work in harmony. It is increasingly likely that in some of the more remote parts of emergency care networks, doctors will have to provide cover across specialty boundaries for emergency cases. Initiatives are forming that include all the competences required for the care of the ill patient. Emergency medicine is working with other Colleges to try and create training programmes that ensure experience and training that will result in the doctors having the skills they need for the best care of the acutely ill patient.

ADVANCING THE SCIENCE OF EMERGENCY CARE THOUGH RESEARCH

A great deal of the work in emergency medicine is based on little published evidence. Fortunately much of the treatment we give is self evident, for example the provision of pain relief to some-one in pain does not require a study. However what might require study is the best methods of pain relief in different clinical circumstances. Emergency Departments have great potential for clinical research. The collaboration of emergency departments in large multi centre trials has the capacity to create world class research. However we do need to expand the academic base of the specialty. There are few professorial departments of emergency medicine. Funding is hard to secure. However the number of trained academic emergency physicians is growing but they do need opportunities and funding to flourish.

HOW DO YOU TRAIN IN EMERGENCY MEDICINE?

After two years general professional training, doctors will enter specialist training. This consists of experience of emergency medicine, acute medicine, anaesthesia/ critical care/ paediatric emergency medicine and musculo-skeletal medicine during the first three years of training. The last three years of training are in emergency medicine departments. There are two examinations, the Membership which tests mainly clinical knowledge, skills and attitudes to an intermediate level. The Fellowship examination tests a wide range of clinical, educational, academic and management skills at an advanced level. Both exams include measurement of ability in communication, decision making and team work and the ability to think about the ethical dimensions of caring for patients with complex problems.

SUMMARY

Emergency Medicine is a young energetic and growing specialty. Huge numbers of patients attend emergency departments. They are "open all hours" and provide a vital safety net for the ill, injured and those who may have difficulty in accessing health care.

Emergency care has undergone a transformational change over the past five years. This has required a great deal of management effort and focus on the major problems that were embedded in previous ways of working of the whole of the emergency care system. These changes have shown the importance of all parts of the system working together. They have shown different ways of working can make a difference to the timeliness of patient care. Resources have been required and more will be required to underpin the continuing success of the changes. Emergency medicine will remain the core at the heart of the emergency care system.

REFERENCES

1. Platt H. *Report Of The Standing Medical Advisory Committee, Accident And Emergency Services*. London: HMSO, 1962
2. Joint Consultants Committee (Chairman: Sir John Bruce). Report Of A Joint Working Party, 1971.
3. Sakr M, Wardrope J. Casualty, accident and emergency or emergency medicine, the evolution. *Emer Med J* 2000;17:314–319.
4. A&E Quality statistics. Department of Health, London. www.dh.gov.uk/PublicationsAndStatistics
5. *Reforming Emergency Care*. Department of Health, London. 2001
6. *Way Ahead 2005*. British Association for Emergency Medicine and the College of Emergency Medicine. London 2005.
7. *Our heath, our care, our say: a new direction for commissioning services*. HM Government and Department of Health. London 2006.

CHAPTER 9
FUTURE OF GERIATRIC MEDICINE

Professor Peter Crome

INTRODUCTION

The increase in life expectancy that has been seen over the last 100 years or so has been a triumph for humankind. Worldwide, the number of people over the age of 60 is set to double in the next 20 years. The majority of this increase will occur in the developing world. In the United Kingdom the increase will largely be seen in the over-75 age group. It must now be regarded as normal to live well into ones 80s with death before this being regarded as premature. These demographic changes are the result of general public health measures, better access to health care of a higher standard, improved education as well as socio-economic factors. However, in contrast to these health gains, it tends to be the negative aspects of the ageing that make the headlines – the crisis in pensions, the extra costs for caring for older people and the "drain and burden" of the increased demands that are made on the health service. Although older people are reaching retirement age fitter and able to play an important and developmental role in society, it is an unavoidable fact that most chronic illnesses increase in prevalence with age as does the likelihood of developing a disability. This in turn leads to the need for some type of support, be it at home from family, carers or in alternative accommodation. It is against this background that geriatricians and their associated health care teams of nurses and allied health professionals, seek to ensure that older people are not discriminated against in terms of access and quality of health care.

THE SUCCESS OF GERIATRIC MEDICINE

The United Kingdom was the first country in the world to establish geriatric medicine as a recognised medical specialty. The British Geriatrics Society was formed in 1948, the same year as the National Health Service, and has steadily grown ever since. Today, geriatric medicine is the largest specialty within the Royal College of Physicians of London with over 1000 Consultants nation-wide. This contrasts with the situation in many other countries where specialist services for older people are patchy and often non-existent. For example, in Canada last year, only one new Geriatrician graduated from their training programme; in the UK it was 90! In recent times there has been the realisation of the importance of the comprehensive geriatric assessment, being the core activity of the older person's multi-disciplinary team. Acting on the findings of such assessments will reduce length of stays, improve clinical outcomes thus reducing future demand and improving the overall functional efficiency of the secondary care system. Put another way, getting it right for older people, makes it easier to offer high quality services for all.

Geriatricians have played the major role in the development of services for older people and have subjected them to rigorous evaluation and proved their benefits. The development of specialist services in falls, stroke units, and rehabilitation for older people who have suffered fractures, have all been led by geriatricians. They have now been accepted as models for the provision of treatment both in this country and elsewhere in the world. Such developments are characterised by mulitdisciplinarity and involvement of carers alongside links with community services. Although, by no means without their own problems, they have resulted in genuine health gains and improvements in care. For example, on my first ward round as a consultant, I found patients tied to chairs or tipped back in "Buxton Chairs", toilets had no doors and bathing was undertaken communally. These gross insults to human dignity are no longer seen but there is till much to do.

NATIONAL SERVICE FRAMEWORK FOR OLDER PEOPLE – AN ACHIEVEMENT SO FAR?

In 2001 the Department of Health published its National Service Framework for Older People (NSFOP) some of the key standards of which are detailed in Table 1.

Standard 1	NHS services will be provided, regardless of age, on the basis of clinical need alone. Social care services will not use age in their eligibility criteria or policies.
Standard 2	NHS and social care services treat older people as individuals and enable them to make choices about their own care.
Standard 3	Older people will have access to a new range of intermediate care services at home or in designated care settings, to promote their independence by providing enhanced services from the NHS and councils to prevent unnecessary hospital admission and effective rehabilitation services to enable early discharge from hospital and to prevent premature or unnecessary admission to long-term residential care.
Standard 4	Older people's care in hospital is delivered through appropriate specialist care and by hospital staff who have the right set of skills to meet their needs.
Standard 5	The NHS will take action to prevent strokes, working in partnership with other agencies where appropriate.
Standard 6	The NHS, working in partnership with councils, takes action to prevent falls and reduce resultant fractures or other injuries in their populations of older people.
Standard 7	Older people who have mental health problems have access to integrated mental health services, provided by the NHS and councils to ensure effective diagnosis, treatment and support, for them and their carers.
Standard 8	The health and well-being of older people is promoted through a co-ordinated programme of action led by the NHS with support from councils.

Table 1 Standards of the National Service Framework for Older People[1]

[1] Department of Health (2001). National Service Framework from Older People http://www.dh.gov.uk/assetRoot/04/07/12/83/04071283.pdf

There was little within the NSFOP with which one could disagree, although many areas, including drug misuse, were not covered. The main criticism of the NSFOP approach has been that it is essentially a "tick-box" approach to the improvement of services rather than looking right to the heart of the matter, and producing a real change in attitude to older people and their health problems. Extra funding was not provided for training or service development, except in the area of intermediate care facilities. Thus, it is one thing to create a stroke unit and hire the staff to work within it. However, one needs funding for training and team building if one wants to develop such units into a patient-centred therapeutic community.

The first standard relates to the abolition of age discrimination. All types of discrimination, including age-discrimination are complex in causation and even more difficult to counteract. In many hospitals this issue was tackled by reviewing all existing policies and deleting reference to specific ages. Obvious examples might have included limits of 65, 70 or 75 for admission to coronary care units. These limits never had any scientific validity. Indeed older patients often have more to gain from specialist services because of their higher risk. An interim report on progress in implementing the NSF published in 2004 reported rises in the proportion of older people receiving flu vaccination, giving up smoking successfully and being screened for breast cancer. On the other hand many discriminatory barriers continue to exist and some would say that more are being invented. For example, although age is the most important risk factor for impotence, age alone is not a valid reason for the free prescription of sildenafil on the NHS.

It is also important to recognise that the developments outlined in the NSF were not in themselves innovative and were building on changes that were taking place in the NHS and in social care anyway. It is likely that the NSF may have given local service improvers a "boost" in pushing forward their plans.

NEXT STEPS: AFTER THE NATIONAL SERVICE FRAMEWORK

The NSF for Older People will not be implemented within the time scale originally outlined. Whether there will be 2nd Edition of the NSFOP or a different type of policy document or indeed whether there will be any policy at all is not yet clear. However what is certainly required is the urgent implementation of the Framework, coupled with an analysis of the barriers to its implementation.

DIGNITY AND RESPECT

Dignity and respect are placed at the top of the list because it is the most important and without these it becomes impossible for older people and their families to participate fully in decision-making as equal partners. The use of first names without seeking permission, the disregard of patient confidentiality, the lack of staff to assist at meal times and with the promotion of continence have been known and talked about for years. Patients are still being asked to eliminate their waste in semi-public spaces. Too often hospital wards discourage activity, sleep and good nutrition rather than encourage them!

HEALTH PROMOTION

Much is known about the determinants of good health in old age – adequate pensions, decent warm housing, good diet, exercise, avoidance of known adverse health influences such as smoking and low self-esteem. Simply put all possibilities should be implemented – from clean safe streets that encourage outdoor activities to affordable food and accommodation. Health promotion activities should continue when people enter care, for example, even moderate amounts of exercise have been found reduce fall rates. Effort should be concentrated at the more difficult to reach communities such as those who live in deprived areas and those from minority ethnic groups. The media too has its role – the return of feisty role models such as Ena Sharples should be encouraged. The eradication of pensioner poverty should be just as much a government priority as the abolition of child poverty.

REHABILITATION

Too often discharge home is seen as the successful end of rehabilitation. This is only part of the story. Too often older people who break their bones go home never to venture outdoors alone for fear of a further fall. Psychological rehabilitation is as important as physical rehabilitation and there is a need for a greater role for clinical and health psychologists within rehabilitation services.

NEW SERVICES

In addition to the services described within the NSFOP specialist clinics for Parkinson's disease, heart failure, immediate assessment and mental health needs for older people are required. An examination of the role of the consultant geriatrician in an acute hospital illustrates theses wider needs:

- Geriatric Medicine
- Unselected take of acutely ill older people
- Selected take of older people with specific health needs
- Physical illness
- Dementia/delirium
- Disability
- Frailty
- Consultation on above medical problems in other hospital units
- Management of specific services
- Ortho-geriatric rehabilitation
- Stroke (all ages or older people)
- Falls services
- Parkinson's Disease Services
- Continence Services
- Emergency Room
- Medical Admissions Unit Liaison
- Delirium prevention/treatment (jointly with old age psychiatry)
- Liaison with general surgery.

Whether these are provided specifically for older people or alongside those for younger people is not so important, provided that they are established, and are older person friendly.

HEALTHCARE IN CARE HOMES

Numerous studies have shown that the medical care of older people in residential and nursing homes is sub-optimal with both under-and over-treatment being common. Agreement needs to be reached for care home staff to access specialist (including consultant) services directly. Accreditation of trained and competent GPs as *nursing home specialists* might be a way forward. For example, this specialty is recognised in the Netherlands.

OLDER PEOPLE AND MEDICINES

There is overwhelming paucity of information about the effectiveness of medications for most common conditions in those aged 80 and over, those living in care homes and those with cognitive impairment. This is despite regulatory authorities requiring that trials should be carried out in populations who are likely to use these drugs. Government and industry need to work together to remedy this issue so that the aim of the NSF that all older people receive the medication they need will become the reality. The misuse of drugs and alcohol is emerging as a serious issue in older people and will need specific therapeutic interventions tailored to this age group.

NEW TECHNOLOGY

The development of new diagnostic and therapeutic technologies will continue but not all new technologies are necessarily or high-tech. The simple telephone call to monitor the health of people with chronic disease linked to new systems of intervention is relatively low-tech whilst sensors to detect if an older person has fallen or if the ambient temperature is high enough are examples of a more sophisticated technologies that are presently available and could be implemented more widely.

CHRONIC DISEASE MANAGEMENT IN THE COMMUNITY

Regular monitoring of high-risk patients in the community with the aim of optimising health and preventing hospital admission has recently been promoted and the first ranks of Community Matrons have been appointed. It is important that they work in a collaborative fashion with secondary care using evidence-based protocols for interventions and referral. The creation of elite community nurses should not be at the expense of undermining or devaluing the role of traditional district nursing.

GERIATRIC MEDICINE AND PRIMARY CARE

The shift of emphasis from secondary care to primary care affects the treatment of older people as it does other client groups. The basic thrust being that only those people who need specialist advice, investigation or treatment will be referred to hospital. Those who are seen by specialists will be transferred back for onward management by primary care as soon as possible. This trend is likely to continue and is supported *provided* that primary care has the capacity, capability interest and continuity to respond to this challenge.

The development of General Practitioners with a Specialist Interests (GpwSI) could represent a new pathway in the UK. Opportunities exist for such doctors (with their primary care team) to take on specific areas of work: supervision of in-patients in community hospitals, chronic disease management of older people, diagnosis and management of specific syndromes in older people (e.g. falls, osteoporosis, dementia). The key to success will be agreed collaborative agreements between primary and secondary care as to who does what.

GERIATRIC MEDICINE AND THE HOSPITAL, SECONDARY CARE

In the United Kingdom, the overwhelming majority of Consultant Geriatricians work for the greater proportion of the week within their District General Hospital. Over half also work as general physicians treating emergency admissions of all ages. Finding sufficient time within the working week, to devote to the development of specialist services for older people, is limited by conflicting pressure. These pressures include the growing number of medical admissions, the need to clear Accident and Emergency Departments rapidly to meet four-hour waiting targets, the withdrawal of certain specialties such as cardiology from general take and the reduction of junior medical support consequent upon the European Working Time Directive.

In addition to their work in acute hospitals, Consultant Geriatricians' expertise is called upon outside the hospital and one of the other developments has been the recruitment of new posts of Consultant Community Geriatricians. The duties of these post-holders not only include the traditional ones of a Consultant in the Community Hospital (ward rounds, in-patient and out-patient consultations) but include supervision of intermediate care schemes, liaison and review with primary care clinical staff (e.g. Community Matrons) and visits to residential and nursing homers. Time can be spent with local authorities and voluntary services to develop preventive strategies.

THE NEW NHS

During my professional life-time I have been employed by a Board of Governors, a Hospital Management Committee, an Area Health Authority, a District Health Authority, a NHS Trust and soon it will be by a NHS Foundation Trust. All of these organisation changes have been designed with a view to improving patient care and decentralising decision making to be nearer the patient. Most geriatricians would say that these changes by themselves have had little impact on the development or non-development of services. The one thing these organisations had in common was that they were all firmly within the NHS. The present Government's desire to move service provision into the Independent sector (whether for profit or not) is considered threatening – not only on a personal level, but also because of worries of cherry-picking, disruption of plans to make services comprehensive, short-termism and reductions in standards. Furthermore, as a marker of commitment, most geriatricians work only within the state system and have little or no experience of the independent sector.

The challenge for geriatricians will be to engage with these new organisations. The British Geriatrics Society has started this process and will need to seek to influence their development in the same way as it engages with Government. Looking to other countries which have more diversity in their supply of healthcare for older people is vital so that the effective services can be emulated and worst services avoided.

Services for older people, particularly for those who are frail, are the responsibility of both health and social services and within health across the primary-secondary care divide. The possibility of establishing Care Trusts which integrate health and social care functions appear an attractive way of improving both the commissioning and the delivery of services. However, this process seems to be stalled. An alternative, and probably more effective way at the present time is the creation of "virtual" directorates which cross organisational boundaries but have integrated management functions. These might be on a whole health economy basis or based on smaller areas such as practice-based commissioning clusters.

RESEARCH AND EDUCATION

The need for a link between service development, research and education is obvious yet co-ordination is often lacking. It is impossible to set up effective services without staff who are trained to deliver that service and without the evidence that service is likely to be effective.

CONCLUSION

Optimising the health of older people is no small task and requires investment and co-ordination at all levels. The requirements for the next decade or so are clear. A greater emphasis on health promotion by education, greater involvement of older people themselves in health decisions and providing a societal infrastructure that is health promoting rather than health damaging. A greater evidence base on the role of health interventions, particularly in the very old, the frail and those with mental illness is required. Effective interventions need to be implemented be this in general practice (e.g. osteoporosis prevention) or within the hospital (e.g. delirium prevention). A co-ordinated and trained workforce that knows what it is doing and which is willing to question dogma and effect change is vital. Finally (and most importantly) is the need to treat older patients as individual people, to respect their rights, opinions and feelings and to treat them with dignity and humanity however ill and seemingly incapacitated. Leadership for all this is required both centrally and locally. Geriatricians are well equipped to provide this role.

CHAPTER 10

FUTURE HEALTH SERVICES FOR CHILDREN

Professor Alan Craft and Dr Simon Lenton

"Children are the living message we send to a time we will not see"

Over the last few years we have seen that children are a high priority for all the government of the UK. The recognition that the future of our nation depends on the education of children was highlighted by the Prime Minister's assertion of his priorities: "Education, education, education". Our child friendly Chancellor of the Exchequer has been trying hard to end child poverty and to reduce the gap between rich and poor. Youth offending, safeguarding and challenging behaviour have all been the target of much action. But what of the health of children, and their health services?

There is an increasing recognition that the wellbeing of the pregnant mother, foetus, and growing child are important determinants of health in later life. However, the benefits of the investment may not become apparent until at least the age of 50. Although Churchill said that one of the best interventions a government can make is to put milk into the stomachs of children, it would be a brave and farsighted political party that would invest in something which was not going to show any real benefits within a parliamentary time scale or two – that is, a maximum of 10 years. Even Sir Derek Wanless in his recent economic reviews for government could not be persuaded to take more than a 20-year view.

Health care systems in the developed world face similar questions.

* how to finance, and then commission healthcare,
* how to deliver healthcare effectively, efficiently and equitably, and

- how-to inspect/regulate in a way that improves healthcare systems.

All this needs to be achieved against a background of changing demography (an increasingly elderly population), rapidly changing lifestyles, exponentially increasing access to information, constant technological and scientific advances and the need to balance investment in improving the determinants of health versus interventions to correct health problems. Superficially children themselves have never appeared to be healthier, but what about the health systems to support children and families, do we really have a first-class service or can we do better?

The reports following the failures such as the Bristol Children's heart controversy and the death of Victoria Climbie, both demonstrate a lack of leadership, lack of joined up thinking, no mechanisms to identify problems in the system and put them right, and little parental involvement in the design and delivery of services.

Because there are few measures of child health, and few performance indicators for children's services they rarely cause concern to government. There are no major waiting lists, children usually get priority in A & E departments and although it may be difficult for an adult to get to see a GP, children are seen without undue delay, at least during the hours of 9–6, Monday to Friday. However, waiting times to see a speech therapist, or access to a wheelchair service, or many child and family therapy services tell a different story.

In 2004 the National Service Framework (NSF) for Children and Young People was produced in England weighing in at 2.4kg. A much slimmer, lighter, 2 language NSF for children in Wales was also produced. Neither came with clear targets for any hypothecated money. In England implementation has no priority for cash strapped NHS trusts. There are standards which are expected to eventually be achieved over 10 years but no clear investment or implementation strategy, no challenging targets, or even milestones to be achieved before then.

So are children really as healthy as they seem? It depends on your perspective, comparisons with our European neighbours suggest that health is not improving as rapidly as it might. Despite the efforts of the Chancellor inequalities in health are actually widening. It is really difficult to get an accurate comparison of health across Europe given the very different health care systems. In particular, it would be interesting to understand whether those countries that have direct access to specialist care, rather than going through the "gate keeping" process of primary care, have different outcomes.

We know of 2 pieces of evidence which suggest that primary care specialists do benefit children. The average age of diagnosis of muscular dystrophy is almost a year earlier in Germany than in the UK. There is little that can be done for children with muscular dystrophy in terms of treatment, but a child who is not walking properly is a great worry to parents and an early resolution of these concerns would be of value and especially important for genetic counselling. The other more important area is that of cancer in children. A recent Eurocare study has shown that children in the UK who have certain types of solid tumour have a poorer chance of survival than those in France and Germany. Interestingly survival for leukaemia is similar across most of Europe. Given that treatment regimes are similar, if not identical, and professional expertise very similar, one has to look for another reason. Children with leukaemia usually present quite acutely and the diagnosis is unlikely to be missed for long. However, for solid tumours, such as bone tumours, there is often a more indolent development of the tumour and it is not unusual for a child in the UK to present to specialist care with a long history of many visits to a general practitioner. It is tempting to suggest, although we have no proof, that the better outcomes in some European countries for childhood cancer, and indeed for an early diagnosis of muscular dystrophy are due to direct access to a primary care specialist.

Therefore one of our key questions for the future provision of care for children in the UK is how primary care for children can be improved. In 1976 Court suggested a new breed of "general practitioner paediatrician". However, this was unpopular with GPs and was the only part of his report "Fit for the Future" which was not implemented 25 years later. Children do consult their GP regularly during childhood and they make up at least 40% of the workload for most practices. In spite of this, historically, fewer than 50% of GPs have had a formal paediatric training. They used to be able to opt to undertake child health surveillance and promotion but the new contract does not make it financially attractive to do so and many are opting out.

The advent of the new GP contract, especially abrogation of responsibility for out of hours cover, has meant that many parents are either being sent to secondary care by NHS Direct or opting to use their local A&E Dept. for emergency care. Acute referrals have increased dramatically and on Christmas Day 2005 many paediatric units reported a 50% or more increase in activity.

Access to an acute paediatric service is a hot topic. In the 60's and 70's most District General Hospitals developed paediatric units with inpatient beds. At the time the beds were often fully occupied with an average length of stay of at least 7 days. Now the beds in many smaller units lie empty for much of the time. Although the total number of admissions has gone up the average length of stay has plummeted to just over 1 day. Most children attending hospital as an emergency require a short period of observation – 4–6 hours – during which time serious disease can be excluded, parents can be reassured and the child sent home. In the past this function was undertaken by a GP who would visit a child at home and revisit 4 hours later. Home visits are now exceptional and even out of hours primary care facilities have little medical continuity so that the only way to achieve a short period of observation is to send the child to hospital. Most paediatric departments have responded1 by setting up assessment units within wards. But due to mainly daytime referrals, many beds remain empty overnight. The pressures of the European Working Time Directive and the shortage of professional staff have made it uneconomic and sometimes impossible to continue to provide 24 hour care at all sites where inpatient care has been delivered in the past. Reconfiguration of services, sharing resources with neighbouring hospitals and developing real managed networks would seem to be the only logical solution. There are now many examples of new ways of working, often using nurses to provide care previously undertaken by doctors.

However, for a local hospital to appear to be losing their paediatric department, and often obstetrics too, is a political hot potato. Across the UK sensible reconfigurations of services have been worked out and agreed by professionals and managers only to be thwarted at the last moment by politicians, concerned about losing votes.

We really do need to find a way that is politically acceptable to redesign our services. Working on the principle of providing the best possible care, as close to the patient's home as possible, with competent staff, but also having a clear pathway to access the next level for those few who really are ill. We must therefore concentrate our scarce resources in fewer centres but ensure that we also strengthen local day time services.

Managed networks of care are vitally important for all children with either acute or long-term conditions or disabilities. Parents of disabled children will very often talk about the very disjointed services that they are offered or have to fight for. Both the Kennedy and Laming reports identified a lack of strategic planning/joined up thinking and that this led to disjointed service delivery. The Audit Commission report into disability highlighted a lottery of provision and individual families will describe the large number of professionals involved in a child's care and that none of them seem to co-ordinate with each other. One of the important innovations over the last few years has been the concept of a "lead professional" for disabled children. This does not need to be any particular profession but someone who has the time to act as the families guide and advocate through the maze of services. Children and their parents want clear, safe, effective and convenient journeys through services. Commissioners want the maximum impact with resources available.

Clear values, pathways of care which define the patient journey and managed clinical networks are all concepts which are evolving across medicine and when properly implemented could lead to a huge improvement in delivery of care to children.

Managed clinical networks are defined as linked groups of profes-sionals at primary, secondary and tertiary levels working in a co-ordinated manner, unconstrained by existing organisational boundaries (and this includes commissioning) to ensure equitable provision of high quality effective services. Managed networks can be applied to both acute and long-term conditions. An acute example would be as follows:

> Take a child with meningococcal septicaemia. The intended outcome of services generally is to improve the life chances of all children, and one element of this is to reduce the incidence of infectious disease and its associated morbidity/mortality. For meningococcal disease, there needs to be a pathway that extends from prevention, through early iden-tification, assessment, acute interventions, long-term support and for a few through to palliation.
> At the population level there needs to be an immunisation program-me, probably delivered in schools for adolescents, programmes to raise awareness of parents and young people of the significance of a

non-blanching rash, and training for those in primary care in the early assessment and management of meningococcal septicaemia. Emergency services need to effectively resuscitate, possibly transport to hospital, and hospital services provide an effective range of interventions to maintain life until antibiotics and immune systems overcome the infection.

For a proportion of children (about 10%) there will be an ongoing disability (mainly hearing impairment) that will require management by rehabilitation services with implications for social care and education. Then sadly, for a minority palliative or bereavement services may be needed. The commissioning process should ensure a balanced mixture of services between prevention, interventions and long-term support to ensure the maximum number of children benefit from the resources available. This whole pathway needs to be considered in the wider public health agenda of improving the determinants of health for example reducing poverty, improving living conditions and reducing inequalities of access to services.

The outcomes for the child are only as good as the weakest point in this pathway, which may be at any stage. Quality improvement is about identifying this weakest point and improving the service at that point. Inspection and regulation processes should focus on ensuring that there are systems to identify the weak points, and corrective action is taken. Because of the many agencies involved in the pathway, this needs to be done across networks, rather than for organisations.

The Association for the Care of Terminally Ill Children and their Families (ACT) have recently produced a pathway of care for children with terminal illness. This is already beginning to bring about change in the way in which commissioners think about how best to provide excellent care for those for whom they are responsible.

Pathway thinking seems to have an intuitive appeal and makes sense to a wide range of people, and it is a logical way of providing information about conditions or describing services. Pathway thinking therefore both supports the individual's journey through services, and the commissioning and quality improvement of those services.

There are many good reasons for developing care pathways:

- Are family centred and clinically driven
- Provide a structured framework for organising evidence to support parents and practitioners
- Support the development of competence and skills transfer between professional groups

- Are a tool to support continuous improvements, learning and patient care
- As a conceptual model that underpins many key local and national agendas simultaneously.

One of the big challenges that we face in developing better services for children, through managed networks, is the fragmentation of commissioning. For any child's "journey" there could be up to 7 different commissioning bodies (across health education social care and the community/voluntary sector) responsible for purchasing "bits" of a journey. The principles of commissioning have great potential for improving services if a way can be found to commission whole pathways across organisations, rather than contracts with individual organisations.

Once we have networks of care we need to quality assure and improve them. The principles of quality improvement are:

Quality improvement is merely about knowing that you are doing:

- the right things
- to the right people
- in the right order
- at the right time
- in the right place
- with the right outcome
- all with attention to the patient experience
- and to compare planned care with care actually given.

It is about preventing crises through an active and systematic process of identifying, and rectifying potential problems. All components of a care pathway should be covered and it is therefore everybody's business.

The key component in most pathways is the competence of practitioners, whether health, education or social care, as it is they that make decisions. The next essential is that families and professionals have information to aid their decision-making, often called "decision support". Regular and relevant information is also required to assess the performance of the whole pathway/programme. Further components include equipment, environment and other resources, and also remembering the whole pathway may take place in a wider social/physical environment that may either promote or hinder the process e.g. poverty, poor housing, family breakdown etc.

Children's health and well-being is dependent on multi-agency services, the outcome of which is only as good as the weakest link in the child's journey. Services should be planned and delivered around the child's journey – sometimes called a pathway, or programme and delivered within a network of providers. Children's services should be needs based, outcome orientated, and delivered through managed networks to provide a seamless service for users. Commissioners and providers need to work together to achieve this, involving children and parents in both the planning and delivery process.

CONCLUSION

All aspects of the care of children need to be strengthened. In primary care we need better training of all general practitioners, and development of more specialists in primary care. The latter could be developing community children's nursing in primary care and by helping general practitioners develop a special interest in children (the GPSI). The recent White Paper *Our Health, Our Care, Our Say*, provides a new direction for community services by encouraging the movement of all specialist care out of hospital settings.

It is no longer possible to continue to provide inpatient care on every hospital sites as we do now. Politicians need to be persuaded to allow reconfiguration of services which will strengthen local care whilst at the same time ensuring access to more expert services when children need them.

It will be vital for these changes to be tied into pathway thinking and managed networks which should guarantee every child to have access to the right care, by competent people, in the right place and at the right time.

The future focus has to be on developing methods, and a culture for continuous improvement. We could do worse than to adopt the mission statement of National Initiative for Children's Health Care Quality (NICHQ), an improvement and research organisation based in the USA. "To eliminate the gap between what is, and what could be, in health care for all children."

CHAPTER 11

THE ORGANISATION OF NHS MATERNITY CARE

Professor Jim Thornton

INTRODUCTION

Three organisational features distinguish NHS maternity care from that in most other West European countries.

1. Britain has the most centralised system. Not only do we have a low rate of home births, typical of all other countries except Holland, but we also have the lowest proportion of small delivery units <1000, and the highest proportion of large ones >5,000 deliveries.
2. Doctors, and in particular senior doctors, are relatively uninvolved in labour and delivery. They leave the normal deliveries largely to midwives and senior doctors leave complicated deliveries, forceps and caesareans, to doctors in training.
3. Probably as a consequence, Britain is unique in having the majority of normal births conducted by midwives, at least nominally acting as independent practitioners in their own right. However, midwives have also expanded their role outside labour and delivery and their numbers, measured as whole time equivalents, have not kept pace with these new developments.

All these differences may partly be caused by historical contingency, geographical accidents, or the personality of the British – things health planners cannot alter much. However, I will argue that they are also an unintended consequence of the nature of the NHS – something which could be changed.

Britain is the only West European country to have almost all (99%) maternity care not only funded from taxation but also delivered by a single government provider, the NHS. All the others fund it through some sort of social insurance model and have a much larger role for private and charitable providers.

NHS MATERNITY CARE

CENTRALISATION

There has been a steady fall in the number of maternity units in England since 1973 (*Table 1*). The fall has occurred entirely among smaller units, those conducting less than 2,000 deliveries annually and as a result a much greater proportion of births takes place in larger units. Over this period birth rates have remained stable at around 640,000 per year.

	< 999	1,000-1,999	2,000-2,999	3,000-3,999	4,000-4,999	5,000-5,999	6,000-6,999	7,000-7,999	8,000+	Total
1973	310	121	58	25	13	0	0	0	0	527
1996	147	104	63	28	31	0	0	0	0	341
2003	16	27	56	49	27	9	2	0	1*	186

*Liverpool Women's Hospital with 8,084 deliveries in 2003.

Table 1 The number and size of maternity units.[1]

England Scotland and Wales now have the highest proportion of large maternity units in Europe (*Table 2*). There are 12 units in England delivering more than 5000 births per annum and the largest Liverpool Women's hospital, delivers over 8,000.

	<500	500-999	1,000-1499	1,500-1999	2,000-3999	>4,000
Austria 2001	14%	39%	17%	9.5%	17.5%	0
Belgium (Flanders 2003)	13%	60%	17%	6%	4%	0
Denmark 2000	4%	3.9%	23%	13%	41%	14%
England 2003	10%	2%	8%	13%	56%	21%
France Entire 2003	15%	34%	23%	12%	17%*	'
Germany 2000 (nine Bundeslander)	17.5%	39%	27%	11%	5.7%	0

	<500	500-999	1,000-1499	1,500-1999	2,000-3999	>4,000
Luxembourg 2000	16%	23%	61%	0	0	0
Spain (Valencia) 2000	2%	7%	21%	32%	23%	15%
Sweden 2000	2	9.6%	14%	15%	59%	0
Scotland 2000	2.4%	7.1%	7.4%	9.5%	44%	28%
Wales 2000	2.1%	0	16%	23%	56%	0

Table 2 European comparisons of maternity units[2]

In contrast the largest Maternity unit in Germany, the Humboldt maternity department in Berlin, after the closure of two smaller units nearby, now has just over 3,000 deliveries per year. Few other units in Germany have more than 2,000 deliveries per year. The Höchst hospital, the largest maternity unit in Frankfurt had 1,800 deliveries in 2004. The Jeanne de Flandre Hospital in Lille, the largest Maternity Hospital in France, has just over 4,000 births a year. The largest unit in Belgium (Flanders) conducted 2,641 deliveries in 2004.

The explanation for the difference must be the NHS. In the rest of Europe many maternity hospitals are either private or charitable, albeit funded through various state or employer based social insurance schemes. They naturally resist merger with their competitors. In England all hospitals are part of the NHS and small ones can relatively easily be persuaded to merge with larger ones. Mergers in the NHS rarely result in any forced redundancy, and are in fact often popular with senior staff since they ease the organisation of staff rotas. Since NHS hospitals have not had to compete for women to deliver in them, managers find it easier to override campaigns to save local hospitals since they do not lose income if dissatisfied patients go elsewhere.

CONSULTANT INVOLVEMENT IN LABOUR

It is difficult to overemphasise the importance of close consultant involvement in labour. Although maternal and perinatal deaths are now both uncommon, the day of delivery remains the most dangerous in most individual's entire lifespan. Deaths in childbirth also have an importance well above the level implied by the raw numbers when measured as healthy years of life lost.

It is generally accepted that severe asphyxia at the point of delivery and severe premature delivery can both cause some types of cerebral palsy, and that some of these cases may be avoidable through good maternity care. In most NHS hospitals the potential medico-legal claims arising from alleged negligent care in labour causing brain damage now dwarf all other medical claims.

Modern medical and midwifery care is perhaps even more important for the mother. In a typical UK maternity unit conducting 3,000 deliveries per year no less than 15 maternal deaths will be prevented every year.[3] Their lives will often have been saved by a relatively minor or routine intervention, a course of antibiotics, a blood transfusion, some antihypertensive drugs or a timely Caesarean delivery. Often neither the staff involved nor the patient will realise that a young mother's life has been saved.

However, the provision of a safe environment for mothers and babies in labour is not easy to achieve. It requires leadership, discipline, and constant efforts from all staff. It requires senior staff not only to be available on call, but to closely monitor the skills of the juniors. To develop local guidelines, ensure that everyone knows them, to audit compliance and take steps when it is found to be lacking. To make sure that emergency drills not only happen, but are conducted sufficiently carefully to ensure that everyone who participates can deal with the emergency correctly. This requires real senior staff commitment to the labour ward. It is not clear that the NHS always achieves this.

Although the evidence is largely anecdotal, few doctors, midwives or patients with experience of maternity care in Britain and another European country would dispute that compared with the rest of Europe, women rarely see any consultant in labour, let alone the one nominally responsible for their care. Even if complications occur doctors in training now conduct the vast majority of such deliveries. The National Caesarean Section audit[4], for example, does not give direct figures for consultant involvement at caesarean section. However it set consultant presence at 10% of potentially complicated caesareans (e.g. placenta praevia, placental abruption, at full cervical dilatation, in obese women, for premature deliveries less than 32 weeks for multiple pregnancy and women with multiple previous Caesarean sections) as an auditable standard. This modest target was achieved in most hospitals, with overall a consultant present in theatre for 21 percent of these complicated cases.

In 1999 an anonymous consultant in an NHS district general hospital calculated that over the preceding three years (out of about 9,000 deliveries, around 750 of them assisted) he and his three colleagues had done six normal deliveries 19 instrumental deliveries, two vaginal breech deliveries and 26 emergency caesarean sections between them[5]. His letter provoked a reply from the president of the Royal College of Obstetricians and Gynaecologists[6] who argued for an expansion of the number of consultants but did not dispute the truth of the original observation.

In contrast in the rest of Europe consultants see their patients personally and regularly, and attend them in labour. In Belgium or Holland it would be almost unthinkable for a consultant not to be present for a Caesarean delivery, let alone a complicated one.

The reason for the difference lies partly in the role of the NHS consultants. They have always been very powerful. Their numbers are relatively low, but their salaries are high by European standards. They are allowed to supplement these salaries by private practice, while giving up only a small fraction of their NHS salary. As a result NHS obstetric consultants have had little financial incentive to compete with midwives to conduct normal deliveries. This is probably a good thing.

However, it is also convenient for consultant obstetricians to delegate abnormal deliveries to junior doctors in training. This allows them to concentrate on other aspects of the specialty such as prenatal diagnosis or on the linked specialty of gynaecology. This is a bad thing.

Although consultant numbers have risen steadily in England over the last 10 years (*Table 3*) there is still a considerable shortfall in consultant labour ward presence. According to the Royal College of Obstretrics and Gynaecology (RCOG) only 80/207 maternity units in England and Wales even claim to have 40 hours consultant presence on the labour ward (Medical Workforce in Obstetrics and Gynaecology 2005), and even this is probably an over estimate because only 18 out of 151 maternity units in the NHS who participate in the clinical negligence scheme for trusts (CNST) achieved 40 hours consultant cover in 2004. It is relatively unlikely that a unit would have genuinely achieved the 40-hour standard and then allow itself to fail on some other standard.

	Specialist registrars head counts	Consultants head counts
1994	806	892
1999	1,001	1,057
2000	939	1,146
2001	950	1,219
2002	1,014	1,308
2003	973	1,353
2004	1,099	1,413

Table 3 Numbers of obstetric staff England 1975–1999[7]

MIDWIFE INVOLVEMENT

Midwives are different. Britain is unique in having the majority of normal births conducted by midwives, at least nominally acting as independent practitioners in their own right. In all other Western countries most normal hospital deliveries are either directly conducted by doctors, or under the close direct supervision of doctors, assisted by an obstetric nurse. Holland is a partial exception in that 30% of deliveries are conducted at home by an independent midwife. However, even there the 70% of women who give birth in hospital are all delivered by a doctor.

The high rate of midwife involvement in normal delivery is a good thing. It is popular with parents and tends to lower intervention rates. There is good evidence that if the midwife can provide continuous one-to-one care in labour that a range of adverse outcomes are reduced[8]. Unfortunately this has been difficult to achieve[9].

One reason is that midwives have many other duties besides delivering babies. They have always performed antenatal and postnatal checks and advised on breast feeding, but now they increasingly get involved in screening for fetal abnormality, mental illness and domestic violence, in giving anti-smoking advice and in counselling. There has also been a considerable increase in the number employed in management roles including risk management, and dealing with patient complaints. All of these activities are important but they take staff from the main work of delivering babies.

At the same time as these new midwife tasks have appeared, and UK birth numbers have remained stable, the numbers of midwives have hardly risen at all. Since 1997 there has been only a modest rise in the total headcount in England (*Table 4*). This minimal rise in numbers is of longstanding. Before 1997 figures were collected differently and are not directly comparable with later ones. Nevertheless Macfarlane and Mugford report midwife-staffing levels as whole time equivalents rising slightly in the 20 years from 18,579 in 1975 to 19,548 in 1996.

	Head count
1997	22,385
1998	22,841
1999	22,799
2000	22,572
2001	23,075
2002	23,249
2003	23,941
2004	24,844

Table 4 Numbers of midwives[10]

Increasing part time working exacerbates the problem. The ratio of full to part time working changed from 60%: 40% in 1994 to 39%: 61% in 2004 (*Table 5*). The net effect has been a 14% reduction in the total number of hours worked by midwives over a period when the role of the midwife has expanded considerably.

	Working full time, per cent	Working part time, per cent	Total number of working midwives
1994	59.5	40.5	35,127
2004	38.6	61.4	33,687

Table 5 Ratio of midwives working full and part time between 1994 and 2004, Nursing and Midwifery Council register, August 2005

COMPARISON WITH CONTINENTAL EUROPE

Many of the centralising changes in the UK maternity service have been introduced with the aim of improving safety. The idea being that large units are better able to provide high quality neonatal and maternal intensive care without the need to transfer sick babies or mothers around the country. A paper from Germany which showed threefold increase in neonatal mortality between the smallest and the largest hospitals in 2002 is frequently cited in support of the closure of small units[11]. However, "small" and "large" are relative terms. The German units were much smaller than UK; 39 had under 500 deliveries per year, 33 had 500–1000, 14 had 1,000 to 1,500 and only five so called "large units" had 1,500 birth per year. The actual size of the "large" units was not given but all five combined delivered only 96,000 women over ten years, i.e. an average of less than 2,000 deliveries each per year. In England they would be classified as "small" (see *Table 1* above).

Larger units may also be more difficult to manage efficiently. Staff may avoid taking responsibility for clinical decisions or for aspects of organisation in the hope that others will do it for them. In this next section of the report I compare the NHS with maternity care elsewhere in Europe.

CRUDE MORTALITY COMPARISONS

The NHS maternity service has not generally achieved better perinatal or maternal mortality figures than other comparable European countries according to OECD Health Data from 2005 (*Tables 6, 7, 8*).

	2000	2001	2002	2003
France	6.8	6.9		
Germany	6.1	5.9		
Netherlands	7.8	7.9	7.6	7.4
Switzerland	7.8	8		
United Kingdom	8.1	6.7	6.9	

Table 6 Perinatal mortality – Deaths/1000 births

	2000	2001	2002	2003
France	6.5			
Germany	5.6	3.7	2.9	
Netherlands	8.7	6.9	9.9	4
Switzerland	6.4			
United Kingdom	7	7	6	8

Table 7 Maternal mortality – Deaths/100,000 live births

	2000	2001	2002	2003
France	17	18		
Germany	21	22	24	
Netherlands	12	14	14	14
Switzerland			24	25
United Kingdom	22	23	22	22

Table 8 Caesarean section rates %

However, it is probably unfair to use routine maternity statistics to make meaningful comparisons about the quality of care. These statistics are often collected in different ways, and with different degrees of accuracy and many maternal and fetal deaths are either unavoidable or related to social factors outside the control of the maternity system.

AUDITS OF SUB-OPTIMAL CARE

A better method is to compare the frequency of less than optimal or "sub-optimal" care. In 2003 the Euronatal Working Group compared the frequency of sub-optimal care leading to perinatal death in a range of countries[12] . An independent audit panel blindly reviewed 1619 perinatal deaths in regions of ten European countries. Sub-optimal care was defined on the basis of the same agreed "evidence-based" criteria for all countries. They compared the percentage of cases graded as having sub-optimal factors present, which either might, or probably did, contribute to the bad outcome, are shown in *Table 9*.

Country	Total deaths evaluated	Substandard care might have caused the death	Percent	95% CI
Finland	163	52	32%	25–39%
Sweden	129	46	36%	28–44%
Norway	139	55	40%	32–48%
Spain	102	45	44%	35–54%
Netherlands	157	76	48%	41–56%
Scotland	85	43	51%	40–61%
Belgium	188	96	51%	44–58%
Denmark	260	133	51%	45–57%
Greece	105	54	51%	42–61%
England	215	115	54%	47–60%
Average	1543	715	46%	44–49%

Table 9 Numbers and percentages of evaluated cases of perinatal death graded as "Suboptimal factor(s) identified which *might* have contributed to the fatal outcome" or Suboptimal factor(s) present which are likely to have contributed to the fatal outcome.[13]

The NHS appeared to have the highest rate of sub-optimal care, which might have contributed to the deaths. The authors rightly caution against making the inference that substandard practice is really more common in England than other countries. Nevertheless this hardly suggests that the centralisation achieved by the NHS has resulted in better care. It is also plausible that poor care in the NHS results from low consultant involvement.

SPECIAL ENQUIRIES

The Kennedy commission reviewed three hospitals in which concerns had been raised about maternity care: Northwick Park in London, New Cross in Wolverhampton, and Ashford St Peters in Chertsey. In all three, serious deficiencies were identified. These included poor reporting of adverse incidents and poor handling of complaints, poor staff working relationships, inadequate training and supervision of clinical staff, services isolated both geographically and clinically, and staff shortages with poor management of temporary employees. It is implausible that similar findings would not have been made in many other hospitals had they been subject to similar detailed review.

MEDICO-LEGAL CLAIMS

Measured by value more than half of the potential claims for negligent injury in the NHS arise from maternity care. These are predominantly cases of brain damage or other birth injury allegedly cause by sub-standard care at delivery. Anecdotally such claims are less common in the rest of Europe although I cannot find any comparative data.

THE SOLUTION

The NHS needs greater consultant involvement in labour. It needs consultants actually doing labour ward rounds, conducting deliveries, assisting trainee doctors in deliveries and otherwise directly supervising the labour ward. A surrogate measure of this is the number of hours when a consultant is rostered to be on duty on the labour ward without any other face to face patient commitment such as a clinical or operating session. The lowest level standard for this set by Clinical Negligence Scheme for Trusts is 40 hours per week.

In theory the 1303 whole time equivalent consultants in England and Wales should be able to provide this level of consultant presence on most of the 207 labour wards (RCOG figures). An average 6.3 whole time consultants per labour ward provides 233 hours of consult-ant work per week (37×6.3), albeit about half of it spent doing gynaecology.

Nor should consultant time on labour ward normally be too onerous. An average English unit of 3,000 births per annum will have less than nine births per day, i.e. rarely more than four or five births between 9 and 5 on weekdays, and often less. A unit of such a size would also have at least one doctor in training to assist. It should therefore be possible for the consultant to do a ward round, get some paper work done and still directly supervise one, two or three operative deliveries. However, in practice it seems to be difficult in the UK. According to the RCOG less than half of units achieve this level of cover and according to CNST only 18 out of 151 did.

MATERNITY UNIT MERGERS

The solution that has been followed to date has been maternity unit mergers, with the idea that this makes more consultants available to join the labour ward rota. The process is ongoing. A number of large 2-5,000 delivery maternity units are currently considering merging to form super giants like Liverpool.

However such mergers may simply allow consultant labour ward hours to be nominally achieved by dividing the hours among a larger number of consultants rather than by changes in working practice. They also reduce women's choice of hospital of delivery which will frustrate government efforts to raise standards by allowing funding to follow women's choice of delivery unit.

Fortunately two other drivers for change are available to maternity unit managers; the clinical negligence scheme for trusts (CNST) and the new consultant contract.

CLINICAL NEGLIGENCE SCHEME FOR TRUSTS

In 1990 as a result of a dramatic rise in claims for negligence, particularly in obstetrics, the NHS assumed responsibility for paying any damages resulting from negligence by doctors working on their contracted NHS duties. In 1995 the NHS litigation authority introduced the clinical negligence scheme for trusts (CNST) as a way of controlling this financial risk. Currently all maternity Trusts make contributions to a fund for paying out claims in proportion to the number of deliveries they conduct. In addition to this the scheme classifies trusts into three "levels" on the basis of the quality of obstetric care provided. Trusts which achieve success at level one receive a 10% discount on their CNST contributions, with discounts of 20% at level 2 and 30% available to those passing the higher levels.

One of the CNST maternity standards is clearly designed to address the problem of low consultant involvement in labour. Maternity units which wish to achieve the higher grades are required to provide evidence of minimum numbers of hours of consultant presence on the labour ward for units of different size.

These savings may be quite substantial in large units. For example a 5,000 delivery unit achieving 40 hours per week consultant labour ward cover and moving from level 1 to level 2 will have an annual CNST premium reduction of about £235,000. This is more than sufficient to pay the salaries of two whole time consultant obstetricians. Since only 18 out of the 151 maternity units in the NHS who participate in CNST, achieved Level 2 in 2004 there is considerable scope for this lever to be used to force change.

THE NEW NHS CONSULTANT CONTRACT

Until recently NHS consultant's contracts specified their duties only in general terms. It was common for consultants to be appointed to spend say a day a week on the labour ward and, over time, to alter that part of their work to gynaecology without formal managerial approval. This should not now happen.

Since 2004 all new NHS consultants have been appointed to a contract which specifies precisely the hours they are to spend on specific duties and which can only be altered with formal agreement of the managers. The unit of consultant work in such contracts is a programmed activity (PA) which generally consists of four hours work. A full time contract thus consists of 10 PA's per week.

The majority of existing consultants also signed these new contracts. However, since many of them, particularly in obstetrics, were already working over 40 hours per week they were given temporary contracts with typically one or two extra PAs per week.

The widespread agreement of such 10+2 contracts is one of the causes of the current financial difficulties in the NHS but it also gives the opportunity for improvements in consultant's working practices in future.

In the short run these PAs over 10 can be removed unilaterally by managers so long as they can identify another consultant to take on the duties. For example a maternity unit which needed to increase its consultant hours of labour ward cover by say 16 hours per week to achieve 40 hours in total, might create a new post funded partly through CNST premium savings and partly through re-deploying PAs from existing consultants. In the long run consultants appointed to such posts will not be able to unilaterally alter their work patterns from covering labour wards to undertake other duties.

This combination of CNST premium savings and re-deploying sessions from existing consultants means that where necessary hospitals can often employ new obstetricians at no extra cost.

Of course there are some difficulties. Pure obstetric jobs without any gynaecology have generally not been popular with senior doctors and have often been difficult to fill. However, the recent rise in NHS doctors has not occurred elsewhere in Europe where the number of qualified doctors is higher. It is therefore often possible to fill pure obstetric posts with well qualified English-speaking doctors from Germany, Holland and Belgium.

SUMMARY

Maternity care in the UK is the most centralised in Europe. Consultants are relatively uninvolved in care, which they leave to midwives or doctors in training. Although there is no clear evidence that outcomes as measured by maternal or perinatal mortality are worse in the UK, there is some evidence that patients are less satisfied and that substandard care is more common.

The recent expansion in consultant numbers, reduced gynaecological workload, the new consultant contract, the clinical negligence scheme for trusts, and health reforms which allow funding to follow patient choice over place of delivery all provide an opportunity for improvement.

Health care purchasers should resist further maternity hospital mergers. These frustrate patient choice and allow consultants to nominally achieve targets for labour ward presence without actually altering their working practices.

REFERENCES

1. MacFarlane A, Mugford M, Henderson J, Furtado A, Stevens J, Dunn A Birth Counts 2nd edition. 2000. The Stationery Office London.
2. Wildman K, Blondel B, Nijhuis J, Defoort P, Bakoula C. European indicators of health care during pregnancy, delivery and the postpartum period. Eur J Obstet Gynecol Reprod Biol. 2003;111 Suppl 1: S53–65.
3. Assumes a conservative estimate of 500 per 100,000 for maternal mortality ratio without medical treatment. Women from religious groups in America who refuse all medical care in

pregnancy have a maternal mortality ratio of 872 per 100,000. Kaunitz *et al.* (1984) AJOG 150: 826–32.

4. Thomas J, Paranjothy S. Royal College of Obstetricians and Gynaecologists Clinical Effectiveness Support Unit. National Sentinel Caesarean Section Audit Report. RCOG Press; 2001.

5. Anon (1999) Consultants are stretched to their limits BMJ 1999; 319: 256 (24 July)

6. Shaw RW (1999) Reply from Royal College of Obstetricians and Gynaecologists BMJ 1999; 319: 256 (24 July)

7. Source Table A 7.8.1 McFarlane and Mugford, (years 1975–1998) and HCHS medial and dental consultants and registrars (SpR after 1996) by specialty group Department of Health 1994–2004. Note that the data are counted differently before and after 1998.

8. Hodnett ED, Gates S, Hofmeyr G J, Sakala C. Continuous support for women during childbirth. The Cochrane Database of Systematic Reviews 2003, Issue 3. Art. No.: CD003766. DOI: 10.1002/14651858.CD003766.

9. Ball J A, Bennett B, Washbrook M, Webster F. Birthrate Plus Programme: a basis for staffing standards? British Journal of Midwifery: Vol 11, no. 5 pp 264–266 May 2003.

10. MacFarlane A, Mugford M, Henderson J, Furtado A, Stevens J, Dunn A Birth Counts 2nd edition. 2000. The Stationery Office London.

11. Heller G, Richardson DK, Schnell R, Bjö rn Misselwitz B Wolfgang Kü nzel W Schmidt S Are we regionalized enough? Early-neonatal deaths in low-risk births by the size of delivery units in Hesse, Germany 1990–1999 International Journal of Epidemiology 2002; 31: 1061–1068.

12. Richardus JH, Wilco C. Graafmans, S. Verloove-Vanhorick P, Mackenbach JP, The EuroNatal International Audit Panel, 2003 Differences in perinatal mortality and suboptimal care between 10 European regions: results of an international audit BJOG: An International Journal of Obstetrics and Gynaecology 110: 97–105.

13. Richardus JH, Wilco C. Graafmans, S. Verloove-Vanhorick P, Mackenbach JP, The EuroNatal International Audit Panel, 2003 Differences in perinatal mortality and suboptimal care between 10 European regions: results of an international audit BJOG: An International Journal of Obstetrics and Gynaecology 110: 97–105.

ADDITIONAL READING

Cammu, H, Martens G, De Coen K, Van Mol C, Defoort P (2003) Perinatale Activiteiten in Vlaanderen. Published by vzw Studiecentrum voor Perinatale Epidemiologie (SPE). Pp 57.

Direction de la Recherche des Etudes de L' Evaluation et des Statistiques (DREES) Etudes et Resultats No 225 Mar 2003.

House of Commons Select committee on Health – Ninth Report. 10th July 2003.

Department of Health. Changing childbirth. London: HMSO, 1993.

RCOG (2005) Medical workforce in obstetrics and gynaecology. 15th Report. RCOG. London.

Tyler S Comparing the campaigning profile of maternity user groups in Europe – can we learn anything useful? Health expectations (2002) 5: 136–147.

CHAPTER 12
THE FUTURE DEVELOPMENT OF ANAESTHESIA

Dr Peter Simpson

INTRODUCTION

Anaesthesia is a relatively young speciality and was only introduced in its present form into the UK and indeed the world in 1846. Since then rapid advances in the quality and safety of anaesthesia have revolutionised surgery in a way that most would not have thought possible even fifty years ago. Advanced techniques which facilitate cardio-pulmonary bypass, neuro-and thoracic surgery or major orthopaedic and eye surgery in patients with severe co-morbidities are now commonplace. Everyone expects to be anaesthetised for whatever they need and the concept of "unfit for anaesthesia" is viewed with incredulity. Patient and indeed surgical expectation is very high and almost invariably anaesthetists oblige.

It is not only in the field of general, regional or local anaesthesia that today's anaesthetists excel; intensive care medicine and pain management being our two main subspecialties. Although both physicians and anaesthetists become full time intensivists, it is anaesthetists that provide the vast majority of consultants with an interest in intensive care medicine. Indeed we provide the lion's share of postgraduate training in intensive care medicine for trainees from all specialities. A similar pattern has developed in pain management, and even fewer pain specialists come from any speciality other than anaesthesia.

We are also facing increasing demands from other specialist areas such as obstetrics, cardiac and neuroanaesthesia, for dedicated twenty-four hour cover, all of which erodes the time that anaesthetists actually spend in theatre administering anaesthesia. Indeed most hospitals now have three anaesthetist doctors on call every night, one covering anaesthesia, one obstetrics and one intensive care.

A report by the Audit Commission showed that an anaesthetist is involved, at some stage of their treatment, with the care of 65% of all patents admitted to hospital. This is because of the breadth of our involvement in the care of acutely and critically ill patients. Moreover most doctors in training feel that spending some time in acute care, linked to anaesthesia and intensive care medicine is valuable for them. Junior doctor anaesthetists are usually the toast of the town in the hospital mess, just because they can do all the invasive measures needed to support and stabilise acutely ill patients and can bale their colleagues out of problems. To many, anaesthetists are the general practitioners of hospital care and the areas in which we work seem to be increasing all the time. Indeed some say that by 2020, the only consultants present in hospitals on a twenty-four hour basis will be anaesthetists and A&E consultants.

SO WHAT WILL ANAESTHESIA BE LIKE IN 10 YEARS TIME?

A number of key considerations will influence the future development of anaesthetic techniques, including patient acceptability and safety, cost, lack of morbidity, hypersensitivity and mortality and pollution. It is hard to envisage a major change to our basic techniques and it is therefore advances in pharmacology and equipment that will tend to encourage innovation and changes in practice. In essence for general anaesthesia, we use either inhalational or intravenous techniques and regional or local anaesthesia as alternatives. New drugs may well improve what we have available at present, but the fundamental principles and techniques are unlikely to change. Alterations in monitoring, particular if continuous "loss of consciousness" monitoring becomes reliably and widely available will increase the precision of drug dosage and therefore hopefully improve the quality of and recovery from anaesthesia, which in turn improves patient throughput. Administration of anaesthesia will still be the province of medically qualified staff albeit assisted by other, non-medical practitioners as is beginning to happen now.

Although patients will be fitter, they will of course be older, and expectations are increasing all the time. Surgery, which at present is not normally contemplated in patients above a certain age, will become more common; with all the attendant anaesthetic problems. And of course in shortest supply will be critical care and high dependency beds, equipment and staff, who will increasingly have to deal with sick, elderly patients in an increasingly invasive way to meet their and their relatives' expectations.

WHAT WILL THE ANAESTHETIC WORKFORCE AND OUR ANAESTHETIC DEPARTMENTS LOOK LIKE IN 2015?

The Royal College of Anaesthetists now has a total of nearly 14,000 Trainees, Members and Fellows, making anaesthetists a very significant clinical group within the NHS. 1 in 6 hospital consultants is an anaesthetist. We carry out detailed workforce planning with the Government and the Department of Health on a regular basis and have put considerable effort into attempting to profile our specialty and future requirements over the next 10 to 15 years. Although there appears to be an inexhaustible need for additional anaesthetists with cries that we should simply provide as many trainees as possible, this would be a very short-sighted approach. Once anaesthesia becomes a consultant-delivered specialty, as many aspects of critical care and pain management already are, the need for vast numbers of additional anaesthetists will decline rapidly.

Despite advances in anaesthetic techniques and the large number of trainees going through the system to become accredited specialist anaesthetists, there is no doubt that the staffing balance within most departments will be very different in ten years' time. Irrespective of the reasons, the potential and inevitable changes to the anaesthetic workforce of the future will have a considerable effect on training. At present it takes approximately nine years to train an anaesthetist from initial qualification and although competency-based training should not be strictly time limited, rotating a trainee through all the necessary training modules will inevitably take a similar length of time. We produce approximately 200 Certified Credited Training (CCT) holders annually over and above the number necessary to replace retirement vacancies and these all help to increase the consultant anaesthetic workforce (including intensive care and pain management), so this expands by about 1000 every 5 years. At present we have about 5,800 consultants and to reach our estimate of the 8,500 staff required for a wholly consultant delivered service will therefore take 13-14 years, and will be achieved in 2018-19. Admittedly this is in whole time equivalent (WTE) terms, but the argument is still valid, in that once the speciality is "full", we will only need to replace consultant vacancies. This means that instead of the 320 or so trainees who get their CCT each year, we will only need half that number, unless we are going to deliberately overproduce. 2018 may seem to be an impossibly long way off, but given the length of training, nine years earlier is actually 2009, or three years from now.

The consequence of these workforce projections and the provision of a consultant delivered service by 2020 with the inevitable reduction in trainee numbers, leads to major changes in the staffing balance of departments, which will vary according to the size and workload of the hospital. We could allow trainees to be spread more thinly, but, while training would not necessarily suffer and may even be improved, they would certainly be unable in terms of their numbers, to sustain the multiplicity of on call rotas which exist at present. This then begs the question as to whether the structure of anaesthetic departments should change with more emphasis on the European model of a tiered structure of career grade staff, with individuals appointed with specific competencies to work with defined responsibilities and in limited areas of care. This is not in any way to say that we should have a "two or more tiered consultant" system, but rather to recognise that while some would want to be specialists with managerial responsibility, others could have academic or teaching roles, and some would be happiest undertaking reduced amounts of service work without some of the other additional responsibilities, i.e. working part time. Competency based training, which has existed throughout anaesthetic training for some years, allows this and such a model is very sensitive to the changing medical workforce and the fact that many more women are entering medical school. If we are to populate departments of anaesthesia with happy and professionally satisfied career grade medical staff, we must provide a variety of jobs for them and also the opportunity during their careers, to gain additional competencies and change their career direction as a result.

SO WHY IS ANAESTHETIC WORKFORCE PLANNING SO PROBLEMATIC?

Although we are able to adjust workforce numbers in line with current service and training requirements, recent experience has shown the variety of unpredictable influences that will affect even the best laid plans. We may understand what the projected workforce needs, but to predict the profile of the future staff in terms of their gender, nationality or indeed the way in which they wish to work is far more difficult. The intake into UK medical schools has increased significantly, and this will take time to percolate through the system to produce accredited specialists, but when it does, the 70+% female intake will undoubtedly influence things.

WHAT WILL BE THE INFLUENCE OF EUROPE AND BEYOND?

Although output from medical schools is increasing, of those currently entering anaesthetic training, 50% are graduates of overseas medical schools. Some European medical graduates wish to continue their postgraduate training in the UK. Free movement of trained EU specialists also has the potential to radically affect anaesthetic workforce planning in the UK. Current regulations allow an EU National doctor, who has his/her primary medical qualification in the EU and who is on the specialist register of an EU state, to transfer that registration to another EU state as they wish. Many such doctors are working in the UK and have helped enormously in areas where recruitment has been difficult, but it is the unpredictability of the size, the sustainability and specialist expertise of this workforce that has made planning difficult. Many will come to work in the UK for a few years before returning to their own country and some will commute to the UK on a weekly basis. Many of us of course did this in the past, particularly to Holland and Sweden and anaesthesia is a very trans-ferable speciality. We should welcome the diversity and positive challenges to training and knowledge that this brings, but for those trying to workforce plan, it is an additional headache!

WILL ALL HOSPITALS CONTRIBUTE TO TRAINING IN THE FUTURE?

An alternative consequence and an inevitable question which arises from all that I have written is whether it will be feasible to sustain trainees in all hospitals in the future. There is no doubt that unlike almost every other country, trainees are present in about 95% of all hospitals in the UK. Given that many of these hospitals do not offer unique training opportunities, this inevitably, has to be largely linked to trainees being relied upon for service delivery, particularly out of hours. The question that is yet unanswered is whether a number of hospitals would actually prefer to run without trainees, allowing them to be consolidated in a more limited number of training hospitals.

This however, requires that service delivery in those hospitals without trainees will have to be delivered by another group of staff. Although different, this is certainly not impossible, in that a number of anaesthetic departments now exist very happily with consultants and new anaesthetic Senior House Officers (SHOs), who inevitably cannot contribute to the service. Out of hours work between consultant anaesthetists and consultant surgeons is perfectly well organised and excellent training opportunities are provided for the SHOs who are essentially employed in a supernumerary capacity. Furthermore, thus far I have only considered medical anaesthetic training and as we all know, anaesthetists contribute to the training of numerous different groups, medical students, foundation trainees, cross-speciality training and non-medical groups such as paramedics, nurses, Operating Department Practitioners and anaesthetic practitioners.

If this change is inevitable, and I believe it is, should we not be trying to plan logically for it, rather than allowing it to occur by a process of attrition? Currently training seems to come a distant third to service work and sustaining the on call rota. While we are certainly sympathetic to problems that Trusts have in trying to balance all their priorities, in some of these situations we are paying lip service to anaesthetic training and actually using trainees to sustain the service. With proper planning, understanding and acceptance of the problem by all those concerned and responsible, together with a positive approach, we can still provide good solutions for the quality and safety of patient care.

WHAT WILL ANAESTHETIC, INTENSIVE CARE AND PAIN MANAGEMENT TRAINING LOOK LIKE IN 10 YEARS TIME?

The result of European Working Time Directive (EWTD) implementation is that approximately 80% of all anaesthetic trainees now work full shifts and this in turn has undoubtedly had a serious effect on anaesthetic training. However, this has had the knock on effect that trainees are not available during the daytime to be taught and is unsustainable in the long run.

Apart from EWTD implementation, developments in training and accreditation are currently dominated by two major initiatives, Modernising Medical Careers MMC and the setting up of the Postgraduate Medical Education and Training Board that are further discussed later in this book.

THE CONFLICT BETWEEN TRAINING AND SERVICE DELIVERY

Recent years have seen enormous changes in the way in which training takes place and importantly, the amount of time in which trainees are available to be trained. Both the implementation of the EWTD and the development of MMC began with a firm emphasis on the need to continue to deliver high quality training, but inevitably, as reality bites, service issues have come to the fore. Complying with EWTD hours and in particular those imposed by the SiMAP and Jaeger judgements, means that trainee's work load has become even more concentrated out of hours sustaining service rotas, with full shift work being the norm in many specialties. Although many of us emphasised that the solution could not simply be a redistribution of trainees across on-call rotas to comply with EWTD regulations, but rather a more wholesale look at the way in which a department delivered out-of-hours service, the former has it fact become reality in many hospitals. While we acknowledge that service work is undoubtedly an integral part of training in an apprenticeship style programme, this must not be its prime aim. Unlike many other specialities, anaesthetic SHOs and Specialist Registrars also make a major contribution to daytime service delivery and many departments depend on this to ensure that routine operating takes place and targets are met. Hospitals are required to meet daytime targets for elective surgery and as such, these take priority over other areas of work and more importantly, away from training. When this is combined with maintaining out-of- hours on call rotas, training sometimes comes a distant third.

MODERNISING MEDICAL CAREERS (MMC)

Foundation Year training, the first part of MMC, began in 2005. This two year period is fundamentally concerned with developing the generic skills of a doctor and their ability to care for critically ill patients, while anaesthesia and critical care has a key role to play in teaching many of the competencies, actual anaesthetic attachments have not been included.

Hence we are introducing a common stem introduction to specialist training in anaesthesia, critical care, acute medicine and emergency medicine, on the basis that many of the competencies will be sufficiently similar to allow the creation of a generic curriculum with transferable skills. Trainees will spend the first two years of specialist training in such a post, rotating at six monthly intervals through these related specialities and achieving common competencies. We believe that this alternative to making an immediate and ultimate career choice at the end of foundation would be very popular with some trainees and prevent them opting for something for which they are subsequently found to be unsuited. It would also be well suited to those training programmes such as intensive care medicine, which require complimentary speciality training.

SO WHAT SHOULD WE BE TEACHING OUR TRAINEES?

While we can be very proud, and grateful to those who designed it, our competency based training programme is the envy of many other specialities, we must not let it rest there. Extensive discussions are taking place about whether, in every speciality, we are preparing our trainees for the role of consultants in the future NHS. This "extended role" of the Consultant comprises many areas beyond our clinical abilities and for which we all need appropriate training. The basic elements of this could and should be included as generic elements of all training programmes. Incorporating not just anaesthetic skills but also how to critically review an article, how to design clinical trails, academic medicine, how to understand the basic elements of research and clinical audit and have the opportunity to undertake research to higher degree level. Incorporating having an understanding of ethics and the issues behind informed consent, understanding departmental management and organisation, teaching, assessment and medical education to be included in all training programmes which will subsequently allow those with these specific abilities and interests to develop them further during their careers.

TRAINING AND TREATMENT CENTRES

The growth and development of independent sector treatment centres has posed a number of problems for the College related both to the practical aspects of delivering anaesthesia and also importantly to the quality and safety of anaesthetic training. We feel strongly that, although such centres that are outside the health service, they should also take part in the training for which we are responsible.

A FACULTY OF PAIN MANAGEMENT

Over recent years Pain Medicine has become a major interest of many anaesthetists. There is already an Intercollegiate Board that supervises specialist training in Intensive Care Medicine and we recognise that aspects of the training of pain management also fall outside the normal jurisdiction of College Tutors and Regional Advisors in anaesthesia. For example, advanced trainees in pain management will be learning about cognitive-behavioural pain programmes, spinal cord stimulation and palliative care.

As a result, two years ago, Council approved the appointment of Regional Advisors in Pain Management and this year approved the establishment of a Faculty of Pain Management within the Royal College of Anaesthetists. A Founding Board is now advising Council on the Terms of Reference of the Faculty and work is underway already on achieving this. We have ensured that other Colleges with a potential interest in pain are aware of our plans and there has been nothing but encouragement from other specialities. This important development for our specialty will emphasise that anaesthetists make massive contributions to healthcare outside the operating theatre and it will ensure that trainee anaesthetists can obtain excellent training in all aspects of pain management.

WHERE ARE WE WITH ANAESTHESIA PRACTITIONERS?

The anaesthesia and critical care practitioner concept has become divided into anaesthesia care practitioners (ACPs) and critical care practitioners (CCPs) but, importantly, the College, working with the Association, has retained very close control and involvement with the project. During the first year, Phase 1 of the pilot programme was undertaken in a small number of Trusts involving two separate initiatives. In the first, trained anaesthesia practitioners were recruited from Europe and worked as part of the anaesthesia team to see if the project was feasible and, indeed, if their presence enhanced the quality and safety of patient care. In the second, locally recruited practitioners were introduced to the programme and continue to be trained to work within the anaesthetic environment.

Although very small, both these projects have been successful and the considerable feedback from them has informed the second wave of pilots which are now being undertaken. In these, groups of interested hospitals are clustered together, each providing a small number of selected trainees who are undertaking the full anaesthesia practitioner training programme. Significantly, in one cluster, all the trainees are science graduates without a healthcare background. The curriculum for this was designed by the College, initially under the umbrella of the NHS University and then developed into its final form by the University Department of Anaesthetics in Birmingham. It is franchised to local universities to use in the theoretical teaching and practical assessment of anaesthesia practitioners. They undertake a full two year, four month programme with continuous assessment, at the end of which they will obtain a Masters level qualification. There will also be a national, voluntary registration programme under the umbrella of the College. The key to the success of the whole project has been close and collaborative working between the Royal College, the Association, the NHS Modernisation Agency and the Department of Health right from the start. All parties are only too aware that the ultimate success of anaesthesia practitioners depends upon a significant buy-in by anaesthetists and that to allow individual Trusts or Strategic Health Authorities to go their own way, against the support of their current anaesthetic staff would be disastrous. Ultimately, it will depend on local implementation and take up by individual hospitals and Trusts, to establish the true value of practitioners within anaesthetic departments, working with anaesthetists in all aspects of their work.

CHAPTER 13
THE FUTURE OF OPHTHALMOLOGY

Mr Nick Astbury

The eye is a discreet organ, highly visible both in function and social context, and through its nervous and vascular connections, its pathology is intimately associated with the rest of the body. Its wide-ranging study encompasses the whole gamut of medicine, surgery, pathology, genetics, molecular biology and public health. But despite this absorbing potential for interest and variety, ophthalmology remains a somewhat 'Cinderella' specialty which in part stems from undergraduates having such a brief exposure to the subject. As a result many clinicians are unsure how to manage 'eye' patients and struggle to understand the complex and sometimes obscure ophthalmic terminology.

Nevertheless, entry into ophthalmology is competitive, as its popularity has steadily increased; and for those who have overcome the hurdles, and for whom the mysteries have been revealed, the rewards are great, but so are the challenges as ophthalmology enters the 21st century. Huge changes in practice have taken place over the past twenty years as technology and the pace of change has accelerated. Working hours are shorter but productivity has increased and standards are now higher than ever. Government demands that targets are met but annual efficiency savings must still be made. The public and press have increasingly high expectations which every once in a while are dented by a high-profile medical scandal which sets back the whole profession.

One constancy in a fast changing health service is our collegiate system, which although seen by some as irrelevant, champions quality and professionalism and the importance of a service centred on patients' needs. The Royal College of Ophthalmologists was formed from the Ophthalmological Society of the United Kingdom (founded in 1880) and the Faculty of Ophthalmologists and received its Royal Charter in 1988. The Charter forms the bedrock of the work of the College and states clearly its purpose to advance the science and practice of ophthalmology, maintain proper standards for the benefit of the public, to educate and to train. Through its work, the balance between service and training is monitored and maintained, in order to ensure that patients now and in the future receive a safe and professional service from competent doctors.

THE OPHTHALMIC WORKFORCE

The future of ophthalmology is intimately dependent upon the workforce employed to deliver the service. Predicting that workforce is an art which requires an exact knowledge of existing numbers whilst taking account of numerous and sometimes unpredictable factors. These include the number of medical school graduates, the gender mix of medical students, changes to European working time legislation, training capacity, demographic trends (such as an ageing population), new treatments especially for degenerative conditions, constantly changing government targets and increasing sub-specialisation.

The College has agreed with the Workforce Review Team that there should be, based on an evaluation of the above factors, a 5% consultant expansion year on year. This of course is dependent upon funding new posts and an acceptance that the service should be 'consultant-led'. In reality there has been a reduction rather than expansion of consultant posts, a situation that needs to be reversed in order to make sense of the entire workforce planning process. In future we will see an increasingly female workforce with more ophthalmologists working part-time as new medical students qualify and working hours further reduce. More ophthalmologists will opt for community ophthalmology, as the ratio of surgical to medical activity reduces and more therapeutic and genetic treatment options become available. A range of non-medically qualified 'practitioners' will emerge to complement the medical workforce.

OPHTHALMIC PRIMARY CARE

Community-based multidisciplinary teams have been a much-heralded answer to capacity problems in the health service and ophthalmology has been at the centre of an intense debate as to the roles of the many professionals involved in delivering the service. These include ophthalmologists, nurses, orthoptists, optometrists, general practitioners, photographers and technical staff. Optometrists heavily outnumber ophthalmologists and are actively pursuing an increased clinical role, which will be backed up by the acquisition of prescribing rights, in common with nurses and pharmacists. Aspiring technical staff will be able to undertake a new foundation degree in Ophthalmic Science and Technology which will open the door for many wishing to work within a multiprofessional environment.

In future we will see a medically led and more varied professional workforce, organised in 'clinical networks' and providing a service less centred on hospitals. This will particularly apply for patients who currently attend overcrowded ophthalmic outpatients or accident and emergency departments and for whom a more locally based and accessible service would be welcome. However, in order to be effective, ophthalmic primary care in the community will need to be fully integrated with secondary care, cost-effective and not duplicate existing services. Sharing of information and IT support will be essential as professional barriers are broken down.

'PLURALITY' AND 'CONTESTABILITY'

For some time, government focus has been on increasing the capacity and efficiency of the NHS in order to meet the growing demands of an ageing population for whom new and expensive treatments have become available. Words such as 'plurality' and 'contestability' have been added to the ministerial lexicon and private independent sector treatment centres (IS-TCs) and overseas providers have been brought in to tackle waiting time targets, in the belief that without competition, the NHS would not by itself be able to pull up its corporate socks and deliver the necessary activity.

The debate about plurality of providers is particularly relevant in ophthalmology, as cataract surgery is the most commonly performed elective procedure in the United Kingdom, and the restoration of vision to those affected makes such a fundamental difference to their lives. The specialty has been leading innovation and development ever since the 'Action on Cataracts' programme, which was a highly successful initiative conceived by the College in partnership with the government. NHS staff, by embracing new technology and working practices and introducing modern high-throughput day case cataract surgery and new patient pathways, have dramatically reduced waiting times.

The future does not lie with commercially driven IS-TCs staffed by overseas doctors on working vacation, who to date have carried out just 2.5% of the cataract throughput, at considerably greater cost. Experience has revealed that well-founded concerns have been realised in the form of adverse impacts on junior staff training, the local health economy, staff morale and consultant recruitment. We should in preference be investing in our own hospital departments that are more than capable of delivering an excellent, innovative and local service.

The massive increase in NHS funding seen in recent years is not sustainable and unless contributions rise or alternative (private insurance) funding streams are put in place, the pressures on the service will continue to mount. Apart from several billion pounds invested in IS-TCs, the additional revenue has been largely absorbed by staffing costs and private finance initiatives that have enabled new hospitals to be built more quickly but at enormous long-term cost to the tax-payer. Given that funding will always be an issue, the government has used the strategies of plurality, increased competition and choice to drive up efficiency. However they risk fragmenting and destabilising the NHS unless training can be protected and recognition is given to the importance of the treatment of long-term diseases (glaucoma, diabetic retinopathy, age-related macular degeneration) compared to profitable short term surgical targets.

CHOICE

The question of choice affects us all, as ophthalmologists are patients as well as doctors. I would prefer to go to my local hospital and receive a first-rate service and if a specialist service was not available I would be prepared to travel to a regional centre. This simple concept appears to have been by-passed and instead the powers that be have it in mind to offer a variety of choices to every patient even if it means travelling to Macclesfield or Morecambe to receive treatment.

The 'Choose and Book' initiative is a vastly ambitious project that is intended to give every soul the choice of 5 different service providers when they consult with their GP who will have available an on-line Directory of Services Data Collection Template and a Service Definer Web Interface. Only time will tell whether the patient (elderly or otherwise) will benefit from leaving their doctor with a unique booking reference number, a date by which the appointment must be made, a priority indication, a HealthSpace website address, a booking service telephone number and an 8 character password.

It does not need to be so complicated though. Information technology at its best has already transformed our lives and has improved the way in which we work particularly when it has been introduced on a small scale and properly piloted. Ophthalmology now enjoys the benefits of digital imaging and storage and in time all units will have a fully computerised patient record. Connecting for Health (CfH), formerly known as the National Programme for IT, is strengthening the clinical input into the design, development and implementation of the IT programme. To this end the Knowledge, Process and Safety Directorate of CfH is working with the profession and the College to develop a national dataset and care pathway for cataract, glaucoma and the management of diabetic eye disease. This is an exciting project to which every ophthalmologist will have an opportunity to contribute.

EDUCATION AND TRAINING

The future of ophthalmology, although bound up with IT progress, will above all depend upon the training of ophthalmologists and other practitioners who come into clinical contact with patients. A change in legislation in 2003, which established the Postgraduate Medical Education and Training Board (PMETB), was introduced to develop a single, unifying framework for postgraduate medical education. At the same time 'Modernising Medical Careers' has led to the establishment of a two year post-qualification generic 'foundation' programme followed by 'run-through' specialist training (with clinical and academic pathways). In future we will see ophthalmologists selected from the second year of foundation training with no requirement for examinations or previous experience in ophthalmology, but practical skills and communication skills will form part of the assessment. Selection directly from foundation programmes and the current over-supply of Senior House Officers (SHOs) in ophthal-mology pose particular challenges for transition. Any solution will need to ensure that there is equitable entry between the two groups for career progression.

The Royal College of Ophthalmologists together with other Colleges and Faculties is working closely with PMETB and has developed a new web-based curriculum for specialist training in ophthalmology which describes the outcomes of 7 years of postgraduate training, which will lead to the award of a Certificate of Completion of Train-ing (CCT). The essential or core requirements are described by a series of learning outcomes derived from a description of what a consultant ophthalmologist should be able to do and how he/she approaches his/her practice. The concept of an ophthalmologist who is core trained but who has developed a special interest is the model on which the curriculum is based. In future this requirement may change in response to patients' service needs and undoubtedly different areas of special interest will emerge.

Examinations have also been 'modernised' so that the new syllabus corresponds with the new curriculum. Ophthalmic Specialist Training in the UK will in future be assessed by two formal examinations rather than the current four; in addition there will be further assess-ments locally in the form of work-placed based assessments that will form part of a more structured Record of In Training Assessment (RITA). The trainee will have a portfolio of attainments achieved that he/she will need to accumulate during training, many of which will correspond with learning outcomes as defined in the new curriculum.

Those that are not in ophthalmic specialist training in the UK, including overseas doctors, may also sit the new examinations with-out the local work-placed based assessments and therefore achieve a Fellowship of the Royal College of Ophthalmologists. It is to be stressed, however, that this will not allow the trainee to gain a Certificate of Completion of Training in the UK.

The new legislation will broaden the routes under which qualified and/or trained specialists from anywhere in the world, including the UK, can be assessed for entry to the General Medical Council's Specialist Register. Under Article 14 it will be possible for experience to be considered, as well as qualifications and training, when assessing a doctor's equivalence and eligibility for the Specialist Register. For ophthalmology we will see an increase in applications, both from overseas doctors and from UK Staff and Associate Specialists, some of whom will require 'top up training' in order to gain specialist registration. The acquisition of transferable competencies gained either in formal training, parallel streams or even in complementary specialties will facilitate this process.

Opportunities for employment for overseas doctors will be radically reduced as a result of recently introduced legislation which will require any NHS trust wishing to employ a doctor from outside the EU to prove that a 'home-grown' doctor cannot fill the vacant post. This will regrettably put an end to current permit-free training arrangements for overseas doctors and result in the loss of international goodwill that has been built up over the years.

WORLD BLINDNESS

The future of ophthalmology cannot be considered without reference to those afflicted by visual impairment worldwide. They number some 124 million of whom 37 million are blind and approximately 90% live in the developing world. Three quarters of these blind people could have their sight restored, or are blind from diseases which are exacerbated by poor diet or hygiene and can be prevented. An immense amount of work is carried out by charitable organisations with which UK ophthalmologists are associated. VISION 2020 or 'The Right to Sight' is a global initiative which aims to help eliminate avoidable blindness by the year 2020, jointly launched by the World Health Organization and the International Agency for the Prevention of Blindness together with more than 20 international NGOs.

There is an active Vision2020 LINKS Programme developed by the International Centre for Eye Health which is designed to give teaching eye institutions in developing countries the capacity to develop high quality programmes for eye care professionals. The VISION 2020 Links Programme will work with an overseas partner institution (initially in Africa) to identify its main needs and priorities and then match those requirements with a suitable UK training eye unit that best meet those needs. Each link may continue over a period of 3 to 5 years or longer depending on the defined priority.

CONCLUSION

In the developed world, technology will continue to advance and cures will eventually be found for major blinding diseases, either through pharmacology or gene therapy. Age related degeneration will continue to be a burden for health services and demands for cosmetic and refractive surgery will increase. Ophthalmologists will rely more on machines but will still need 'good hands' and well developed communication skills.

The future rests in all of our hands to a greater or lesser extent. What we do today directly affects our patients and those around us; we can set a good example to others or lead them astray. But there will always be events over which we have no control and governments that impose change for change's sake rather than building on existing good practice.

We can counteract these outside influences by reflecting on the rewarding nature of ophthalmology and remember that the profes-sional doctor-patient relationship is essentially the same as it always has been. It is one of trust that depends on ophthalmologists following Hippocrate's advice from 460 BC: practise for the benefit of patients, do no harm and abstain from mischief and corruption.

CHAPTER 14

THE FUTURE OF CARDIOLOGY WITHIN THE NHS

Dr David Stone

The prediction of cardiological development is always fraught with uncertainty, because the discipline crosses many borders and is associated with technological development in very rapidly changing fields. The basic questions to be addressed are: *what* will we be doing and *where* will we be doing it?

I will firstly address the question of the changes in the discipline itself. In recent years there has been a revolution in the delivery of therapeutic treatment in terms of tablet treatments such as with statins and ACE inhibitors, which has reduced the incidence of heart attacks and seems to be lessening the demand for other interventions such as balloon angioplasty (PCI). Nonetheless PCI has been the single most potent factor in the reduction of the demand for coronary by-pass surgery. In conjunction with this the investigation and treatment of patients with heart beat irregularities (arrythmias) has become more aggressive, in other words, there has been a shift towards invasive treatment with ablation techniques for many conditions and a huge increase in the availability of implantable defibrillators and their application. The rapid evolution of chip technology has allowed the fantastic development of radiological techniques and the ability to view images at a distance and instantaneously. Cardiac Magnetic Resonance Imaging and Multi-slice CT are displacing cardiac catheterisation from its pole position as the key investigation technique for patients with heart disease. The demand for nuclear scans is high, but their availability low. Patients with heart failure are receiving enhanced medication treatment and where appropriate, imaging techniques play a vital part in revascularisation techniques such as angioplasty or surgery.

On top of these changes, we are dealing with an increasingly more elderly population and thus with patients with more complex multi-system disease. Many of the vascular diseases involve vessels in all of the body and heart investigations and treatments are taking place within a broader context. In particular, diabetics have a very high incidence of cardiac problems. Smoking remains the single biggest health risk in terms of cardiac disease. There is a clinical as well as a political need to deliver care as quickly as possible, particularly when it comes to the treatment of heart attacks.

Which brings us to the issue of *where* cardiac care is to be delivered and the clinical and political drivers that determine the decision. As I have implied the nature of cardiac disease requires expeditious and in some cases immediate treatment. The National Service Framework for heart disease has revolutionised cardiac care and where it is given. Catheter laboratories are now available in most large District General Hospital's where treatment for heart failure is being administered locally, often by specialist nurses. Because of this, the emphasis has been on local provision of services and the natural extension of this is the greater involvement of cardiac primary care health professionals into the process. Many of these changes have been initiated and organised by cardiac networks, which have provided forums in which decisions can be made about how and where to deliver care.

The landscape in which all this has been talking place is however far from simple. In recent years there have also been major alterations in professional roles, the training of doctors and others and the financing of the whole process. The role of the specialist has altered and the position of the generalist has become threatened, affecting the delivery of emergency acute care and referral patterns. The shorter training, albeit with much improved assessment and appraisal processes, has resulted in a less experienced newly appointed consultant, and with respect to specialist services a more focussed specialist with more knowledge but mainly in a highly specialised field. This is not an insurmountable problem but has implications in terms of patient perception and expectation.

The most fundamental change is in my view an alteration in the ethos of the NHS as a whole. In summary, there has been a shift from an all encompassing organisation, with joint rights and responsibilities being assumed by patients and staff (but, I agree far too paternalistic in attitude and behaviour) towards what might be called 'The Selfish

NHS', with much more emphasis on individual needs and wants and far less consideration being given to others. Examples of this are legion but key indicators and influences would be Foundation Trusts, Agenda for Change, Patient Choice and the new Consultant Contract. All of these initiatives, while praiseworthy in themselves, and while dealing with fundamental and crucial issues, encourage individualism, which is at odds with the earlier NHS. The modern patient is not expecting to allow for the effect of her Choice on others; the consultant will not take on extra work or struggle into the evening without it being costed and paid for; the nurse has fought for his grading on the basis of what he does and been expected to demonstrate and justify that; the Foundation Trust is to be aggressively competitive and to attract patients in innovative ways that may not fit in with other health care organisations.

There are also inherent dichotomies and divisions that inhibit the making of health care provision decisions. I think that many of us are used to contradictions engendered by being part of a complex organisation led by political imperatives that may change or suddenly be imposed upon us. Nonetheless, at the moment there appear to be significant internal contradictions that make life challenging. For example, there is a clear clash between Patient Choice and Cardiac Networks. Does the patient choose where it is best to go for heart failure treatment or should the network decide? Do you go to your local District General Hospital for your balloon angioplasty or your local – but perhaps more distant – cardiac centre? If the centre is a Foundation Trust or part of one then do they not need to go out and tout for your business and perhaps 'threaten' the District General Hospital cardiology service set up following the NSF initiative?

All of this is all the more apposite, because we are talking about specialist high profile but expensive services. And now we come to money. The final enabler but one, which is underlying many of the current issues. There is no doubt that specialist services present additional problems for a cash limited NHS. They are often high profile and deal with life threatening conditions. And of course cardiology is a paradigm for the specialist and expensive service plus heart disease is very common. The introduction of Payment By Results is having a destabilising effect and there is great concern that the system is not making sufficient allowances (as yet) for the costs relating to complex and expensive pathways and procedures. For cardiology services to remain viable, more sophisticated and responsive methods of payment have to be instituted. Once this has been achieved it will become clearer where and how to provide the most cost effective and efficient care. It is my belief and understanding that the process is still developing and this problem at least will be solved in the short to medium term.

What, then, is my vision for cardiology in the NHS of the future? In order to summarise my views I will divide, perhaps somewhat artificially, the specialty into sub-divisions.

ISCHAEMIC HEART DISEASE

The effect of improvements in imaging on the provision of cardiac services will be to change the face of diagnostic testing. Multi-slice CT scanners will allow screening for coronary artery disease and the newer scanners are already able to delineate coronary anatomy in most cases. Currently nuclear scanning is the main screening modality once the patient has had an exercise test that is inconclusive or unsatisfactory. I would anticipate that the use of cardiac catheterisation to diagnose whether or not there is coronary disease will die out, and be displaced by non-invasive testing, particularly CT. Instantaneous image transfer will enable testing to take place locally, with reporting done centrally. While it is likely that most District General type hospitals will be doing balloon angioplasty (PCI), the inter-relationship with cardiac centres will be critical, both for advice and peer support. The more entrepreneurial centres will no doubt seek to attract patients directly.

The place of PCI versus thrombolysis (clot busting therapy) in acute heart attack will depend on logistics. Where PCI can be performed expeditiously it is will become the prime method of treatment otherwise the location for this will be an acute cardiac care unit.

The multi-vessel and multi-system nature of cardiac disease will mean that cardiac centres will be co-located with other specialities, particularly diabetes and neurology, and that coronary angioplasty will be performed at the same sitting as peripheral vessel PCI. It is likely that there will be less coronary by-pass operations performed, but due to their age and concomitant diseases, the patients will be sicker and have longer lengths of stay.

HEART FAILURE

The delivery of chronic therapeutic agents will continue to take place near home, led by nurses either in the environment of the local District General Hospitals or specialist General Practice. Screening will continue to be dependent upon echocardiography availability; once again either in outreach practices or the local hospital. The ability of sophisticated imaging techniques, MRI or PET, will enable patients with so-called hibernating myocardium (i.e. those with poor left ventricular function that would improve with revascularisation by PCI or coronary surgery) to be more easily identified. It is likely that this will take place in the cardiac centre due to its complexity. However, the extremely poor ventricle will be treated by transplantation or ventricular support as now, but in fewer centres spread over the country.

HEART RHYTHM DISORDERS

There is no doubt that the expert treatment of rhythm disorders is the most rapidly developing area of cardiology. The use of ablation techniques has revolutionised the treatment of atrial arrythmias, and the number and demand for electrophysiologists carrying out the specialist techniques, has escalated. Similarly, the use of device therapy such as cardiac defibrillators for malignant arrythmias and, to a lesser degree, biventricular pacing for heart failure, has mushroomed. The key questions, as yet unanswered, are whether ablation techniques for atrial fibrillation will become permanently and widely established and whether the use of implantable defibrillators will prove efficacious in the management of patients with impaired left ventricular function without proven arrythmias. Both of these issues will have a profound financial and logistic implication. In general, device based treatments could take place in the local District General Hospitals, but the ablation procedures will need to be administered by a trained electrophysiologist in an appropriate environment.

VALVULAR HEART DISEASE

The diagnosis of patients with Valvular heart disease rests on clinical assessment and early availability of echocardiography. Nearly all GPs have access to echocardiography and in some cases echocardiograms are performed in the practice environment. The major pathologies now being treated are aortic and mitral valve disease, with or without impairment of left ventricular function. There has been a shift in mitral valve surgery from replacement to repair and it is likely that specialist surgical valve centres will develop with full imaging – particularly echo – support. Percutaneous aortic and mitral valve surgery is being mooted but is unlikely to replace conventional surgery. Similarly, atrial septal closure by percutaneous techniques is being performed regularly and if small hole in the heart closure proves efficacious in the treatment of migraine, this will become an important component of interventional cardiology.

OTHER AREAS

It is difficult to cover everything in a short article but other areas of major concern include the management of patients with Grown Up Congenital Heart disease, Maternal Medicine during pregnancy and the use of stenting and percutaneous techniques in patients with aortic diseases of the aorta (the vessel, not the valve). These will require focussed training but are of critical importance and need to be instituted appropriately as soon as possible.

AND NOW TO THE FINAL QUESTIONS

WHAT HAVE WE FORGOTTEN AND WHERE ARE WE GOING WRONG?

There is s certain element of short termism in working within a system at least somewhat dependent on an electoral system with a (maximum of) 5-year cycle. If imposed upon what is a financially based health service that is at the same time undergoing major changes in training and reimbursement, it is little wonder that the future is uncertain and that there is a retreat into a defensive position. Yet all concede that there are certain functions that contribute to service, that are the foundations of our future and which are essentially an investment in our children and their children.

These functions are research and education.

Fortunately the warning bells about research have been ringing for some time and steps are being taken to redress the undermining of research in cardiology and indeed all disciplines. It is vital that the issue is resolved and that there is a renewal of the link between clinical, translational and basic research.

Similarly education and training are under threat. There is no obvious immediate financial or indeed clinical benefit in terms of education and training for any given institution or for those who purchase health care. For the first time in my career, senior clinicians are questioning the worth of providing training for junior doctors. After all, it is expensive in terms of hours of preparation and consequent reduction in availability for front line patient care. Nurses cannot be freed because of service pressures and their training is becoming more and more difficult to achieve. In order to attract and develop front line technical staff a formalised and inspirational programme of learning is essential. Technicians are a valuable and increasingly difficult to find resource – yet absolutely crucial for the provision of the cardiological service – now and in the future.

I do not feel that there is a lack of concern about these issues, more an inability to fully allow for them in our health service as it is developing. They must not be allowed to become marginalised and our future sacrificed for our present.

CHAPTER 15

THE CRYSTAL BALL OF CANCER CARE

Professor Karol Sikora

The global incidence of cancer is set to double from 10 million to 20 million over the next twenty years. In Britain the incidence is increasing at 2.5% per year because of earlier diagnosis and an aging population. Remarkable recent advances have been made in our ability to treat cancer with both radiotherapy and drugs. We have also seen a greatly increased basic understanding of the molecular abnormalities that cause cancer driven by an explosion of genomic knowledge. This will lead to the creation of more effective and less toxic therapies given for longer periods of time.

The public is more frightened of cancer than any other illness. Many avidly seek increasing amounts of information about novel conventional and alternative therapies. The increasing use of the internet as an effective information source has empowered patients to seek out optimal care. The media are bombarded with press releases from cancer charities, the biotechnology and pharmaceutical industry about breakthroughs. These often result in confusing but positive stories in the written and broadcast media, which are read avidly by patients and their families. The recent frenzy over the use of Herceptin as adjuvant therapy for early breast cancer has led to legal action and the Health Minister taking the unusual step of overruling NICE for political expediency.[1] We're not very good at presenting balanced views as everyone has a vested interest and calm analysis is not front-page stuff.

State run health services around the world have not anticipated the dramatically increasing costs associated with high quality cancer care and many have developed complex systems of overt and covert rationing which cause widespread inequity. The NHS in its current form is no exception. Elected politicians are keen to join initiatives to improve cancer care but cannot provide additional revenue without increasing taxation or reducing other healthcare services. This has led to much confusion amongst patients who rarely get adequate explanations of the options available. The cancer budget has increased dramatically under the NHS Cancer Plan since September 2000.[2] The accounting wouldn't pass muster with my tax collector, but over £2.5 billion extra money has apparently gone into a traditional public sector model for improving services through the Cancer Plan. But there are too many people trying to get their fingers in the till – the Department of Health, the 14 Strategic Health Authorities, the 34 Cancer Networks, the 302 Primary Care Trusts and the 124 cancer treatment centres in provider trusts of which 61 provide radiotherapy. Mike Richards, our cancer czar, has done an excellent job in providing strategies but their implementation has been poor and patchy as judged by a recent House of Commons Public Accounts Committee report.[3] Basically, the existing system just can't cope even when massive amounts of taxpayer's money is thrown at it.

The icon of the next decade for cancer treatment is the exponential curve. New surgical methods will be developed causing minimal damage to normal tissues. Robotic excision using minimally invasive techniques will lower the impact of cancer surgery on patients and lead to shorter hospital stays. Radiotherapy techniques are now available which allow the delivery of a high dose volume precisely conforming to the shape of a tumour. But this takes time, money and equipment. Yet the NHS still has intractable delays for standard radiotherapy with waiting times of greater than 3 months in many areas. Despite a huge spending spree using National Lottery funds our capacity is still far lower than any other western European country. The 2005 QUARTS study[4] considered the actual number of radiotherapy units, to their requirement, in 12 different EU countries. England is third bottom above only Poland and the Czech Republic and this is after a huge spending spree using funds stolen from the National Lottery, which I thought was a charity.

The increasing accuracy of medical imaging, novel techniques which detect molecular characteristics of a tumour and the ability to use superimposed images obtained from diverse techniques will make radiotherapy more precise but more costly.

New drugs specifically tailored to the molecular abnormalities found in cancer cells in an individual will revolutionise therapy. The dramatic increase in the pace of discovery of new molecules with potential clinical benefit will require novel approaches for their development in the clinic[5]. Tumour profiling based on genetic changes will be needed to identify those patients likely to respond to specific, logically based novel therapies. This will require integrated molecular solutions for the stratification of patients in addition to conventional pathological criteria. But all this comes at a cost. McKinsey's estimate of global cancer drug budget will triple from US $25bn in 2005 to over US $75bn by 2015.[6] Yet we are still lagging far behind Europe on the uptake of new cancer drugs and the long delays imposed by NICE are causing serious alarm amongst the oncology community.[7]

The necessary technology will not be widely available outside those clinical centres with considerable basic research capabilities, so presenting huge logistic challenges. The completion of the human genome project, novel surrogate endpoints for measuring the response to cancer drugs and radiotherapy and the ability to design optimal therapy programmes for an individual will transform the interface between diagnosis, therapeutic choice and prognosis. During this time of considerable technological turbulence the expectation of patients will increase but the NHS in its current format will simply not be able to meet the surge in demand for innovative cancer care.

WHAT DO CANCER PATIENTS WANT?

Numerous studies using a range of methods have demonstrated consistently what people with cancer want.

- the best chance of cure with good quality of life
- honest, clear information on available options
- to have the diagnostics fast-tracked and treatment started in 14 days
- to see the same specialist at every visit
- convenient, streamlined services close to home with dedicated car parking
- to be treated in a decent environment with dignity
- to get the best care without worrying about its cost

Currently the NHS struggles to deliver all this. There are simply no incentives for hospitals to increase their attraction to patients. More patients mean longer waiting times for both diagnostics and therapy and a higher consumable bill. Payment by results will hit cancer shortly but the capacity is simply not there. There are no processes in place to motivate the staff. Therapy radiographers, for example, are in extremely short supply and yet little imagination has been shown by Trust HR departments to motivate and develop this highly skilled group. Physicists are needed to plan radiotherapy and yet their NHS pay-scales are pitifully low. No attempt has been made to imitate the centralised planning services set up by enterprising US Cancer Centres to allow a more distributed model of high quality care.

I believe its time to get the independent sector to drive the cancer delivery agenda. We have moved the NHS from a military period into the propaganda rich, target driven approach of a Stalinist era. We now need to move it into the consumer age where people can vote with their feet. As one NHS commentator said memorably 'money talks, preference walks'.[8] The problem for cancer patients today is there's nowhere to walk to. The NHS is the last bastion of communism in Europe.

DELIVERING CARE IN THE NEW ORDER

So let's stop whinging and design the new order from scratch. We need a template for the rollout of a network of outpatient 'cancer hotels' in many cases linked to existing hospitals. They will be open from early morning until late with a social as well as medical function. Their structure will be simple. A relatively small, but architecturally pleasing environment, fully equipped to deliver radiotherapy and chemotherapy will provide a focal point for all non-surgical treatment of cancer. As organ preserving surgical techniques become more commonplace, the role of surgery will continue to diminish. But effective post surgical care will become the essential component in determining clinical outcome. Because the diagnosis of cancer is devastating we must create a unique environment, completely focussed on the patient and yet accessing the emerging high technology normally associated with a leading academic institution.

From the moment of entry, the atmosphere is quite unlike a hospital. Each patient will have a single professional guide to take them through their cancer journey. The guide will be a health professional with considerable experience in cancer management. They will provide general counselling as well as written, video and web-based information on their illness. They will act as the patient's friend – a go between – with the world of high technology on one side and the practical need for hope on the other. Web based contact will be encouraged from the start.

The management of each centre will be in the hands of a group of 6–10 consultants in either clinical oncology (radiotherapy) or medical oncology (chemotherapy). A centre director will provide operational and strategic support with links to an HR function to recruit and retain nurses, radiographers and other health care professionals. The consultants will take equity in the centre and be rewarded with a sessional fee, a fee for service or productivity bonus and options to purchase further equity at an attractive discount. City investment bankers are tripping over themselves to fund such developments. Money is not the problem. The patients will be attracted from both the private sector and the NHS where the emergence of enlarged Primary Care Trusts will almost certainly encourage entrepreneurial models of care delivery and not simply local squabbling. The poor, the socially excluded and the elderly will gain as well as the rich.

There will be no loss of identity of an individual who will be guided through a series of evaluations. These will include a history and physical examination using a combination of nurse practitioner and consultant oncologist. Specific sessions with a complementary therapist – who will be able to access a boutique of popular therapy modalities in the centre – and a nutritionist who will address questions on optimal diet will be available. Following this initial visit any further clinical data, radiology and pathology will be requested and reviewed. Diagnostics – pathology and imaging will be completed within 5 working days and treatment options discussed at a second consultation and started within 14 days from diagnosis.

Two detailed reports will be prepared and given to the patient. The first will explain the situation in lay terms with web information links – local, national and global. The second will be a formal medical report, which will also be sent to the patient's general practitioner and other consultants. Both reports will contain clear therapeutic options with their rationale.

These options might include services not provided at the current time by the NHS tariff such as sophisticated conformal radiotherapy or drugs not yet approved by local funders and NICE. Such services could be purchased through co-payments. However, as much as the leaders of both main parties wish to avoid this issue, it is a box we simply have to open at some point. You can just hear the howls of inequity but at least access becomes transparent and less of a lottery and avoids patients having to bear the full costs of their care by buying themselves out of the NHS into fully private systems. Focus groups have recently suggested that cancer patients are not as alarmed by co-payment as our political masters.

Particular emphasis will be taken to ensure that the content and implications of the reports are clearly understood by the patient. The patient's guide will act as an interpreter to explain the options available and their chances of success. Immediate implementation of the chosen treatment plan will then occur. The current NHS target of 62 days from diagnosis to treatment is just unacceptable. Cancer doesn't take a holiday but continues to grow and spread for the two months. In the USA, people would sue.

Competing groups of franchised centres using this model adapted to local circumstance could be strategically placed in cities throughout the UK and subsequently internationally. Such branded global networks of high quality individually tailored cancer centres could provide a leadership role across a range of economic environments. These franchises would create a drug and equipment distribution centre with massive purchasing power. Novel patient management schemes using a combination of web based technology, tailored drug distribution systems and linked radiotherapy centres will provide politically attractive solutions to many countries struggling to contain the economic consequences of their rising cancer incidence.

The NHS needs a revolution. We need to demolish the icons of the past – waiting times, targets, restrictions to access, propaganda and mindless bureaucracy – cracking them apart like the statues of Lenin around Eastern Europe. When they fall, the new Phoenix of a consumer led healthcare system will emerge. Britain could then lead the world in cancer care rather than vying with rapidly improving Poland and Czech Republic to be bottom of the EU league.

REFERENCES

1. *Panorama* BBC Channel 1, Sunday 5th February, 2006
2. *The NHS Cancer Plan* Department of Health, London, 2000
3. Mayor S Many cancer networks fail to improve services *BMJ* (2006); 332:193
4. Bentzen S et al Towards evidence based guidelines for radiotherapy infrastructure and staffing needs in Europe: the ESTRO QUARTS project *Radiotherapy and Oncology* (2005) 75; 355–65
5. Cancer 2025 Expert Rev *Anticancer Ther.* Suppl 1 2004
6. McKinsey Consulting, New York *Report on Cancer*, 2003
7. Wilking N and Jonsson B *A Pan European comparison regarding patient access to cancer drugs* Karolinka Institut, Stockholm, September 2005
8. Spiers J *Patients, power and responsibility* Radcliffe Medical Press, Oxford 2003

CHAPTER 16
THE FUTURE OF PUBLIC HEALTH

Professor Griffiths

DEFINITIONS OF PUBLIC HEALTH

In 1988 the Acheson Committee[1] defined public health as 'The science and art of preventing illness, promoting health and prolonging life through the organised efforts of society'. In 2002 Derek Wanless[2] suggested a refinement 'the science and art of preventing disease, prolonging life and promoting health through the organised efforts and informed choices of society, organisations, public and private, communities and individuals.' Why the difference, most probably because the Acheson Committee was describing the specialty of what was then Public Health Medicine, whereas Wanless was describing the end point of the health of the population. It could be argued that the last sentence of Wanless's definition does little more than expand what society consists of and emphasise informed choices as the end point of organised efforts.

The important thing about both definitions are that they set out three aspects of public health. The first that public health operates in three domains.

- Health promotion, efforts to persuade people to make choices which will reduce their risk of disease;
- Health protection, measures to reduce the risk of exposure and contain infections and other hazards;
- Service improvement, efforts to prolong lives through the provision of health and other services.

The second key aspect is that public health is both a science and an art and the third is that it involves influencing or organising society in some way in order to optimise health. These three aspects define the areas in which public health professionals are trained and they create a framework through which the success of efforts can be judged.

THE SCIENCE OF PUBLIC HEALTH

The most fundamental science is epidemiology and with it statistics. Making sense of the pattern of illness in a given population and creating hypotheses about possible causes of ill health or likely successful interventions lies at the back of most public health programmes. Unravelling apparent associations between possible hazards and diseases has to be done with care, caution and skill, there are too many examples of false clues and unlikely discoveries for any other stance. It is salutary to recall that Sir Richard Doll originally included smoking in his study with no expectation that it was the cause of lung cancer. That is why good science is so important.

In recent years techniques for bringing many studies together and critically appraising evidence have been added to the armoury of public health sciences along with health economics. While there may be individual experts in any of these subjects who do not see themselves as part of the specialty, public health specialists are expected to be able to bring them all together around assessing population health.

THE ART OF PUBLIC HEALTH

Public health issues and public perceptions of them are beset with irrational fears, complex risk assessments which involve predictions of likely behaviour and both local and national politics. Any one who doesn't think there is an art involved should try explaining to a few hundred people why their local hospital ought to close in order to improve service quality and safety.

The phrase 'organised efforts of society' goes further, recognising that many different actions may improve health. Studies linking urban planning policies to the prevalence of obesity, or housing and energy policies with winter deaths are good examples of the way in which society can be organised to create or undermine health. Historically we are familiar with the impact of urban pollution, hazardous occupations, unsafe foods and many other threats that are under some sort of control. Society may be organised through a variety of means, legislation is obviously important but information may be enough on its own. Education of food workers is as likely to be effective as threats to prosecute or actual fines. Changing consumer preferences can be achieved by a variety of means. No legislation has been necessary to increase the consumption of low fat spreads or in the last year dramatically reduce the consumption of potato crisps. Skills in using the media, making effective alliances, fostering community development may all be relevant.

PROGRESS IN PUBLIC HEALTH

The health of the population, as measured by life expectancy has steadily improved in the UK but priorities have changed as different threats have been understood and opportunities for intervention have been identified. One common theme over the last 25 years has been the need to identify groups in the population who suffer because they cannot access effective services. In some cases this has been particular client groups, such as the mentally ill or those with learning difficulties, at other times the priority has been sections of the community such as the socially deprived, who have shorter life expectancy for a variety of reasons. The public health task has been to identify the populations concerned, work out ways of getting the right services to them, plan how resources can be developed and monitor their effectiveness.

Some of the major gains over the last few years have been made in both the prevention and treatment of major killers such as cancers and heart disease and they provide good examples of the way that public health works.

Cancers are of course caused by many different things and present a range of opportunities for intervention. Advances include the clear identification of those cancers caused by smoking, the identification of the association between the lack of fruit and vegetables in the diet and a number of cancers, the possibilities of screening and the steady advance in effective treatment, particularly since randomised control trials became the norm. Each of these advances shows a different side of public health in action.

Screening for cervical cancer by smear tests was well described and widely practiced by the early 1980s but the death rate from cervical cancer in the UK did not fall very much, a few hundred less deaths at most despite two and a half million smears per year being taken. The reason for this was simply that the wrong women were being tested and in many cases tested too often. Later in the 1980s a call and recall system was devised where women were called for screening from the population register designed to support general practice. The screening interval was based on the best evidence available at the time. The result was that death rates for cervical cancer started to fall. Adopting a policy based on sound public health science probably saved two or three times as many lives as an opportunistic policy based on patient and clinician choice alone. Despite these gains it is still the case that the poor are more likely to get the disease and more likely to die of it.

These lessons were learned when breast cancer screening was introduced. A multidisciplinary committee reported, screening was driven from the population register with call intervals based on evidence, based on technology that had been evaluate. Each element of the programme was involved in a quality assurance programme and mortality has fallen since the programme has been established. A similar process has been followed in order to evaluate whether colo-rectal cancer screening looks like a good buy and the programme is expected to start soon.

The steady improvement in treatment service owes less on a day to day basis to public health but the pressure for all new interventions to be subjected to Randomised Control Trials (RCTs) began with Archie Cochran, the first president of the Faculty of Public Health. Cancer registration, particularly population based registration, another public health activity, has been an essential underpinning in helping to evaluate whether results from trials could be translated into effective services.

Progress on diet and smoking has been slower. Comparisons between different countries led to the hypothesis that a diet high in fruit and vegetables was associated with lower rates of heart disease and some cancers but it has proved difficult to produce this difference in intervention trials. It has also proved difficult to persuade some of the food industry to market product that fit with the recommended diet. There is no doubt, however, about the trend towards increased obesity in developed countries. Diseases that would be expected to be associated with obesity, particularly type two diabetes, are showing parallel increased with a time lag of a few years. It is widely assumed that this is 'caused' by excess food consumption but is equally plausible that there has been a reduction in calories burned each day as both industry and home life are mechanised and we exist in heated buildings. An imbalance between food intake and calories burned of less than 100 calories per day can equate to a gain in weight of 5 kilos every decade. It is no surprise that obesity has proved to be a difficult problem.

Smoking is different. No-one is now in any doubt that smoking is dangerous and probably kills about half of any group of people who continue to smoke all their life. The tobacco industry has resisted every attempt to restrict smoking and promoted the habit through every means possible. Somehow the issue has been made one of personal freedom and the freedom of individuals to engage in dangerous activities has been equated with a licence to aggressively market a dangerous product. The recent parliamentary vote in the England to ban smoking in all enclosed public places was a landmark and may be an indicator that opinion is finally moving to really combat this menace. It has been half a century since Doll and Hill showed that smoking caused lung cancer and its role in heart disease and other cancers has been known for many years yet the tobacco industry shows no hesitation in aggressively marketing its products to the developing world, killing vast numbers of Chinese, Indians and others as it does so.

Progress with heart disease has been equally good and again there has been a combination of action across the domains of public health. Reduction in smoking, opportunistic screening for hypertension, cholesterol lowering drugs, early thrombolysis and secondary prevention measures have all contributed. Each measure has been shown in the level when it has been implemented through an epidemiologically driven strategy with appropriate monitoring and incentives within the health system.

Every society has its blind spots, and often failure to deal with excess deaths that might be prevented by societal action is equated with some sort of argument about freedom. This is advanced in the USA to avoid action on firearms and in many countries to avoid action on motor transport deaths. Public health workers have to continue to put the epidemiology and possible solutions in front of society until attitudes change, as they did over the last century in relation to industrial accidents and air pollution and many other issues. These examples show why the crucial phrase 'through the organized efforts of society' is included in the Acheson definition of public health.

The other element of the organised efforts are of course publicly funded health systems which usually deliver health protection and in the UK delivers the majority of health care.

HEALTH PROTECTION

This involves both surveillance of infectious disease and environmental hazards and interventions intended to control outbreaks and incidents. In England health protection is now the job of the Health Protection Agency (HPA), established by its own act of parliament, in the devolved administrations slightly different arrangements liaise with the HPA. Personal protection through immunisation is provided through primary care but monitored by Directors of Public Health in Primary Care Trusts. Protection against environmental hazards is more complex, with responsibilities spread across the Environment Agency, Local Authorities and the Health Protection Agency.

Controlling an outbreak of infectious disease involves several different kinds of work, isolating and identifying the infectious agent, determining the exposed population, arranging treatment for those infected and prophylaxis where it can prevent infection, giving advice to the general population to assist control and reduce anxiety, reporting on the incident and comparing it with others to ensure that lessons are learned and future outbreaks can be better controlled. The Health Protection Agency brings together several important areas of expertise; local and regional services who provide the day to day cover of expert advice to health services and local authorities; national reference laboratories who can provide expert typing services to help identify infectious agents; research laboratories who also provide connections to other international resources through the World Health Organisation (WHO) and other collaborations. The HPA also covers radiation and chemical hazards. Bringing all this together into one agency in 2003 was a major change designed to put health protection in the UK in a leading position in the world. Only the Centres for Disease Control in the USA provides a larger collection of expertise in these areas. While most local work is concerned with local outbreaks and chemical spills the importance of international collaboration has been made clear by the work on SARS and on avian influenza where a WHO collaboration around the world identified these new infectious agents in a matter of weeks and greatly assisted control measures.

WHO ARE THE PUBLIC HEALTH WORKERS

Public Health may require many skills. While there is a core of medical work, simply because sickness in people is at the heart of it, there are many other disciplines that may be important. Training in the UK has been changed over the last decade so that it is now possible for any graduate to compete for a place in public health training. Most of those coming into the specialty are from related disciplines, having first degrees in subjects such as statistics, epidemiology and social sciences but graduates from the arts are equally welcome provided that they are able to acquire the relevant knowledge and skill. This influx of workers from a variety of backgrounds has enriched public health enormously, the challenge has been to make sure that training and assessment of competencies is entirely consistent and standards are maintained. There is now a system of specialist registration for other graduates which is equivalent to General Medical Council (GMC) specialist registration, in due course it is likely to become a statutory requirement.

ORGANISATION OF PUBLIC HEALTH

Because it is so closely involved in statutory activities and the deployment of publicly financed resources it is inevitable that public health workers are mostly employed in statutory organisations with a population responsibility. At the moment in England that is Primary Care Trusts and Strategic Health Authorities with some workers in Regional Offices of Government and the Department of Health. In the other devolved administrations in the UK public health is situated in equivalent organisations close to health service management with links to local government. Joint appointments with local government are encouraged, though not yet compulsory. This close relationship with statutory organisations makes public health vulnerable when politicians decide to reorganise the system. So far it has proved difficult to show any association between changes in the organisation and any health indicators. Death rates from heart disease or cancer do not suddenly fall as a result of NHS reorganisation but public health is disrupted and this can lead to loss of capacity. Employment law gives people who are reorganised certain rights and it is no surprise to discover that some people in public health take the opportunity of early retirement when it is thrust upon them. The rapid succession of reorganisations in the early part of the century have been associated with a net loss of public health capacity. The changes taking place in 2006 may allow a more stable pattern of authorities to be retained for a longer period, especially as there is more effort to ensure co-terminosity with local authorities. Stability over a few years would allow the training programme to catch up and would ensure that public health was an attractive career option.

REFERENCES

1. Public Health in England HMSO 1988.
2. *Securing Our Future Health: Taking a Long Term View* Final Report Derek Wanless HM Treasury April 2002.

CHAPTER 17
PLASTIC, RECONSTRUCTIVE AND AESTHETIC SURGERY

Mr Peter Butler

Plastic surgery is an innovative speciality that has developed techniques for the treatment of a wide range of conditions at every conceivable anatomical site. The five main areas of work are trauma and burns, cancer, congenital deformities, reconstruction of degenerative conditions and appearance related surgery.

Through innovation, plastic surgery has developed many specialised techniques to correct more and more complex reconstructive challenges. The speciality has faced a problem of provision of adequate manpower. It is estimated that there should be one consultant per 100,000 to 125,000 per head of population, this would require doubling of present consultant numbers. This lack of provision has meant that these specialised techniques cannot be provided by trained plastic surgeons. Consequently other surgical specialities have adopted these techniques with variable standards and have achieved mixed results due to the lack of standardisation of the skills required to perform the reconstructive techniques.

These standards are further threatened by the shortening of training time on account of compliance with the 'European Working Time Directive'. The reduced exposure to the number of cases during training has been highlighted in plastic surgery and other surgical specialities. This has implications for the quality of graduates from plastic surgical training programmes in the UK. Development of training courses by the British Association of Plastic Surgeons and Royal College of Surgeons will address some of these issues but as with any craft speciality it is very difficult to replace practical experience. Development of basic and advanced skill courses in plastic surgery can maintain minimum standards but these require validation to make them meaningful.

Despite inadequate numbers of plastic surgeons to deal with the patient workload there is an increasing demand for plastic surgery provision in most units. This is in part related to developments in anaesthesia and intensive care, which have made possible plastic and reconstructive surgery on more and more complex congenital and acquired conditions that before now would have been deemed untreatable. Pressures on plastic surgery services are further compounded by an ageing population with increasing numbers of patients needing plastic surgery for degenerative conditions, wound management problems and cancers. Plastic surgery activity in some units is also unrecorded when performed as the reconstructive part of an ablative procedure carried out by another surgical speciality. This can account for a significant workload. 'Action on Plastic Surgery' addressed this in a survey of 'Hidden Activity'.

Demand for surgery for normalisation and improvement of appearance has increased pressures on plastic surgery services. This is in part related to increased patient demand and increased awareness due to television programmes such as 'Extreme Makeover'. Increasingly general practitioners refer patients to plastic surgery units for this type of surgery. In response to this demand most plastic surgery units either do not offer this service or restrict its provision. 'Action on Plastic Surgery' addressed this issue by suggesting nationally agreed 'Cosmetic Surgery Referral Guidelines'. The most common cosmetic surgery procedure performed on the NHS is bilateral breast reduction. This procedure is beneficial in reduction of cervical spinal problems in later life and when measured in quality of life outcome data outperforms hip and knee replacement surgery, coronary artery bypass surgery and cataract surgery. Provision of cosmetic surgery is not driven by evidence-based medicine but subjective opinion. Rationing of this type of surgery is politically expedient as the public perception of cosmetic surgery is that it is unnecessary. GP referral is further compounded by a number of factors. GPs knowledge of plastic surgery is very variable with GP surveys showing that they have a poor understanding of what plastic surgery as a speciality provides.

Poor understanding of the nature of plastic surgery begins in medical school education; in surveys it has been shown that medical students believe plastic surgeons perform predominantly cosmetic surgery, which is not surprising since very few have exposure to plastic surgery as undergraduates. This is likely to increase in the future as surgery as a subject is moved out of the undergraduate curriculum. Lack of understanding will become apparent as 'Patient Choice'; 'Payment by Results' and 'Practice Based Commissioning' becomes a reality. This can be addressed by education and engagement as well as the use of Specialist Commissioning Groups within Primary Care Trusts (PCTs).

Practice Based Commissioning (PBC) also presents an opportunity. Plastic surgery as a speciality is innovative and can react to challenges, which is its strength. It can adapt as the models of health care delivery change. PBC will drive community-based services and provision of plastic surgery in local facilities may be deemed more economic by PCTs. This however may undermine the larger hospitals leaving them to treat the more complex and costly cases.

Plastic surgery as a speciality has by its nature and the challenges that it faces developed new methods of medical care. The research originating within the speciality benefits all surgical disciplines. Transplantation as a speciality developed out of plastic surgery. Transplantation of skin was used in treating severe burn injuries in World War I and World War II. Accelerated rejection seen when skin from the same donor was re-transplanted onto the same recipient spawned understanding of rejection and is the basis for modern transplant immunology. Microsurgical techniques allowing vessels as small as 1mm in diameter to be joined were developed by plastic surgeons. These techniques are now used by other surgical specialities. Research, therefore is an important part of the future of plastic surgery but as a speciality has difficulty obtaining research grants from grant giving bodies as it is clinically applied research and not basic science research.

Plastic surgery as a speciality is extremely resourceful and will adapt to the challenges it faces in an ever-changing healthcare environment. It has done so in the past and will do so in the future.

FURTHER READING

1. *The Way Forward; The Future of Plastic Surgery.* British Association of Plastic Surgeons. 2003.

2. *A Strategic Approach to Delivery of Plastic, Reconstructive and Aesthetic Surgery*. Action on Plastic Surgery, NHS Modernisation Agency, Department of Health. 2005.

CHAPTER 18

THE FUTURE OF PSYCHIATRIC SERVICES IN THE NHS

Professor Peter Tyrer

Mental health services are conventionally regarded as Cinderella services in comparison with other medical disciplines; scrabbling for resources after the big players from cancer, cardiology and acute medical disciplines have had first pickings. This is certainly true of many countries, but much less so in the United Kingdom, where mental illness services have gained significantly from being associated with the National Health Service. It is sad to be reminded that one third of the population of the world (around 2 billion) live in countries which spend less than 1% of their income on mental health[1]. Research into mental health, which often anticipates general service funding, shows a similar split between rich and poor countries, reinforcing what is often called the 10/90 divide (90% of the world's resources are consumed by 10% of the world's population) and this gross imbalance shows little sign of change[2].

In Europe (excluding the UK) around 8.1% of the gross national product is spent on health[3] compared with 6.3% in the UK, with about 9% of that going to mental health. Similarly, in the NHS between 8 and 20% of funding for primary care trusts is currently spent on mental health[4] and for several years mental health has been earmarked as a priority for funding and special initiatives, recognised by the appointment of a mental health Czar (an inappropriate autocratic epithet for a position that argues for consensus), a position currently occupied with some distinction by Professor Louis Appleby. There is little prospect of this proportion going down and, as will be argued below, a significant case for its increase in future services can be made.

LIKELY DEVELOPMENTS IN NEED FOR MENTAL HEALTH SERVICES

There are several important changes in the demographics of illness that have an important message for mental health services. In the last 15 years there has been increased recognition that mental illness incurs a heavy burden on populations and it is very unwise to ignore this burden. In the past it was convenient to ignore mental illness when examining the impact of allegedly more serious medical illnesses but, largely due to the influence of the World Health Organisation, and of the World Bank, the morbidity and economic costs of mental illness have been measured against those of other illnesses. This has been done by a useful development, the calculation of health-adjusted life years (HALYs) in whole populations, and these carry the advantage that both morbidity and mortality can be simultaneously described within a single number. They are particularly useful for estimating the total burden of disease and for comparing the relative burden of specific illnesses in populations and also lend themselves to economic analyses. The two main measures are quality-adjusted life years (QALYs) that constitute a measure of positive health and disability adjusted life years (DALY's) that are calculated by combining prevalence and incidence of illnesses as well as estimating the impact of illnesses on life expectancy and health.

Disorder (*indicates a mental disorder primarily)	% of DALY's
Ischaemic heart disease	10.5
Cerebrovascular disease	6.8
* Unipolar depressive disorders	6.1
*Alzheimer and other dementias	3.0
* Alcohol use disorders	2.9
Hearing loss, adult onset	2.6
COPD	2.4
Road traffic accidents	2.4
Osteoarthritis	2.4
*Self-inflicted injuries	2.0

Table 1. Leading causes of disability-adjusted life-years (DALYs) in Europe, estimates for 2000 (reproduced with kind permission of the World Health Organisation and the British Journal of Psychiatry)[5]

In Europe (there are variations between regions of the world) the top ten illnesses in terms of accounting for disability adjusted life years (DALY's) are shown. Four of the 10 are primarily mental illnesses accounting for 34% of disability. Governments need to be highly conscious of these figures at all times, because although they can be ignored they will not go away and all predictions are that they will increase. The population is getting steadily older, mainly as a consequence of improvements in both prevention and treatment of common diseases, and as the incidence of Alzheimer's disease increases markedly with advancing age,[6] and depression somewhat less so,[7] the need for appropriate services is likely to increase. There is also reasonably good evidence that a significant proportion of DALY's can be averted by treatment, probably about 10–30%[8], so this is not merely an aspirational exercise.

The economic costs of mental illnesses are also very large. As Gro Harlem Brundtland, the Director-General of the World Health Organisation summarized it on World Health Day in 2001, "If we don't deal with mental illnesses, there is a burden not only on the mentally ill, on their families, on their communities, there is an economic burden if we don't take care of people who need our care and treatment". Large numbers can sometimes be perceived as so large that they pass by our conscious minds and get lost in the forgotten corridors, but in England alone it has been estimated that the total costs of adult depression (that is excluding child and adolescent depression which also constitutes a significant burden) in one year is over £9 billion, of which £370 million represents direct treatment costs, with 109.7 million working days lost and 2615 deaths due to depression.[9] A large proportion of these costs are hidden costs – the impact on friends and relatives – and these are several times larger than the direct NHS costs of illness.

Clearly, if we are less effective in finding new ways of preventing and treating a specific illness it will create a greater burden than those which can be dealt with successfully. Alcohol and substance misuse, in which our interventions are generally of limited efficacy, is likely to rise further in the DALY league table in the future, and when we consider its impact on other mental illness such as schizophrenia[10] interventions to reduce its incidence become even more pressing. The same applies to self-harm, where we remain limited in the value of our interventions[11] and in which there remains a strong link to completed suicide.

FUTURE DEVELOPMENTS IN MENTAL HEALTH SERVICES

The last fifty years has seen dramatic changes in the settings in which mental health services are delivered. In 1946, at the dawn of the NHS, there were more patients in hospitals for those with mental illness and mental handicap (169,000) than there were in acute general hospitals.[12] There are now less than 10,000 beds in general psychiatry and learning disability (http://www.performance.doh.gov.uk/) (a fall of over 94%) but their has been an increase in secure forensic beds and use of private hospital beds for psychiatric patients (partly because of overflow from NHS hospitals that have no beds available and partly from specialist provision).

How is this likely to change in the future? Firstly, there is likely to be an increase in the number of beds *under the control* of mental health services, even if they are not hospital ones. I deliberately emphasise the italicized words because, despite the attempt to integrate mental health and social services, there remain a yawning gap between the ability of non-NHS staff in supported accommodation and those in mental health services, and a similar one in the funding streams of health and social services. Thus, for example in the assertive outreach team in which I work, we may be very clear about the right placement for a patient under our care, but whether the patient is allocated a place depends on a system run by people in social services who have no coal-face clinical knowledge, and who demand a great deal of unnecessary footling data, involving a great deal of work, in an attempt to determine 'priority for funding'. If these beds, however named, were supervised and had their priorities decided by clinical experts in mental health the system would be much more efficient.

Many of these beds would be the equivalent of high support housing schemes, but would offer the chance of better integrated care, be more reassuring to the public and would also satisfy the requirements for the rehabilitation needs of what were called the 'new long stay' in the pioneering White Paper, *'Better Care for the Mentally Ill'* published over 30 years ago.[13] At that time 17 beds per 100,000 population were planned for this population but now rehabilitation services have very few dedicated beds and have not been even addressed in the recent National Service Framework or in National Plans.

This would be a better way forward than what could be described as 'creeping reinstitutionalisation'. Whilst at one end of mental health services there is almost unseemly energy diverted to keeping people out of hospital with the expansion of assertive outreach and crisis resolution teams, at the other there is a great expansion of forensic facilities, a dramatic increase in the number of patients admitted under the Mental Health Act, an expansion of facilities to treat those with severe personality disorder in both private and public facilities, and pressure for more care involving close supervision and support.[14]

What is clear is that some changes will have to be made to the bed base of our psychiatric facilities. At present we have too few beds to manage them effectively and, because we have too few outlets for patients with the potential to be discharged, those that are in hospital often should not be there, and the proportion not needing a bed may be as high as 39% in overstretched places in central London.[15]

DEVELOPMENTS IN MENTAL HEALTH POLICY

Many of the changes anticipated in this chapter will require a change in policy, but not very many. The mental health services of the NHS have suffered an excess of reform in the last few years and a period of consolidation would be welcome. The zeal with which these reforms have been made have many downsides, emphasized cogently recently by Richard Sennett in his analysis of new capitalist structures.[16] The dedication necessary to work in mental health services, an activity in which I have been proud to be involved in the past forty years, depends on long-term commitment, recognizable by patients as continuity of care, and this cannot be achieved by the quick fix management reorganizations that are common, and often necessary, in competitive environments such as information technology. I find it no coincidence that caustic little jokes, pertinent newspaper cuttings, and cartoons poking fun at such energetic reformists, litter the offices of community mental health teams, hospital wards and even management offices in mental health NHS establishments (and others too, as this is not confined to mental health), as they ridicule these apparently worthy attempts to improve performance and efficiency. But things move slowly in mental health, much less rapidly than the managers come and go, and as Sennett comments, who is there to witness the solid work of the mental health worker even if performance is improving, if change becomes frenetic and ill-thought through?

All I would ask in this context, 'please, oh please, do not introduce changes in policy until they have been shown to be evidence-based'. This is the only way in which they can be properly embraced and implemented.

DEVELOPMENTS IN TREATMENTS FOR MENTAL ILLNESS

It is difficult to predict advances in treatment in any medical discipline, but there are several guesses that are more likely to be accurate than not in mental health:

(i) there will be major advances in the treatment of the organic conditions of old age, principally dementia, as new drugs become introduced and the basic neuropathology of Alzheimer's disease becomes understood. Old age psychiatry may move away from mental health into a branch of neurology;

(ii) effective treatments will be developed for substance misuse problems. Our valiant attempts to 'change behaviour' here have been little short of disastrous, and new initiatives that reduce the chemical reinforcement of illicit drugs, possibly the use of vaccines, will be a much more successful alternative;

(iii) more psychiatric treatments will be given in primary care. Although past initiatives to improve liaison in primary care faltered when the move for community teams to develop comprehensive services for 'psychosis only' patients was initiated in the early 1990's, this needs to be, and will be, reversed. The major morbidity of mental health remains in the community and is insufficiently addressed at present;

(iv) there will be an expansion of psychological treatments at the expense of drug treatments for disorders where the alternative of a psychological intervention is at least as effective and preferred by patients.

This last prediction may be realised sooner than the others. Lord Layard gave the first Sainsbury Centre for Mental Health Lecture in September 2005 and made a strong case for the rapid expansion of cognitive behaviour therapy in the NHS (http://www.bps.org.uk/dcp/news/layard.cfm), which he also feels would satisfy that delightful aim in the US constitution, the 'pursuit of happiness'.[17]

In this he argued as much from an economic viewpoint (he is primarily a health economist) as from a clinical one. The logic of his argument has attractions; (a) many of those with common mental disorders are on incapacity benefit and have treatable mental health problems, (b) psychological treatments, particularly cognitive behaviour therapy, have equivalent evidence of efficacy as other treatments[18] but insufficient therapists are available, (c) this poor access, related issues such as stigma, and poor recognition of psychological disorders in primary care mean that there is much unnecessarily untreated mental illness in the community, and (d) if the resources were available the savings made in terms of increased return to work would offset the increased costs of training and paying new therapists. In his talk he estimated that about 10,000 extra therapists would be needed to satisfy this need, most of whom would work in primary care settings.

The changes in mental health care will all have a new element that was absent in the past. They will involve patients or, if you prefer, the less attractive term of service users. This, if properly implemented, would be the ultimate weapon in the battle against stigma and prejudice. At present there is still a great deal of tokenism in the involvement of patients in these developments, but this will have to go if we are to improve the access to care, choice of treatment and adherence to its administration. "We are all socialists now," said George V at a point in the 1930's when coalition blurred party lines. "We are all likely to get mentally ill now", should be the slogan for these new pioneers.

REFERENCES

1. World Health Organisation (2001). *Atlas: country profiles on mental health resources*. Geneva: WHO.
2. Saxena, S., Paraje, G., Sharan, P. *et al* (2006). The 10/90 divide in mental health research: trends over a 10-year period. *British Journal of Psychiatry*, **188**, 81–82.
3. Appleby, J. & Boyle, S. (2001). NHS spending: the wrong target. *Health Care UK (spring issue)*, 94–99.
4. Glover, G.R. (2003). Money for mental health care in 2003/4. *Psychiatric Bulletin*, **27**, 126–129.
5. Üstün, T. B., Ayuso-Mateos, J. L., Chatterji, S., *et al* (2004) Global burden of depressive disorders: methods and data sources. *British Journal of Psychiatry*, **184**, 386–392.

6. Brayne, C., Gill, C., Huppert, F.A., Barkley, C., *et al* (1995) Incidence of clinically diagnosed subtypes of dementia in an elderly population: Cambridge Project for Later Life. *British Journal of Psychiatry*, **167**, 255–262.
7. Bergdahl, E., Gustavsson J.M., Kallin, K. *et al* (2005). Depression among the oldest old: the Umeå 85+ study. *International Psychogeriatrics*, **17**, 557–75.
8. Chisholm, D., Sanderson, K., Ayuso-Mateos, J. L., *et al* (2004) Reducing the global burden of depression. Population-level analysis of intervention cost-effectiveness in 14 world regions. *British Journal of Psychiatry*, **184**, 393–403. **10–30%**
9. Thomas, C. M. & Morris, S. (2003) Cost of depression among adults in England in 2000. *British Journal of Psychiatry*, **183**, 514–519.
10. Arseneault, L., Cannon, M., Witton, J., *et al* (2004) Causal association between cannabis and psychosis: examination of the evidence. *British Journal of Psychiatry*, **184**, 110–117.
11. Townsend E, Hawton K, Altman DG, *et al* (2001). The efficacy of problem-solving treatments after deliberate self-harm: meta-analysis of randomized controlled trials with respect to depression, hopelessness and improvement in problems. *Psychological Medicine*, **31**, 979–988. Tyrer, P., Thompson, S., Schmidt, U., *et al* (2003a). Randomised controlled trial of brief cognitive behaviour therapy versus treatment as usual in recurrent deliberate self-harm: the POPMACT study. *Psychological Medicine*, **33**, 969–976.
12. Webster, C. (1991). Psychiatry and the early National Health Service: the role of the Mental Health Standing Advisory Committee. In: *150 years of British Psychiatry: 1841–1991*, (ed, Berrios, G.E. & Freeman, H.), pp. 103–116. London: Gaskell Books, Royal College of Psychiatrists.
13. Department of Health and Social Security (1975) *Better services for the mentally ill. Cmnd 6233*. HMSO, London.
14. Turner, T. & Priebe, S. (2002). Forget community care—reinstitutionalisation is here. *British Journal of Psychiatry*, **181**, 253.
15. Tyrer, P., Suryanarayan, G., Rao, B., *et al* (2006). The Bed Requirement Inventory: a simple measure to estimate the need for a psychiatric bed. *International Journal of Social Psychiatry*, **52**, in press.
16. Sennett, R. (2006). *Culture of the new capitalism*. London: Yale University Press.

17. Layard R. (2005). *Happiness: lessons from a new science.* London : Allen Lane.
18. National Collaborating Centre for Mental Health. *Depression: management of depression in primary and secondary care.* London: National Institute for Clinical Excellence, 2004.

CHAPTER 19
THE FUTURE OF MENTAL HEALTH PROVISION

Mr Derek Draper

Discussions about mental health policy invariably draw upon statistics. An overemphasis on facts and figures, however, can easily obscure what they are there to represent – the actual experiences of real people. So before we examine the headline statistics for mental and emotional health, I'd like you to imagine an all too typical row of houses in an ordinary British town.

Let's start with the Bakers. They are a couple who argue a lot. Mrs Baker has felt miserable – she won't bring herself to use the word "depressed" – for years. She doesn't know why she always feels so low. Her husband is very moody and often abusive, though he's never hit her. He drinks far too much, but Mrs Baker has learnt to keep her mouth shut about this, as it's not worth the grief she gets in return.

A few doors away lives Tracey with her two young boys, Kevin, 8 and Daniel, 5. The boy's dad hasn't been around since Dan was born. Tracey tries to work part-time, but the pay is poor and the kids demand so much attention. They are always getting into trouble at school, and that takes time to sort out. Tracey usually goes back to bed after getting the kids ready in the morning, and often lies there quietly weeping. Her doctor gave her some anti-depressants which helped a bit, but it hasn't occurred to her to get any other help. After all, she tells herself, "There's loads of people in the same boat as me, I'm nothing special."

Across the way lives Ted. He keeps himself to himself, as he has always been shy and finds other people, if he's honest, a bit frightening sometimes. He spends his time watching TV but his main preoccupation seems to be worrying – about "big" stuff, like bird flu, and "little" stuff, like what he should be doing with the garden. He sleeps badly, and every few weeks he has one of his "turns" where he can't breathe properly and it feels as if his heart is going to explode.

The family next door to Ted are the best-off in the street, but their daughter Becky is painfully thin, and this has caused a lot of rows in the house. Her dad has resorted to shouting to get her to eat, but her mum doesn't think that helps. She suspects she must be in some way responsible for Becky's problems, and feels guilty all the time. The constant worry and arguments are really getting her down.

At the end of the street lives old Mrs Turner. She hasn't been the same since her husband died, and although she probably has a couple of decades of life left, she sometimes wonders if she can be bothered. She's lonely, and hasn't been able to shake off the blues since her son told her his family couldn't get down to visit until the new year.

These fictionalised vignettes should demonstrate that the task of categorising – indeed diagnosing – mental health disturbance is not always straightforward. While some of these people are clearly suffering from diagnosable problems, others are suffering from what I describe as "sub-clinical" problems; conditions that don't quite meet the diagnostic criteria for a particular disorder, but that nonetheless involve a great deal of psychological or emotional unease. Often manifested as a prevailing sense of misery, worry or anger, this profound unease was recently described by the former head of the Downing Street Policy Unit, Geoff Mulgan, as a "quiet crisis of unhappiness".[1]

In this chapter, I'll present a brief overview of the present mental health system, and its recent historical context. Mental health care encompasses an enormous range of treatments, from anti-depressant prescriptions to secure hospitalisation, but the focus of this paper will be "talking treatments" – therapy and counselling. I will explore what improvements are required to provide adequate therapy and counselling care for all those who need it – firstly, by examining the changes that would be necessary to make the current system deliver on its existing standards, and secondly by reviewing recent proposals for a dramatic expansion of therapy services, known as The Layard Proposals. I will argue that such changes, while welcome, would still be fundamentally inadequate to deal with the scale and depth of the problem. Instead, I propose a radical new solution: a "fourth force" of therapeutic volunteers – whom I have dubbed "para-counsellors" – working alongside primary and secondary care and the existing patchwork of voluntary services. Without this new voluntary "fourth force", I believe the millions of Britons in need of mental health treatment will simply never receive it.

According to recent Office of National Statistics (ONS) surveys 9 million adults[2] and 1.1 children under 16[3] are suffering from a clinically diagnosable mental health disorder – a total of 10 million people. The vast majority of those reporting mental health problems in the ONS survey suffered from depressive and anxiety disorders. 9% had mixed depression and anxiety disorder; 4% had generalised anxiety disorder and 3% reported a depressive episode. Phobias, obsessive-compulsive disorder and panic disorder occurred in less than 2% of the population. This survey is the source of the widely reported statistic that one in six people are suffering from a neurotic mental disorder – an arrestingly high figure which still does not, of course, include people suffering from "sub-clinical" problems.

On the other hand, severe mental health problems such as schizophrenia are relatively rare, affecting around one in 200 adults each year. The numbers suffering from personality disorders are also very low. (Though if the category is extended to include those suffering from debilitating traits of disorders such as borderline, avoidant and histrionic, rather than the full blown conditions, then the numbers are higher.)

The National Treatments Agency report over 150,000 people currently in treatment for drug and alcohol related problems and there are obviously many more not in treatment. It is likely that many of these people have accompanying emotional problems, which could benefit from support as their treatment progresses.

As for children and adolescents, a 2004 ONS survey[4] concluded that 10% of 5–16 year olds had a clinically diagnosed mental disorder. Some have more than one: 4% had an emotional disorder (depression or anxiety); 6% a conduct disorder, and 2% a hyperkinetic disorder such as Attention Deficit Hyperactivity Disorder (ADHD). As with adults, furthermore, it is fair to assume that a further large group of children are suffering from sub-clinical problems. According to The Mental Health and Psychological Well-being of Children and Young People report published in October 2004[5], "It is likely a similar numbers of children and young people with less serious mental health problems will need some help."

The ONS study focussed on 5–16 year olds. This is symbolic of the particular problems facing adolescents in mental health services who are often "lost" between the child-focussed and adult service. A recent Social Exclusion Unit Report[6] stated that, "there are relatively few examples of services that address the needs of 16–25 year olds in the round or ensure an effective transition between youth and adult services". Just one statistic shows the scale of the problem: a quarter of the total deaths of men aged 16–24 are caused by suicide.

The policy implications of these figures are clear. Media coverage of mental health issues often focuses on headline-grabbing cases involving violent psychotics, and treatment for such people needs to be expanded, but it is the less dramatic but equally destructive clinical and sub-clinical neuroses that affect many millions of people. Left untreated, these result in enormous human misery and wasted lives, and often the trauma is unwittingly handing them on to the next generation. If left untreated, the numbers of people suffering in this way will only continue to grow.

How do we treat them currently? In the present system, people with problems contact their primary care health team – in practice almost always their GP (between a quarter and a third of all GP appointments deal primarily with mental health concerns). They are then assessed, and sometimes treated within primary care; the number of GP surgeries with at least some cover from psychologists and counsellors is steadily increasing. If those services are unavailable, or inappropriate, the patient will be referred to secondary care – usually the local Community Mental Health Team, and/or a specialized service such as an Eating Disorder Unit. In extreme cases, it would be a psychiatric inpatient department. At present, 10–15 per cent of patients are referred from primary to secondary care.[7]

The history of our current approach to mental health can be traced back to the document "National Service Framework for Mental Health" (NSF), which was published in 1999. This followed a White Paper published in 1998. The then Secretary of State, Frank Dobson, proclaimed at the time that mental health would be a top NHS priority, ranking in importance alongside heart disease and breast cancer.

It was an ambitious declaration of intent, and in December 2004 a comprehensive review of its progress was published, called "The National Service Framework for Mental Health – Five Years On". (Child and adolescent mental health was covered separately in "The Mental Health and Psychological Well-being of Children and Young People"[8].) The National Mental Health Director, Professor Louis Appleby, begins this report with his judgement that: "It is a record of progress and achievement that I believe is unprecedented in the history of NHS mental health care". The government is similarly optimistic; in March 2004, health minister Rosie Winterton declared: "We are making significant progress, not only clinically but also in terms of helping people get the most out of their lives."[9] Professor Appleby concludes his five year review with the statement: "No one would claim that we yet have...the services nationally that service users deserve and that staff can be proud of...[but]...it is an exciting, impressive and promising start".[10]

Certainly, the government has committed unprecedented resources. In 1998/9, spending on mental health services was £4.2 billion.[11] An additional £700 million a year was pledged alongside the National Service Framework (NSF) from 1999 onwards. An additional £300 million was committed in the NHS plan over the three years from 2000/1. Spending in 2002/3 was £5.4 billion (this is made up of NHS and local authority spending – NHS spending alone was £4.6 billion). That represents a 19 per cent increase in real terms from 1999/00 to 2002/3. It equates to spending per head of population of between £108 (the North West) to £144 (London).

Staffing levels have risen significantly. Between 1999 and 2003, the number of NHS psychiatrists rose by 25%, to a total of 3155. Mental health nurse numbers rose by 13%, to a total of 39,383, and clinical psychologists by 42%, a total of 5331. The NHS employs 477 art/music/drama therapists, 13,053 occupational therapists, and 4,200 approved social workers. Nevertheless, the total number of NHS psychotherapists remains relatively tiny: just 633.[12] It is no wonder that Professor Appleby was forced to admit: "Long waiting lists remain in many places."[13]

Even after such a radical injection of cash, conversations with NHS staff working in primary and secondary care reveal deep concern. There is recognition of the increased priority and resources that have been made available, certainly. But the burden on the system is still too great. One psychologist working in primary care told me, "The guilt of your waiting list is with you every day." Another who worked in a Community Mental Health Team admitted that his team could still only really deal with the most extreme of cases. "If a patient is managing to hold down some sort of job and a relationship – of any description at all – then frankly, you'd feel guilty for spending any time with them."

The sums of money being invested are indisputably impressive. However, the overall rate of increased expenditure is not being maintained, and very soon any increased spending on mental health is likely to fall behind general NHS spending increases. Even where it continues to grow, the sums are still inadequate given the scale of the challenge. The government has pledged that Child and Adolescent Mental Health Services will grow by 10% per annum, for example. But spending would have to rise even further still, before the proper level of support became available to every family in difficulty.

The Sainsbury Centre for Mental Health (SCMH) has recently launched a major consultation exercise, "Defining a Good Mental Health Service", to evaluate the levels of resources needed to bring the current system to the level needed to achieve its own aims and standards as set out in the NSF. Even the SCMH's preliminary work[14] shows that resources would have to be increased way beyond what is economically or politically likely. Just to provide adequate provision for the services currently envisaged, the budget would have to, very approximately, double.

In my view, the SCMH project, while impressive in its depth and scope, makes assumptions which underestimate the magnitude of resources needed – though this might change as the work evolves. The model of psychotherapy it assumes, for example, – treatment lasting an average of just 12 weeks – is unduly optimistic. Its assumptions for budgets for mental health awareness campaigns, and for carer and existing volunteer support, are quite conservative. Moreover, the SCMH consultation does not yet address the issue of child and adolescent mental health – a key area in a land of ASBOs and high teenage suicides. The stark truth is that even a doubling of resources would be inadequate.

So what needs to be done? Certain measures are, of course, necessary. We need to maintain the financial priority given to mental health services; build on the involvement of staff and user input into strategy; improve research; develop better clinical guidelines for treatment; continue to ensure departments work better together; and expand primary, secondary and specialized services. However, the focus of this paper is talking treatments, and what can be done to extend their provision.

Under current NHS proposals, expansion of talking treatments is to be tackled by improved therapy skills in frontline staff; the appointment of new staff, including primary care mental health workers; self-help technologies (which involve computer programmes such as the one developed at the Maudsley Hospital, "Beating the Blues", which offers a form of interactive cognitive behavioural therapy on DVD); and a broader choice of providers, both within the NHS and the independent sector. The NHS plan[15] also proposes the appointment of 1000 "graduate workers" who are trained in brief therapies. Another new role is that of Support, Time and Recovery (STR) workers, 3000 of whom are to be recruited by December 2006.

If executed, these plans would go a good way towards making the system deliver on its existing standards. It should be noted, though, that filling vacancies in mental health nursing is more difficult than in other NHS areas and there is accordingly an over reliance on agency staff. But more importantly, the new resources already committed since 1999 have to be recognised as unprecedented. Sadly, it is realistic to conclude that it will require an enormous political effort merely to ensure that steps backward are not taken. The benefits of increased expenditure are clear, and the case for higher spending should be made forcefully, but the likelihood of many more substantial steps forward, requiring even more funds, has to be recognised as slim.

This is why the government is considering the idea that an entirely new approach is required. At present, the most radical idea on the table is a proposal by Professor Layard, a long-standing government economics adviser, for a radical expansion of short-term psychotherapy provision. Drawing on the extensive analysis he presented in his book "Happiness",[16] he envisages the creation of 10,000 new therapists, working in 250 "independent" therapy centres across the land. It is likely that his ideas will be adopted by the government in some form, most likely initial pilot projects.

While the attention Layard has focussed on mental health – what he describes as "our biggest social problem" – is to be welcomed, his proposals have been criticised for exclusively promoting just one form of therapy – Cognitive Behavioural Therapy, or CBT. Respected clinicians Andrew Cooper and Phil Richardson, both professors at the Tavistock Clinic, have commented that:

> "Government backing for Layard's proposals is welcome – up to a point. In treatment trials for mild depression, CBT emerges as no better or worse than other approaches. In a study comparing treatments for people with depression and a range of other problems, the CBT patients

dropped out and this arm of the trial was abandoned. Longer treatments, such as psychoanalytic therapy, have demonstrably better long-term impact. But longer means more expensive in the short term. A significant proportion of working days lost to "mental distress" involve conditions not treatable by CBT. Layard's proposals point in the right direction, but there is an urgent need for more refined analysis of the evidence base, and a subtler account of the interplay between mental distress, produc-tivity data and Treasury economics."

The British Association for Counselling and Psychotherapy (BACP) has been equally frank:

"Lord Layard does not seem to realise that CBT is only one form of talking treatment, it will not suit all patients, there is strong evidence that other counselling can be equally effective and CBT is not necessarily the cheapest solution. Outcome studies of CBT can be more easily eval-uated than other psychological therapies, but although CBT can be valuable it is not always the best choice, nor the patient's choice. As the mental health charity MIND said on August 18th 2005: 'Other treatments such as counselling can also be effective'. Lord Layard says he wants to get away from depression as just a 'health' issue and 'to look beyond the diagnosis' yet his proposals will have the opposite effect. Counselling begins with relationship and NOT diagnosis. Unhappiness is the consequence of more than a diagnosed condition and always arises from a life situation. Counselling isn't deductive; it is holistic and will not merely treat a symptom but look towards the cause of the depression, as any responsible therapist should".[17]

But the greater problem with Layard's proposals is one of cost. In the current economic climate, where public spending will not be growing as it has in the past few years, and demands on resources in the health service for all manner of treatments and drugs (such as those for breast cancer and Alzheimer's) is constantly on the rise, it is highly unlikely that the amount of money needed to make Layard's dream a reality will be forthcoming. Remember: the initial SCMH calculations suggest that budgets would need to double merely in order to properly provide the services currently on offer. Where would the money come from to pay for Layard's proposals?

Professor Layard proposes "independent" therapy centres, without specifying precisely what this means. As both the Labour and Conservative parties now appear intent on increasing private provision of healthcare services – initially some hospital services, but more recently even GP surgeries – it is reasonable to assume that psychological services may soon too become candidates for quasi-privatisation, and "independent" may well mean "for profit".

But poorer and middle-income sufferers are unable to pay privately for the long-term support they need. It is my view that if the huge numbers of people who need and would benefit from therapy or counselling are to be helped, their care will never be adequately funded by the state. Much of the provision will therefore have to be provided by volunteers – well trained, closely supervised volunteers. Whatever the benefits of private provision – in terms of increased cost-effectiveness, efficiency and creativity, we are also going to have to develop a genuinely "not-for-profit" arm of mental health care.

It is a view endorsed recently by Ann Byrne, the chief executive of the Women's Therapy Centre. "It is important that discussions about the provision of 'talking therapies'," she has said, "should include the provision by the voluntary sector, and its capacity to develop its work with the availability of increased resources." Even the government's mental health czar, Professor Appleby, has concurred. In his commentary on NSF – Five Years On, he acknowledged – and was unapologetic – that most of the improvements in the last five years had been in specialist services. "There is now a need," he wrote, "to develop services for people of all ages.... At the heart of this is...the relationship between health and social care and *communitie's responsibility*, not only to tackle illness and vulnerability, but to promote well-being and independence....*Joint working should extend...to the voluntary...sector*." (Author's emphases.)[18]

Professor Appleby was basing this conclusion on figures which did not even include the sub and threshold clinical category I described earlier. If the increased numbers struggling at that level are taken into account, it becomes overwhelmingly obvious that the crisis of "quiet unhappiness" will never be tackled by government-funded services. It can only be addressed with an unprecedented, enormous, programme of new-style, systematic voluntary provision: a massive attempt to build social capital among every community in the area of mental and emotional health.

That is why I propose the development of a fourth force of mental health service. The existing primary, secondary and voluntary sector provision cannot merely be improved; we need an entirely new, distinctive category of provision. It would comprise of a nationally supported, locally based network of centres, where support given to people in the sub and threshold clinical category would be offered by trained, supervised volunteers – a new breed of what might be termed "para-counsellors". It is a bold, and potentially controversial pro-posal – but one I believe is realistic, having witnessed it first hand elsewhere.

While undertaking my psychotherapy training in the US, I worked in a community counselling centre. It is the inspiration for my idea of a nationwide force of "para-counsellors". The centre depended on charitable contributions, but was also paid fees by the local state health insurance body to carry out certain work. It was led by an experienced psychologist, and every volunteer who worked there was supervised by accredited therapists, who offered their services either free of charge or for a standard fee. The people who provided the counselling were trainees, working towards their qualification, and by volunteers. This latter group undertook an intensive course of evening and weekend workshops to learn the basics of counselling and therapeutic work.

While I was there I worked closely with, for example, a retired medical doctor, a former Texaco executive, several women whose children had left for college – bright, successful people seeking a part-time, rewarding activity. Before being accepted onto the course, they had been subjected to psychological testing, extensive interviewing and a thoroughgoing reference procedure. Intensive mentoring and super-vision continued while they worked. There is no doubt that the team of volunteers I worked with provided a good support service to a variety of people with sub-clinical problems.

A typical example of a case I treated was Darius (names and details have been changed):

> Darius was a bright but impulsive eight-year-old who had been sus-pended from school and fought constantly with his 12-year-old brother, Jake, who had started to hang around in gangs and be exposed to petty crime and drugs. They rarely saw their father. Their mother was a former addict who suffered from clinical depression. She had a third child, a toddler, by another man.
> Darius received weekly play therapy with me, while Jake saw a colleague. Their mother was on anti-depressants but also attended coun-selling at a separate site. All three therapists, plus Darius' educational psychologist from school, and Darius and Jake's volunteer mentors, would meet every week at the family's house for a family discussion and

to co-ordinate the family's care. If administration and case management time is included, it meant this one family was receiving eight hours of treatment each week, and the dividend was dramatic. Darius was better behaved at school, relations between the brothers were improving, the stress and chaos for the mother – and hence the toddler – were relieved, and the family's dysfunction, anger and pain were being healed.

None of this work was easy. It was challenging for all of the people involved, and there was no guarantee of continued success. But it meant that there was a real chance that the boys could escape a fate of juvenile delinquency, and that this one family could have a chance of stabilising, and living more happy, productive lives.

Both the mentors and the boy's counsellor were volunteers. I was treating Darius as part of my supervised training, and Jake's counsellor was a retired accountant who had received intense training in parenting skills, play therapy and child counselling. His work was supervised by an accredited therapist. Because of this volunteer aspect, backed-up by the qualified members of the team, the costs of this intense programme of support were reduced dramatically. Without the volunteer component, it simply would not have happened.

Reflected across the centre as a whole, the input of volunteers meant that the work of just one psychologist and a few hours a week from half a dozen therapists enabled 30 volunteers to provide hundreds of hours of support to people each month.

The details of selection, training and back-up for such a scheme here in Britain need to be developed carefully. When devising exactly how the fourth force would work, we could draw on the experience of the hundreds of existing voluntary groups that already provide essential services in every part of the country. At their best, these groups are knitted into the local mental health eco-system, and have good relations with primary and secondary care providers.

For example, thousands of people in the UK are helped every year by the Samaritans, a body relying on volunteers with intensive training, back-up and support. There are also a multitude of other charities that provide befriending services, bereavement counselling and so on. The NSF and NSF Review documents are full of examples of best practice among these vital community bodies. The patchwork of existing volunteer services offers a promising foundation, but it is inadequate given the scale of the problem. The idea of a fourth force of "para-counsellors" would build on their work, but would attempt to build a systematic, multi-problem addressing service in every local community.

Naturally, there will be concerns among therapeutic professionals about delegating care to "unqualified" volunteers. But many already acknowledge the crucial work carried out in the voluntary sector. For example, the leading psychoanalyst Patrick Casement has written about the importance of the work undertaken by voluntary bereavement counsellors. "It is my belief," he says, "that bereavement counselling provides a crucial service to a vulnerable group of people at a time when the rest of life can be at stake".[19] If we recognise that volunteers can provide an invaluable service to people at one critical stage in life – bereavement – then it is surely the case that they could also be valuable at other times.

At its most basic level, the argument for a voluntary fourth force is simple: there is no alternative. The cost of professionally qualified provision on the scale we need is simply prohibitive. But there is also a highly persuasive, sophisticated therapeutic rationale for the scheme. The research on what works in therapy and counselling has consistently highlighted the importance of the quality of the relationship between therapist and client.[20] This has been shown to rank in importance above theoretical approach or levels of experience. If enough people with the right sort of qualities can be identified and well trained, there is an enormous amount of positive work they could do. It might not always be to the standard and depth of the "top" therapists – but it could still be life-changing for those whose lives it touches.

If we return to our "typical" row of houses in our imaginary town, we can see how each person and family might fit into this new model. The following contains, of course, a degree of wishful thinking. The reality, as any mental health worker knows, is that healing psychological and emotional turmoil is a hard, often fruitless task. But, as they would all also say, it is worth the effort, and imperative to try.

> Mrs. Baker might see an article on her local para-counselling centre, and decide to drop-in. She would have someone to talk to about her struggles at home. Her para-counsellor might liase with her GP and ensure she was evaluated for treatment with anti-depressants. Maybe she could try a course of Cognitive Behaviour Therapy in a Layard-style therapy centre. It is likely, though, that she would need ongoing support, and

after a few weeks might have opened-up to her para-counsellor about the abuse she witnessed at home while growing up. Slowly, she could process that trauma, and begin to heal. Maybe she would be able to get her husband to attend some relationship counselling, perhaps at an existing provider like Relate, or with another para-counsellor. Perhaps he could take the first steps to cut down on his drinking. Another para-counsellor, dedicated to him, could provide details of AA meetings and provide additional support.

Tracey and her misbehaving boys could each be seeing their own para-counsellor, the boys for play therapy, where their pain and anger could be expressed and worked through, and where they would have an additional role model in their lives. Tracey could get some non-critical support and understanding. Maybe her para-counsellor could encourage her to attend some parenting classes, and offer her continuing support when these are over.

Ted would be hard to reach, but if he dropped into his local para-counselling centre he could slowly begin to build a relationship of trust with another human being, possibly for the first time in his life. He would probably drop-out repeatedly, but he would be welcomed back, and might gradually become able to commit more. Eventually, options for further, intensive therapy for anxiety could be explored, and perhaps he could see a doctor to be evaluated for anti-anxiety medication. The crucial thing would be the provision of a long-term, safe relationship where he could learn new ways of relating to people and the world.

Becky's mum might start by talking about her struggles with her daughter and her husband. Maybe the para-counsellor might be able to begin encouraging her to take Becky to a local Eating Disorder Unit for an evaluation. The whole family could get together weekly with a para-counsellor, to talk through their dynamics and explore new ways of communicating with each other. The family's stress, worry and guilt might dramatically reduce.

Mrs. Turner could find her weekly sessions a way of expressing some of her disappointments. Her para-counsellor might put her in touch with local groups she could join. She could explore her past and her present with someone who – and she'd never have believed this possible until she started coming along – was always there for her.

Of course, one could argue that each of these cases deserves the attentions of professional, fully trained mental health professionals. But this is the demand for help on just one street. It amounts to around 10 hours of direct client contact a week, which would require several more hours of accompanying administration, supervision and case-management. Just a handful of such streets could occupy an NHS clinical psychologist or psychotherapist for several months to several years. And think how many such streets there are in a typical town.

Sensitive, well-informed GPs, community mental health teams, new psychotherapy treatments and specialised services are all vital. But so too is a new layer of community-based, ongoing support for sub-clinical and threshold clinical problems. It is a delusion to imagine that support for Britain's millions of mentally and emotionally disturbed can ever be provided by paid, tax-payer funded services alone. The demand is too great, and the supply – however much we fight for its expansion – will always be too small. A fourth force of volunteer para-counsellors may be a radical, challenging proposal, but it is the only viable solution.

REFERENCE

1. Porcupines in winter: The Pleasures and Pains of living together in Modern Britain, The Young Foundation, January 2006.
2. Surveys of Psychiatric Morbidity among Adults in Great Britain, Office of National Statistics, 2000.
3. Mental health of children and young people in Great Britain, Office for National Statistics, 2004.
4. Mental health of children and young people in Great Britain, Office for National Statistics, 2004.
5. The Mental Health and Psychological Well-being of Children and Young People, Department of Health and DfES, October 2004.
6. Young Adults with Complex Needs, Social Exclusion Unit, ODPM, November 2005.
7. Defining a Good Mental Health Service, Sainsbury Centre for Mental Health, November 2005.
8. The Mental Health and Psychological Well-being of Children and Young People, Department of Health and DfES, October 2004.
9. London Mental Health Chief Executives' Group conference: mainstreaming mental health, March 2004.
10. National Service Framework Five Years On p. 74.
11. National Service Framework Five Years On p. 38.
12. National Service Framework Five Years On p. 45.
13. National Service Framework Five Years On p. 72.
14. Defining a Good Mental Health Service, SCMH, November 2005.
15. The NHS Plan – a plan for investment, a plan for reform, July 2000.

16. Happiness: Lessons from a New Science by Richard Layard, Allen Lane, March 2005.
17. BACP Press Release, September 2005.
18. National Service Framework Five Years On p.68.
19. Mourning and Failure to Mourn, Patrick J. Casement, Ph.D, Fort Da, Fall 2000, Vol. VI, No. 2.
20. *The Heart and Soul of Change: What Works in Therapy*, American Psychological Association, 1999. (See esp. Chapters 1 & 2.)

CHAPTER 20
THE FUTURE OF NURSING

Sylvia Denton and Jane Naish

INTRODUCTION

This chapter examines the future for nursing. Unlike some of the other areas of discussion within this book, nursing is not confined to a particular area of specialism or population group so we have provided an overview of a general direction of travel we believe nursing should follow in the future.[1] We start by exploring what nursing actually is and some of the challenges it currently faces, including the very practical challenge of maintaining the numbers of nurses in the health care workforce. We then set out three key principles for the development of nursing fit for the future which are:

- inclusivity and the development of a family of nursing;
- patient centred care;
- integrated nursing care that spans health care settings.

WHAT IS NURSING?

Before we examine the future of nursing, we should perhaps start with a discussion of what nursing actually is. For many members of the public the image of a nurse still largely conjures up a picture of a (female) health care worker in uniform working in a hospital dealing with imminent death or acute illness. This is akin to TV soaps such as *E.R.* and *Casualty*. In fact the reality is somewhat different and out of the RCN membership – which reflects the composition of the nursing workforce – approximately:

- 50% of nurses work in NHS hospitals;
- 15% are based in community settings outside of hospitals;
- 7% work in the area of mental health;
- 25% work outside the NHS in the independent health care sector such as nursing homes for the elderly or private hospitals.[2]

Nurses work in every setting in which the public comes into contact with health and welfare services – from schools, general practices, community centres and clinics, telephone help lines, and workplaces through to hospitals. And they don't necessarily wear a uniform either!

But what is a nurse? In this chapter we refer to nurses as those who have undertaken the minimum three year period of higher education to become registered nurses. However we recognise that others – still predominantly women – undertake caring work that has links with nursing such as looking after babies and young children or elderly relatives and neighbours. In addition health care workers other than registered nurses are employed to undertake some nursing care, for example health care assistants. Even though registered nurses work in a range of different environments with different population groups such as children, adults, and the elderly, there are common-alities that underpin what they do and why they do it.

The Royal College of Nursing (RCN) definition of registered nurses (RCN 2003) describes nursing as:

> "the use of clinical judgement in the provision of care to enable people to improve, maintain, or recover health, to cope with health problems, and to achieve the best possible quality of life, whatever their disease or disability, until death."
>
> (RCN 2003 p3)

The following characteristics are seen integral to nursing practice:

- a particular purpose to promote health, healing, growth and development, and to prevent disease, illness, injury and disability;
- a particular mode of intervention that is concerned with empow-ering people, and helping them to achieve, maintain or recover independence;
- a particular knowledge domain about peoples unique responses to and experience of health related events;

- a particular focus on the whole person and the human response rather than a particular aspect of the person or a particular pathological condition;
- a particular value base which is expressed in a code of ethics and professional regulation;
- a commitment to partnership with patients, carers, communities and other members of the multi-disciplinary team.

These characteristics are of course shared to a greater or lesser extent with other health and welfare workers but are unique to nursing in the way they combine together. They translate in practice to the responsibility of registered nurses to maintain all aspects of the health environment so that it is conducive to improving health, facilitating recovery from illness and rehabilitation, and where appropriate achieving a dignified death. This therefore encompasses:

- essential nursing care including personal hygiene and activities of daily living such as bathing, eating, toileting and so on – and patient safety;
- treatment and technical procedures;
- social and emotional health support;
- population health and health promotion;
- managing the environment in which care is delivered.

The way in which nurses deliver care and work with patients forms a major part of how patients and others experience health care. Nursing teams are the main 'front line' workers and deliver about 80% of direct patient care. We know from research and patient and service user survey s that how patients are spoken to and looked after – for example treated with kindness and respect – really matters. What is less well known is that the numbers of registered nurses and their level of skill and experience has a relationship with *clinical* outcomes. 'Gold standard' research[3] demonstrates that higher numbers of registered nurses in acute hospital settings are associated with:

- lower patient mortality
- reductions in the numbers of (hospital acquired) respiratory, wound and urinary tract infections
- reduction in numbers of patient falls
- reduction in drug administration errors

- increased patient functional independence and speed of rehabilitation from illness
- better patients experience of health care and health services.

That is, it is not just the skill and experience of the surgeon or the use of the latest drug therapy which has a bearing on how-or whether-patients recover, the number and skill of registered nurses is critical too. This is an important point as health services are under increasing financial pressure and the nursing workforce is a major budget expense.[4]

CHALLENGES TO THE HEALTH AND SOCIAL CARE SYSTEM

Key challenges facing the UK health and social care sy stem over the next decade include:

- increasing the efficiency and effectiveness of health and social care
- changes in population demography, including a decline in the birth rate and predicted rise in the numbers of older people
- changes in patterns of disease especially non-communicable disease and chronic and long term illness, for example diabetes
- changes in lifestyle patterns that impact on health, for example diet, exercise and sexual activity
- changes in public expectation and demand for quality and personalised care
- inequalities in health status and health care outcomes
- reconciling access to, and demand and need for health care with safety and quality issues.

Patterns of demand and need for health and social care are changing, and will continue to change in the future. The central challenge is how to match effective, appropriate and efficient provision of services now and in the future to available resources. In part this will be shaped by other changes already taking place in the way in which care and treatment is delivered such as:

- advances in medical and information technologies, for example tele-medicine or developments in genetic science
- a focus on services rather than settings so that the hospital is not necessarily the central place for treatment

- new care settings including telephone consultations, walk-in centres and treatment centres in some parts of the UK.

The numbers of people employed within the health care workforce and how they contribute to the provision of heath care services is of course critical within all of the above since health care is – and will remain – labour intensive and dependant on skilled health personnel for its delivery.

NURSING WORKFORCE CHALLENGES

There are shortages in almost all categories of health care workers across the spectrum of health care. The numbers of registered nurses in the UK has been a concern for successive governments and the Royal College of Nursing for a number of years. The key features of the registered nurse workforce profile[5] are:

- recruitment and retention is a significant problem.
- general nurse shortages in addition to shortages within particular specialities and in particular parts of the UK.
- an ageing nurse population and predictions that more nurses will leave the nursing register than will join in the future.

In summary there are not enough registered nurses in the health care system and predictions are that this will continue.[6] Therefore there are clear issues to resolve regarding the capacity of registered nurses to meet demand for health services and provide quality nursing care in the future. There are already practical pressures on nurses' time and the time to nurse appropriately and deliver high quality care is a constant source of frustration to RCN members. Indeed we know that this is a major reason why nurses leave nursing, especially in the acute hospital sector. Nurses feel they cannot provide the kind of care to a high standard that they would like to because there are simply not enough nurses and so leave the profession.[7]

In addition to numbers, changes to what registered nurses do have taken place which impact upon their workload. For example nurses now undertake work previously the domain of others, particularly doctors, for a number of reasons including the reduction of junior doctors hours in order to comply with the European Working Time Directive. But also because nursing as a profession has grown and become more sophisticated as a result of improved education *and* changes in the pace and type of medical treatment available. Nurses have developed expertise in all areas of health care both as generalists – for example nurse practitioners in primary care who see, diagnose and treat people in general without recourse to a doctor – and as specialists and experts in particular areas of health care. Breast care nurses who work with patients with breast cancer are a good example of the latter and over the last 25 years have developed expertise and clinical decision making skills in breast care that covers new technologies such as genetic screening and new treatments such as hormone therapy as well as emotional support and counselling skills.

Increasing numbers of nurses are working at advanced or specialist levels of practice (for which there is additional education and preparation over and above the three year education period to qualify as a nurse) in all health care settings. There is a range of evidence which suggests such nurses are popular with patients and at least as effective as doctors for many conditions.[8] This is a trend that is likely to continue but does have implications for the nursing workforce and the nursing workload. We are well aware that there have been calls – particularly in the populist media – for nurses to abandon some of the treatment and technical procedures they now undertake and only carry out essential nursing care. But this is simply not feasible – not least because the NHS is now dependant upon nurses to do this work – as a recent joint Department of Health and RCN survey reveals[5] – and who else could, or is best placed, to step in and undertake this? It is also not realistic and premised on a notion of fixed health care roles and a return to a 'golden age' in nursing when in fact what nurses – and other health workers – do has never been static and has evolved over time. For example not so long ago the measurement of blood pressure was the sole prerogative of doctors which is in contrast to today when a variety of people – nurses, physiotherapists, health care assistants to name but a few – will undertake this as part of their routine contact with patients!

The solutions to workforce shortages and pressures do not lie in recreating boundaries between health care workers, or indeed viewing health care as a series of tasks to be passed between different groups in the workforce. We need to recognise that the boundaries between health professions and health care workers have blurred and will continue to do so in the future. Workforce issues, and the nursing workforce issue within this, needs a whole system approach that is not amenable to a single or 'quick fix' solution. There are three key strategic options for attempting to balance nurse workforce numbers with need, demand and changes to health care. These are:

- increasing numbers in the registered nurse workforce
- changing what registered nurses do
- shaping demand and need for health care.

The first option to increase the numbers of registered nurses is obvious but continued recruitment and retention of nurses is dependent upon ensuring nursing is an attractive career comparative to others. This translates to job satisfaction and the value accorded to the nursing contribution, competitive pay, family friendly policies, and a flexible career structure that enables nurses to leave and rejoin the career ladder with appropriate and accessible educational support.

The second option regarding what registered nurses do and the effective use of their time has several facets. It is in part about decisions made by both the local multi-professional team and individual nurses about what care nurses personally undertake and what they delegate to others and supervise. This is based on factors such as patient choice, expertise, competence and accessibility. However improved administrative and housekeeping support services – for example simple form filling, answering the telephone – are also vital since we know from research that approximately 25% of registered nurse time is spent on such activities.[5] Lastly a more imaginative look at nursing resources is needed, which we will pick up in our vision of the nursing future.

The third option regarding shaping demand for health services is about disease prevention and the early diagnosis of illness prior to the emergence of complications. For example preventing coronary heart disease by reducing smoking within the population or managing diabetes more effectively to prevent complications of the disease and hospitalisation. But it also about:

- supporting patients in self-care and management of disease and illness so that they have less contact with the health services and develop their own expertise
- expert primary care services that provide some acute treatment and prevent and control hospital admissions

- engagement of patients and the public in decisions about health service provision
- greater public responsibility for using the health service effectively.[9]

These three strategic options need to be blended together to form a rounded approach to the workforce problem. How do we see these coming together for nursing in the future?

THE NURSING FUTURE: AN INCLUSIVE FAMILY OF NURSING

A nursing strategy for the future needs to recognise that registered nurses will not be able to personally deliver all the nursing care needed. Therefore nurses must be organised so that they are able to influence, mentor and shape the delivery of nursing responsibilities, whether or not they actually deliver those on a day-to-day basis. Teamwork is the key medium here, both within and outside of nursing. The RCN recognises the valuable contribution to nursing made by health care assistants – who are not qualified nurses – and we need to build an inclusive family of nursing and take responsibility for the support we provide to health care assistants and the quality of nursing care delivered.

We also need to go further than this and acknowledge and build upon the experience and expertise of others who provide nursing care, including extending to the informal setting of the home and neighbourhood outside of health care institutions. For example, care provided by families and relatives, neighbours and volunteers. Nurses do already do this – especially community nurses – but we need to develop this much further into *active* support networks which are easy to access and 'tap into' for patients (self care) and others and which share expertise and education.

THE NURSING FUTURE: PATIENT CENTRED CARE

Alongside the above we most definitely do not want nursing to become either task based or concerned only with technical and treatment procedures. Essential nursing care must remain a central plank of what registered nursing is about even if it is not always s personally carried out by registered nurses. Our vision of nursing in the future is one of 'maxi-nursing' rather than nurses as 'mini-doctors'. Numerous research studies show that this is also what patients want.[10] But more than this patients want care that is integrated and seamless to what they need – that is, they do not want to have to deal with a variety of agencies and workers for various facets of their condition (or at the very least they want to have one health care worker who navigates and puts together a package of care for them). They also want *personalised* or patient centred care which takes into account their individual needs and identity rather than a 'one size fits all' approach, a trend which is set to increase in the future.

Person centred care has two fundamental implications for how health care is delivered which are based on:

- a facilitative and partnership style of interaction between health care workers and patients
- the way health care systems are organised.[11]

Patients want to be partners in their care, at least for most conditions and situations and will require information and support to enable them to make their own informed decisions. Patients and their families/carers are likely to require health practitioners to further adopt this way of working in the future which will mean a step change in professional attitudes to the basis of professional knowledge and expertise.

Health care systems will also need to change to accommodate a patient centred approach so that care is not based on professional boundaries or demarcations, or traditional care settings such as the hospital or general practice. This poses challenges for how health care is commissioned and funded in the future – which is outside the remit of this chapter – but we can paint a picture of how we would like to see nursing positioned within this.

THE NURSING FUTURE: INTEGRATED NURSING ACROSS CARE SETTINGS

We have set out above two of the key tenets of how nursing should develop in the future. The third and complementary aspect which brings together the first two is that nursing and nursing teams must become far more integrated across the different care settings and align themselves to the patient health care journey. That is, they need to span both community and hospital settings and work across traditional boundaries of institutions or indeed professional nursing roles and specialisms. So for example nursing based upon illness care pathways for people with diabetes or asthma, or on population groups such as the elderly or children. There are numerous ways in which this could be organised but it may change how many nurses are currently employed and configured since at present they are usually employed by setting (hospital or general practice for example). There will still be a need for some nurses to work exclusively within say a hospital but as the nature of what hospitals do evolves over time – they are likely to focus much more on the care of the critically ill rather than primary diagnosis or investigations for example – opportunities will emerge that allow nursing to develop integrated patient care that crosses settings. The speed of development will also be influenced by local circumstances since rural environments with an absence of local acute or tertiary care lend themselves to more rapid development, probably within an overarching framework of local clinical networks.

Other health care professions and workers could develop similar models and will certainly contribute to same. But nurses are well placed to lead on this as nursing is very much a generalist occupation that deals with first contact care, chronic or long term illness and health promotion. There is no reason why nurses in the future cannot be responsible for complete episodes of care, whether needed for 10 days or 10 years, drawing on the specialist resources of others such as doctors as appropriate. In fact despite the many myths about the boundaries of what nurses can and cannot do, they are already able to admit and discharge patients to hospitals, refer them to others, or order and interpret tests and investigations (Department of Health 2003); it has simply been custom and practice that they do not do so on a routine basis.

CONCLUSION

We have set out above a general direction of travel for how we believe nursing should develop in the future. Of necessity this has to be a broad brush approach rather than a prescription for practice since nursing spans all areas of health care. Our vision requires investment in nursing resources – particularly education since future nurse leaders will need the additional skills, but importantly also the confidence, to anticipate and respond positively to change, deal with uncertainty and calculate risk and understand and manage effective team working.

REFERENCES

1. This chapter is based on a recent RCN publication *The Future Nurse: The RCN Vision Explained* available on www.rcn.org.uk/resources/publcations/futurenurse.
2. This includes those employed by general practices.
3. West, E., Rafferty, A.M. and Lankshear (2005) *The Future Nurse: Evidence of the Impact of Registered Nurses* London School of Hygiene and Tropical Medicine, University of York and Royal College of Nursing: London.
4. Cairns, J. and Naish, J. (2005) 'What are Nurses Worth?' *Nursing Standard,* Vol 20, No 13.
5. Royal College of Nursing (2005) *Survey of RCN Members in Advanced and Specialist Roles* www.rcn.org.uk/resources/publications/maxinursesadvancedandspecialistnursingroles.
6. Recruitment of nurses from overseas has bolstered the numbers of registered nurses in the UK but there is evidence that overseas recruitment is now in decline (RCN 2005).
7. Royal College of Nursing (2004) *Stepping Stones: Results from the RCN Membership Survey 2003* RCN: London.
8. Laurant, M. et al (2005) *Substitution of Doctors by Nurses in Primary Care: Cochrane Collaboration Review* John Wiley and Sons: London.
9. Wanless, D. (2002) *Securing Our Future Health: Taking a Long Term View* HM Treasury: HMSO. Wanless, D. (2004) *Securing Good Health for the Whole Population* HM Treasury: HMSO.
10. Kendall, L. (2001) *The Future Patient* Institute of Public Policy Research: London.
11. Kendall, L. and Lissauer, R. (2003) *The Future Health Worker* Institute of Public Policy Research: London.

FURTHER READING

Department of Health (2003) Freedom to Practice: Dispelling the Myths Department of Health: HMSO.

Royal College of Nursing (2003) *Defining Nursing* RCN: London.

Royal College of Nursing (2004) *The Future Nurse: The RCN Vision Explained* RCN: London.

Royal College of Nursing (2005) *Past Trends, Future Imperfect? A Review of the UK Nursing Labour Market 2004/5* RCN: London.

CHAPTER 21
INTEGRATING ALTERNATIVE HEALTH

Dr Mosaraf Ali

Alternative Medicine was born in the nineteen sixties as a rebellion against the indiscriminate use of antibiotics and drugs like Thalidomide which caused terrible birth anomalies. President Nixon's visit to China in the late sixties opened up acupuncture to the rest of the world as a group of doctors witnessed demonstrations of surgery performed without the use of conventional anaesthesia. In the nineteen seventies, The Prince of Wales used the word 'Complementary Medicine' to make such subjects like homoeopathy, osteopathy, acupuncture and herbal medicine, amongst other disciplines, more acceptable by conventional or allopathic medicine in general. Research and active lobbing of Parliament (which was followed by statutory intervention) saw osteopathy and chiropractic accepted as a powerful therapy for backache.

In the eighties and nineties, the use of complementary medicine grew by 8%–15%, primarily because of the sales of supplements and health products. Many training schools opened up to teach and regulate practitioners among them aromatherapists, counsellors, naturopaths, homoeopaths, acupuncturists and reflexologists. These practitioners carried out door-to-door campaigns to popularise complementary medicine. People who were curious at first became firm believers. Newspaper columns on health and health magazines began to appear everywhere. Some insurance companies were compelled to accept many of the therapies because of popular demand by clients.

Many doctors seeing the benefits in their patients and the growing popularity began to do courses themselves in homoeopathy, acupuncture and osteopathy. Thus Integrated Medicine was born. It combined the best of conventional, complementary and traditional (ayurveda, acupuncture, Chinese herbal) medicines and practised by qualified medical doctors. Pain clinics for the management of chronic pain with acupuncture or the TENS machine (Transcutaneous Electrical Nerve Stimulator), became part of major hospital facilities. Chinese herbal medicine for the treatment of eczema was researched. The role of meditation for the management of blood pressure and stress-related ailments were also studied. GP practices now receive funding for homoeopathy, osteopathy and acupuncture.

I have been practicing Integrated medicine for over twenty years and now run. The Integrated Medical Centre in Central London with over twenty five doctors and therapists seeing around six hundred patients every week. My first research project was on the effectiveness of Marma, an ancient Indian rehabilitation technique, for the treatment of stroke. A pilot study conducted at The Hammersmith Hospital in 1976 was followed by a comprehensive study at The Royal Devon and Exeter Hospital. The results are due for publication later in 2006 and will clearly show the benefits derived. This will be followed by a further research study on three hundred and fifty cases of stroke. Stroke rehabilitation is the largest single consumer of the UK health-care budget. It costs the NHS approximately thirty nine thousand pounds per stroke bed per annum in hospitalisation costs and much more in maintaining the support system for the long term disabled who account for forty per cent of the one hundred and thirty thousand new cases every year. The proposed research will give these people more mobility and freedom to carry out day-to-day functions at the very least. This will cut current costs drastically.

As Hippocrates said, eighty per cent of illnesses can be cured using Regimen Therapy or Lifestyle Programme, which consists of diet, massage, exercises and relaxation. Just as fractures, bruises, cuts, mild burns and common flu heal on their own; it is possible to lay down those conditions which can lead to self cure. It is generally agreed that many diseases can be prevented and cured by diet, exercises, massage and stress management. At least chronic ailments respond better to such simple therapies than to conventional whose failure led to the diseases advancing from the acute to chronic stage. Backache, osteoarthritis, obesity-related diseases, heart disease, metabolic disorders, and stress-related conditions for example, can be prevented or managed by the above simple approach. Logic and human experience has proved that and Integrated Healthcare demonstrates it with most chronic cases. Why are we looking for more 'evidence' to accept such a commonsense approach?

The very basis of integrated healthcare is the patient's participation in creating their own health. They are encouraged to follow a regimen of diet, exercises (yoga, pilates, tai chi, walking), massages (self, partner, professional) and relaxation (music, tapes, visualisation, meditation, prayers). They feel immensely better for doing it. Excess weight goes, Energy lifts, appearance improves and the 'feel good factor' is restored. This is the basis of self-healing. In addition, time-tested remedies and other treatment modalities such as acupuncture, homoeopathy, and manipulations are used to enhance the body's self-healing mechanism. These treatments have negligible side effects and can be incorporated into healthcare on their face value. If the right parameters of research are set, then one can put them to test to study their efficacy and safety, which in my view will be a time consuming process.

I have trained four batches of NHS doctors over the past four years. Dr. Richard Halvorsen's report, published in the *General Practitioner* Magazine on 25th July 2005, clearly summarises the results. These doctors were trained to use simple diagnostic techniques and observation skills and to use simple methods (some traditional) to treat most common acute and chronic ailments. The doctors are practising very successfully using these methods. Since patients follow the instructions on diet and exercise, the use of medicines is minimal. The reports I get are that they have prevented and cured many illnesses by using Integrated Medical techniques.

The NHS should place emphasis on the training of Primary Healthcare physicians in principles of integrated medicine. Many diseases can be arrested at the grassroots level and there will be fewer burdens on the more expensive hospital and specialised treatment. These primary healthcare centres should have sufficient budgets for group therapies and training in areas like yoga, relaxation and massage, and have advisors on diet and nutrition. If patients had the facility to attend pregnancy yoga class, backache yoga class, weight loss seminars etc, they would make use of such services. Some patients may need reminders but the majority will attend, as they don't want to be ill or continue suffering. Imagine the impact such simple methods of health and stress management will have on the nation's health and healthcare budget.

The NHS should cast aside its reservations about 'old fashioned' therapies just because their advisors are against it. They should embrace them by forming a panel of top integrated health experts and seeking their advice on the best methods. These therapies should be available in conjunction with the general lifestyle programme. Hospitals however, would continue to give specialised treatment, carry out surgery and attend to the acute or emergency medicine. The vast majority of cases that are chronic should not clog the hospitals unless they are life threatening.

If people are health conscious and are offered free guidance and services to improve their health, they would make use of them. The number of hospital visits would drop, the queues would be reduced and the general health of the nation will improve as a result.

There is however, the risk of many losing their jobs in healthcare and the pharmaceutical industry. This is where the stumbling block is. The NHS should take a bold step to make a firm decision. Either they will fail to deliver their promises or earn kudos and save money – that is the dilemma the NHS faces now.

The future of healthcare depends on what decisions are made today.

CHAPTER 22
WHAT DO PATIENTS WANT?

Claire Rayner

Over half a century ago Aneurin Bevan (with, admittedly, the full support of the rest of the Labour Government Cabinet of the time) unveiled his magnificent newly invented wheel. A National Health Service that would at last free the population of these islands from the fear that had constantly dogged them and their ancestors; the fear of illness. Not just the fear of the condition from which they suffered but fear of the ancillary effects. Would it be painful? Would it mutilate them and leave them unfit to lead a normal life? Would it kill them? Would it, above all, damage their ability to earn a living and so send them plus their families into a downward spiral to pauperdom?

As a child I was well aware of these fears. I was born in 1931, and at no time did my mother have any direct medical care. She had no antenatal supervision, and when she went into labour was tended to by an untrained midwife, although the woman had had ample experience as the local East End 'wise woman'. She and my father were extremely young and very poor, and could not afford anything better, not even the few pence a week it cost to join a Hospital Savings Scheme.

As a result neither I nor my two sisters were seen by a doctor until we started school at four plus and met the local authority's school doctor and nurse. In fact, there is evidence that I had contracted pulmonary TB before school entry. When I started my nurse training in 1951 and had my chest X rayed for the first time ever and was given a Mantoux test, the first showed calcified glands attributed by the radiologist to childhood TB, and the second showed a massive reaction which gave me a painful and swollen forearm for several days.

I also knew what it was like to work in a hospital before that beautiful new wheel, the NHS, rolled into our lives. Before I was old enough to start my proper nurse training I became a nurse cadet in 1945 at the age of fourteen by dint of lying like Ananius and telling the Matron of a Cottage Hospital that I was seventeen. Consequently I discovered the constant penny pinching and various stratagems that were needed to give the patients the best care we could, as cheaply as possible.

As I recall it was very good care indeed, with a lot of close patient observation and bedside attention, although staff were thin on the ground (too expensive) and those who were employed were paid very little. I remember £15 per annum and emoluments (board and lodging and so forth) for which we worked an average 12 hour day, usually running well into unpaid overtime, with a day a week off which, we were frequently told by our Ward Sisters, was lavish to the point of extravagance. *They* had to pay for their training and got one day off a month.

By 1951, when I started proper training the pay was not markedly greater An envelope containing £6 was put into our eager hands each month by Matron herself. We worked from 8.30am to 8.30pm each day and had three hours a day time off in which we attended lectures and revised for exams. We had a day and a half off each week, but put in a great deal of unpaid overtime.

Since then, I have worked as a self employed health educator, that is, writing and talking in both the serious and the popular press and TV and radio on health issues, remembering always the WHO definition of health, which is that it is not just the absence of illness but a state of physical, mental and social well being. The literally hundreds of thousands letters I have received over the years from patients of all kinds, and still receive via my involvement with the national charity The Patients Association have greatly informed my mind and given me some expertise in the matter of what today's patients want – and more importantly need – in the future.

And finally, I have in the past couple of decades experienced a good deal of physical illness, and via some dozen or so major surgical interventions have had more experience of what it is to be a patient than I would have chosen.

This lengthy preamble is offered to validate my right to speak for patients, even though much has changed since I worked at the bedside rather than occupied it. And it is clear to me that what patients valued most then, they still do, though perhaps to a more sophisticated degree.

WE WANT TO KNOW THE PEOPLE WHO TREAT US

Many patients complain they see the Consultant to whom their GP has referred them in Out-patients and who decides they need further outpatient care, or need to be admitted, and discover at future out-patient visits, or on admission, that they are then seen perhaps by junior clinician. Even if the Consultant does do his/her own ward rounds, he/she all too often says much less to the anxious patient, than to the people who come on the round as well – Registrars, House Officers, Physiotherapists, perhaps a nurse or two and sometimes medical students, to swell the crowd and make it very formidable to patients' eyes.

Knowing the doctor who looked after you and your family was a great part of the charm of cottage hospitals, where the medical staff were local.

In addition to being unable to develop a patient/doctor relationship in hospital because of the bewildering number of strange faces who come to you, nursing staff are often in a state of flux with agency nurses brought in to provide adequate pairs of hands to cover sickness days, holidays and the various demands on the regular staff which take them away from their wards. So once again strangers who know little about you or even why you are there, make patients feel not only lonely but alienated.

Furthermore, the shift changes of nursing staff, as well as those holidays, and days off sick, mean that even a patient's 'named nurse' who is supposed to be the one who provides continuity "Always seems to be off duty or too busy with another patient to come to me" as far too many patients have reported. (This was an experience that I too had when a patient).

Perhaps the current (at the time of writing) changes will offer patients the security of having at least one health professional they can really get to know and to whom they feel they can talk easily and trust to answer all their questions. We hope so...though there is nothing in the White Paper to bolster those hopes.

The Government, which is constantly reinventing Bevan's wheel, just as previous Governments have over a period of many years (especially the Thatcher regime which started the vogue of putting money firmly before patients' needs, and which has handed on its monetarism to the current administration in a considerably swollen form) is offering for the future, more input from GPs via Primary Care Trusts, which are sometimes extremely large conglomerations of GP practices, as well as smaller local hospitals to deal with bread-and-butter disorders, some of them designated 'Foundation Hospitals', which are meant to be centres of excellence, to deal with the tougher cases and more innovative therapies.

Is this what patient's want? Possibly, if the smaller local hospitals are actually a reinvention of the cottage hospital, with GPs and other familiar primary care staff looking after them and ensuring they are able to see a Consultant if necessary at an Outreach Clinic, These are also to be set up in the brave new medical care world promised for the future. Such clinics may make some of us think it a waste of skilled medical time to have them sitting in traffic jams to get to us, but most will be pleased because they won't need to travel to a hospital and brave its complexities and often unnerving busy-ness.

When it comes to Primary Care Trusts, there are already patients who complain that it is very difficult to make an appointment with the GP they regard as 'their' doctor. If more and more practices merge into big Trusts, surely they will feel even less happy and, just like hospital in- and out-patients, alienated and unable to feel the trust we all need when we consult a doctor.

On the much trumpeted issue of choice, with patients free to say which of four hospitals they elect to go to, we have some caveats.

First, it's possibly a good idea for those who live in large conurbations with several hospitals reachable by local public transport, but risible for those who live in small towns or villages or deep in the country-side. They may already be a considerable distance from their nearest hospital, let alone three others. Their choice only exists if they have some particularly rare condition for which there is a specialised hospital such as Roehampton, Royal National Orthopaedic, or St Marks for gut diseases (and possibly not even then, if their local

Trust refuses to pay for them, which is always possible) They have to be prepared for loneliness, since it would be too costly, expensive and difficult for relatives to visit regularly.

And of course it could be choosing a pig in a poke. What we want is to be referred to a Consultant with whom our GP has worked in the past and been satisfied with the care given to his/her patients. An added benefit; the GP will be able to offer a few comments about the Consultant's personality. "A really nice chap; loves explaining the details of what he's doing for a patient, complete with very clear drawings. I think you'll like him." That sort of recommendation is the best choice every time for us.

WE WANT TO FEEL SAFE

In the past most patients, in my experience, feared the outcome of their illness or the prospect of an operation or being unhappily away from home. Relatives' visits were much curtailed, and children were not allowed them at all until 1959 when Professor Harry Platt published a Report that led to the acceptance of more humane 24 hour visits by parents of under fives.

What patients never feared was the risk of catching a dangerous infection. Hospitals were famous for being exceedingly clean as well as exuding a very familiar hospital smell made up of such cleansers as carbolic, Jeyes' Fluid, soap, beeswax polish and Brasso. The ghosts of Semmelweiss and Lister walked every corner of every ward and department of every hospital, and staff at all levels washed their hands so often that many needed to use large amounts of cold cream under cotton gloves when they went to bed.

Now, as any fool knows, hospitals are a byword for dirt and disorder and above all extremely unpleasant at best and fatal at worst hospital acquired infections (HAIs). Newspapers publish horrid accounts of amputations, long inpatient stays and of course deaths. MRSA is the most important; there cannot be a patient in the country who doesn't know that the letters mean an infection caused by a ferocious bacterium that does not succumb to regular antibiotics. Quite a lot of them also know that Clostridium difficile is also spreading in waves of severe and almost constant diarrhoea and is particularly dangerous when it infects the very young and the old and frail.

There are also newspaper articles about surgeons removing the wrong leg or breast, or one of other paired organs; of staff giving the wrong drugs and thereby killing the patient; of patients being given accidentally a massive overdose of radiotherapy, of patients' notes being lost, so that they do not get the treatment originally written up for them, and sundry other potentially disastrous events. Is it any wonder that there are people now who swear that however ill they may become they will never go near a hospital?

We know full well that modern surgery is amazing in its scope, able to deal with hearts and brains (including minute infants' organs) as well as other not quite such essential organs with a nonchalance that can only come from great skill. We know that the creation of Intensive Care Units and Special Care Baby Units save lives that in my nursing days would have been regarded as completely unsalvageable. But we did not expect we would have to lose basic life-protecting hygiene and cleanliness to pay for these advances.

At the time of writing, efforts to combat the spread of potentially lethal Hospital Acquired Infections are being made from the Department of Health downwards, to encourage a practice, once so ingrained in all staff that no one ever had to think about it – hand washing between attending to each patient. Patients too are involved in the effort. We are encouraged to ask whether a doctor or nurse has hand washed properly before allowing them to touch us. Few, of course, have the courage to do so.

There are also plans in some Trusts to stop sending out the laundry, as it were. Thatcherite thinking deemed it would save money to employ contract cleaning firms; maybe it did, but it left hospitals disgustingly dirty. The contract company's employees tend to lack any real incentive to do a good job and they are rarely paid enough for the effort demanded of them.

When hospitals put cleaners on their payroll as permanent staff, the sense of team membership the workers develop helps to make them much better at the job because they come to regard their workplace as their own fiefdom; even ward sisters have been told by a ward cleaner to 'stay out of my kitchen/sluice/treatment room whatever until the floor's dry – I've just scrubbed it'. That's real devotion to the job and it shows in gleaming floors and dust-free surfaces which add to patients' sense of security. Obviously dirt worries ill people a great deal. I have had many letters about it in the past twenty years or so...

Reports on the progress of these initiatives are showing that doctors are proving much harder to convince of the necessity of hand washing, but it was ever thus. Some tend to develop the notion that they are so special they walk about inside a sterile bubble. And Trust Finance Managers may be resisting the loss of contract cleaning and the recruiting and employment of their own cleaners, claiming the transition costs will negate any savings. Maybe; but they'd get value for their cash and so would we.

As patients we await hopefully the outcome of these efforts, while we yearn for the clean hygienic hospitals that once helped us to feel and be safe.

WE WANT RELIABLE DAY AND HOME CARE

The best promises patients are given in recent diktats from the Department of Health are those that deal with new ways to access professional health care.

Walk-in centres in railway stations, high streets and other busy places, especially outside normal working hours? Great for one-off problems; an injury, an assurance that we're not foolish to worry about a symptom, of *course*, go to see your GP and no, he/she won't be annoyed with that, nor similar matters.

Actually we have that already with NHS direct, one of Frank Dobson's initiatives whilst Secretary of State for Health and very popular and successful it is, if sometimes a little slow, and the Minor Accident Centres tucked into convenient places like old cottage hospitals, but even more convenient access via walk-in centres will improve on them both.

When it comes to hospital based Day Care the picture is a little less glossy for some patients, such as those who are elderly, or who live alone. It's great to be able to have your hernia repaired, your varicose veins stripped, even your hysterectomy, as at least some gynaecologists are offering; much better than going as an inpatient into what you might regard as a pest house.

The problem is, however, what happens at the end of the day. Even if you have a wife or a mother or some other woman to care for you – and at the risk of seeming to be androphobic it usually *is* a woman who is expected to provide any necessary home care – which could add considerably to the burdens many such women already carry.

People who live alone (there are more single person households now than there ever have been) are also vulnerable and they can experience a great deal of anxiety in the depths of the night if something unexpected happens, such as a bleed from the keyhole site of their operation. It is true of course that the Day Care Department issues home-going patients with instruction sheets about what they should or should not do, and a phone number to call if there is any emergency or anxiety, but there are some patients who feel that this sort of care somehow short-changes them.

"Whatever happened to the idea of convalescence?" I have been asked, and it is true that patients may well fail to give themselves enough rest to recover fully from the anaesthetic, which is of course more debilitating than the surgery in many cases and, because it was 'only a day job' believe themselves fully recovered when they are not and go back to work too soon thereby suffering further illness, perhaps in the form of clinical depression and/or an anxiety state. Not common of course, but an avoidable possibility, surely.

If Day Care patients can get anxious and depressed, consider how much more difficult it can be for people with chronic or long term illness who need support and further treatment.

The people who tend to fall into this category are the frail elderly, especially those who add to age a disability perhaps from arthritis or stroke or fractures, which are all too common among long-past-the-menopause women who have osteoporosis. They are all too likely in some areas of the country to get less community support than they need.

When the Royal Commission on Long Term Care for the Elderly produced its report, 'With Respect to Old Age' the Government turned down some of our recommendations (the most important, the great majority of the Commissioners felt) but at least promised to spend a substantial amount to provide Intermediate Care. This was to be a the provision of a series of units, possibly outside the main hospitals, staffed solely by nurses where people not ill enough to need acute beds, but not well enough to go home, would get the care they needed.

Cynics amongst us thought this was not particularly patient centred care; more a wheeze to get elderly patients out of acute hospital beds where they were unpleasantly, indeed insultingly, labelled by management as 'Bed Blockers'

It seems that few of these Intermediate provisions ever saw the light of day. The Patients Association Helpline has never been asked about them or heard from callers who showed any knowledge of them, and we can only suppose that if the money was given to Trusts for the purpose, they found it much simpler to use it to pay off some of their often painfully large overspends.

So, when it comes to long-term home care, the provision is patchy in the extreme. Some Primary Care Trusts are willing to use enough of their funds to supplement what's offered by the Local Authority. Others leave it all to the Local Authority.

If the patients are too old and frail or disabled to care for themselves properly, and have little or no family support, social workers and nurses will visit them to assess their needs, in order to create a 'Care Package' for them.

Unfortunately, in some areas it is suspected, by relatives and friends of patients who have contacted me, that the assessors from social services are well aware of the financial pressures their department is under and make an assessment of need that suits their budget, better than it suits the patient who therefore is provided with a package too limited for their needs.

The people who suffer most in old age are those who are asset rich and cash poor. The scheme that allowed people to buy the council houses in which they lived (guess which Government did that!) made saving money for their upkeep in old age more difficult. So, when the time arrived when they simply would not be safe living in their own homes, the answer had to be Residential Care Homes.

If a suitable one with space for more residents can be found and is run by a charity or the Local Authority, then the patient will be lucky. If they have to go into a privately run Care Home it is a very different story.

First of all there are far fewer of them than were set up by those of an entrepreneurial bent who went into the business (which was regarded by many as potentially very lucrative, as more people lived longer) and also because the same Government that put council houses up for sale also closed virtually all wards for geriatric patients, thus creating a large constituency from which it was possible to make sizeable profits.

But then changes in EU rules about the way Care Homes should be built (very sensible ones) were made mandatory in the UK and a large number of crestfallen entrepreneurs found it all too costly. It was simpler to close down and invest their money elsewhere, and leave the residents – who of course regarded the Home as their own, and had made friends there, and found the prospect of losing it all very painful – high and dry and their families or social workers struggling to find somewhere else.

In effect the NHS has washed its hands of the frail or disabled, whether mentally or physically and sometimes both, and they are in limbo. Many people are campaigning to right this wrong to the people who came back from the War immediately after which the NHS was born, and were promised they would be cared for 'from the cradle to the grave' They most certainly do not have that and too many of them have had to pay, and are still paying, for private Residential Care which costs all they all they have (private Home rates are high; most are over £300 a week and can be more than double that) except for their final £16,000, which doesn't go far over a few years when you want to buy worthwhile Christmas and birthday gifts for your children and grandchildren.

Even more demeaning for many of these elderly people is that in order to pay for their care they have to sell the home they laboured to build (and the chattels they have accumulated and for which they have no space in their Care Home room) all of it wrapped in a tissue of the precious memories of their long lives.

Providing what NHS gurus call Social Care and many others regard as basic nursing care – and I as a nurse am one of them – is not mentioned in the 1946 Act which gave birth to the NHS in 1948. Nor is it mentioned in recent DoH statements. Although living as we do in the fifth richest country in the world, we must face the fact that the NHS will *not* be looking after us to our graves.

WE WANT THE NHS TO CONTINUE TO EXIST

For all its current problems and occasional disasters there is no doubt in my mind that the majority of the people in this country value the NHS highly, and would be deeply dismayed if the current obsession to reduce its costs, which we know is a major problem, takes us back to the bad old days pre 1948.

This is true even for those who have the means to take out private healthcare insurance so that they can be treated in private hospitals by private Consultants, whom they know full well have been trained and validated as truly safe pairs of hands by the NHS.

I have talked with many people who are frank about using the private sector for various problems, but who add that if they ever need exceedingly high quality care, say after major heart attacks or strokes or illnesses or injuries so severe that they need to be admitted to Intensive Care Units, an NHS hospital offers a much greater chance of a good outcome than the glossiest of private establishments. "When it comes to the crunch, the NHS is what you want" is a cliché I often hear.

But will its problems cause a collapse of the NHS in some coming decade?

It is obvious to those who work in the NHS that they will become a great deal worse. Ever larger cost problems loom. The use of Private Finance Initiatives to build hospitals, equip them with hugely expensive equipment like magnetic scanners and machines that count positron emissions, as well as less dramatic but equally costly things like building, maintaining and running car parks – indeed anything a hospital Trust simply cannot afford – will have to be repaid, with interest, some time. In effect the private finance insurance has mortgaged the future NHS; who will have pay it off? And at what cost to the NHS itself as well as to the taxpayer?

So, I return to that almost rhetorical question; will the NHS collapse in the future? I write now not as a spokeswoman for the patients I have known and cared for and listened to during a working life as a health professional that stretches back some sixty years, but as an individual who has built up a considerable body of knowledge.

And I have to say that I very much fear it will.

It has, without many patients and potential patients realising it, already been severely damaged. The promises made in the beginning of free-at-the-point-of-need everything required for a full, healthy and as a result long life, including drugs, dental care, hearing aids, spectacles, wigs and anything else that a patient needs to be well and happy, have mostly fallen out of the NHS larder. Rare indeed is a fully NHS dentist to be found, the cost of prescriptions has risen steadily, with only the over sixties getting their medicines free of charge. The most modern of digital hearing aids are rarely offered to the deaf, and patients made bald by cancer treatment must supply their own wigs.

And of course drugs are getting extremely expensive, especially those used to treat cancer. Some Trusts flatly refuse to supply them, and women with breast cancer have gone as far as suing them, in the hope they will be forced to provide the life saving treatment other breast cancer patients get, simply because others are in the care of Trusts who will pay for it.

This situation is an example of the problem of what has become the cliché most used in NHS and patient circles; the 'post-code lottery' Because the money needed to run the NHS no longer comes from the centre via regional Health Authorities; localisation is the buzzword. That means that hospital Trusts and Primary Care Trusts hold the purse strings today and have to use the money they get to cover everything their patients need.

The result of this has been not only that some Trusts agree to provide expensive drugs for a cancer patient, or similarly expensive drugs for those with Alzheimer's disease or Invitro Fertilisation for those unhappy childless couples who plead for the chance to try to have a child, while the next door Trusts will not. This is repeated all over the country as Trusts running either a hospital or a GP service struggle to make ends meet with many failing to do so and showing overspends – a new word for debts – running into many billions of pounds collectively.

So, we now have not a *National* Health Service but a series of Local Health Services, a net that has many large holes through which patients fall with distressing frequency. Add to that the cost of servicing debts and the future of the NHS is very bleak indeed. Hence, my fears for the continuance of that glorious life-enhancing Aneurin Bevan launched almost sixty years ago. Will it be part of the future? Or will our descendants be pushed back into the past, to one day, die not only unhonoured and unsung, but uncared for.

SECTION III
ORGANISATION

CHAPTER 23
TRAINING FOR A NEW NHS

Professor Shelley Heard and
Professor Elisabeth Paice

INTRODUCTION

Others authors have painted their vision of the future NHS and it is one in which patient care is expert, safe and consistent. People have easy access to information and treatment when they need it, and choices about where and how to get it. They are respected, share in decisions about their care, and are at the centre of a well-co-ordinated team effort to deal with their problem. To reach that vision has huge implications for the way we train doctors, nurses and other healthcare professionals. When Tony Blair asked people at the end of the nineties what they wanted to see improved in the NHS, 'more and better paid doctors and nurses' was at the top of their list. Six years on, we have more and better paid doctors and nurses. The next challenge is to make sure that the supply is sustainable, and that they are trained to deliver the vision of a new NHS. Medical education in the UK has an international reputation for excellence. International medical graduates apply to train here in numbers far greater than can be accommodated; our own graduates are eagerly sought after by other countries; and a recent international comparison showed the UK to have the lowest rate of patient-reported medical errors. Nonetheless, there is plenty to improve about the way we train doctors, and there are powerful drivers to do things differently.

TRAINING EXPERTS

One of the things that sets doctors apart from other healthcare professionals is the depth and breadth of medical education. Medical schools ensure that their graduates emerge with a broad understanding of the basic and clinical sciences that underpin medical practice and have had the opportunity to study selected elements of the course in more depth. This scientific foundation is crucial to a lifetime of increasing specialisation ahead, leading advances in one area and keeping up as needed in others. Research has shown that doctors who developed a deep learning style while at medical school are more likely, when followed up years later, to be coping with their workload, keeping up to date with their professional reading, and finding their jobs satisfying. Whatever else is needed to support the vision of a future better NHS, educating doctors who demand to understand the rationale behind what they are expected to do, who spend their lives questioning received wisdom and who drive as well as adapt to change, must be right up there – uncomfortable though such people may be to have around.

Scientific knowledge and attitudes are not a sufficient basis for specialisation. The public has a right to expect that any doctor, whatever their specialty, has certain basic clinical skills, and can recognise when someone is acutely ill and take appropriate first steps to deal with the situation. Under the new *Modernising Medical Careers (MMC)* policy initiative from 2005 all new UK medical graduates will have to complete a two year postgraduate foundation programme. This is mainly designed to ensure they are experienced in a range of basic clinical skills, centred on the recognition and management of the acutely ill patient in a variety of clinical settings. The programme is based on a well-defined curriculum, which requires doctors to specifically demonstrate the acquisition of 41 competences relating both to acute clinical care and to a range of professional behaviours. The over-riding theme of the curriculum is its explicit emphasis on patient safety. By the end of the programme, doctors will have been formally assessed in these areas, with respect to their actual performance in the clinical workplace in caring for patients and interacting with professional and healthcare colleagues. This will enable a much improved standard of quality assuring our developing medical workforce by demonstrating that 2 years after qualifying from medical school doctors have achieved standards of skills, attitudes and behaviours that should enable them to progress into specialty training. Finally, the foundation programme also provides the opportunity for new postgraduate doctors to work in a range of clinical specialties, including general practice. This will enable them to consider their future specialty options, and to obtain advice about these. They will be supported and urged to recognise the need for flexibility in committing to a specialty so that their career aspirations are aligned to their aptitudes and ability in the face of the workforce needs of the NHS.

Specialty training that follows will have more structured and updated curricula in order to meet the stringent standards set by the new Postgraduate Medical Education and Training Board (PMETB). As in foundation training, competence-based assessment will also be required throughout specialty training which will be quality assured both in terms of the process and the outcomes. Doctors who complete these formal specialist programmes will nonetheless need to develop the skills and attitudes to support life-long learning so that their approach to their careers retain the flexibility required by the rapidly changing medical environment.

SAFER TRAINING

Postgraduate medical training has always been delivered on the apprenticeship model. The young graduate learns the trade through working under the supervision of a master. Huge efforts in recent years have gone into clarifying exactly what knowledge, attitudes and skills constitute expertise in a given specialty, and into strategies for ensuring that the trainee has acquired them, but the basic underlying model has remained that of apprenticeship, with most of the learning on-the-job, supplemented by two or three weeks of taught courses each year. This is set to change. In light of the events in Bristol the practice of "see one, do one, teach one" is no longer sustainable. There has been a huge shift in public attitudes and expectations around patient safety, shared information and decision-making and quality assured and bench-marked clinical care. That a surgeon's 'learning curve' can be a reasonable excuse for poor outcomes for patients is now unacceptable. And yet skills must be learned and indeed, learned in a more concentrated and shorter time-scale than previously. Moreover, the on-going dependence of the health service on doctors in training to supply a substantial amount of the care of patients – a phenomenon which is not unique to UK training but which is the basis of every good postgraduate clinical training programme in the world – will not change. But technology and improved understandings about how adults learn can help ensure that they are better prepared for dealing with clinical situations they have not yet met and for the enormous stresses of clinical decision making, especially in the acute environment.

Rehearsals and drills to develop the necessary skills, familiarity and confidence to participate successfully in these situations are essential to enhance experiential learning while promoting patient safety. There are now numerous opportunities to practice in simulated settings with actor-patients. There are sophisticated dummies which breath, bleed and react to pain in highly realistic clinical environments which enable doctors to practice how to respond in difficult and unexpected clinical scenarios. The public does not expect a pilot to fly a plane full of passengers for a first solo flight. Simulators now ensure that the training pilot has ample opportunity to "fly solo" in virtually real conditions before being entrusted with the lives of people. The vision for training in medicine must be the same – where it is possible to do so, learning through simulation, as faithful to the real clinical situation as possible, should be used to train our doctors.

DEVELOPING THE SKILLS AND ATTITUDES TO SUPPORT LIFE-LONG LEARNING

On the face of it, it is hard to see why anyone would wish to shorten the duration of training when medical advances mean there is so much more to learn. But these advances alter the very nature of practice. Conditions once requiring surgery can now be managed with drugs. Conditions once dismissed as something to be 'lived with' now have effective treatments. Cardiothoracic surgeons have become a glut on the market now that interventional cardiologists can unblock arteries, but there are a significant excess of doctors in training who have committed to training in the specialty. Specialists in care of the elderly may become redundant if patients choose instead to consult specialists in the systems troubling them. Things are changing so fast that the ten to twelve years it now takes to train a specialist – and that is after leaving medical school, and not counting forays into research for the purpose of embellishing the CV in competitive specialties – is just too long. It currently takes longer to train a surgeon than it does to plan and build a new hospital. We need to make specialist training shorter and more flexible, by bringing selection into specialty training forward, and providing the training in shorter modules, with the option to move on or step off the training ladder at agreed way points defined by the competences required to undertake a given job. The old hierarchical firms made up of house officers, senior houses officers, registrars, senior registrars and consultants are already gone. In future doctors will complete their formal postgraduate training programmes and become accredited as specialists sooner, but this achievement will be just one step in a lifetime of gaining formal recognition for new skills learned. The UK needs to develop a serious and sustainable "e-education" strategy for its workforce that will enable professional staff to learn new knowledge efficiently, keep up-to-date with the ever expanding clinical knowledge base, assess their knowledge and practice clinical decision making using validated case studies. Employers will need to invest in their doctors and nurses to keep them up to date. Continuous professional development will mean more than attending the grand round, taking a journal and going to the specialty annual general meeting. Instead, sabbaticals, training modules requiring planned time-out from routine work, international exchanges and other innovative means to ensure lifelong learning and development will be critical to sustained excellence in health care.

SLEEP, SHIFTS AND THE HOSPITAL AT NIGHT

Healthcare is a twenty-four hour business, and it is likely that in the future the public will expect easier access to it more of the time. But the move to a twenty-four hour society has not produced twenty-four hour people. Night working is intrinsically stressful, error-prone and socially undesirable, and no vision of a future NHS as a model employer can ignore the damaging effects of night work on its staff. The European Working Time Directive has proved a powerful driver for change, and weekly average working hours have dropped from 72 to 56 in the last few years. By 2009 doctors in training will work a maximum of 48 hours/week. Shift-work has replaced residence on call at night in most specialties. These changes have not been universally welcomed by doctors in training or their supervisors. In some cases, shortening the hours has simply resulted in excessive intensity of work, with doctors working in series rather than in parallel. Many trainees have found an increasing proportion of their working week is now spent on night or weekend duty, separated from their consultant supervisor, and prevented from attending the clinics, operating lists, seminars, and other training opportunities available by day, even if their night has been undisturbed. Others have been subjected to ill-planned shift patterns that result in chronic sleep deprivation.

Night work is all too often a lonely business, carried out by junior doctors without enough supervision.

The *Hospital at Night* initiative offers a vision of how a different approach may offer solutions for staff, while making patient care safer. Work study research in several hospitals has shown that much that is done at night is work that could have been carried out during the evening or safely left until morning. Life-or limb-threatening conditions do arise and need dealing with promptly, but they represent only a small proportion of the activity at night in most hospitals. The central concept of the *Hospital at Night* is of a multi-professional night team, with the combined skills to deal with the common situations needing attention during the night. Such a team needs a leader whose responsibility it is to direct the activities of team members, and seek more specialised help when necessary. Specialists whose skills might be urgently required from time to time, but where a delay of up to an hour would be acceptable, would be on-call from home. To be successful, the scheme requires increased staffing and specialist input in the evening, so that patients are seen and work completed before the night team comes on duty. It needs consultant-led handovers morning and night, carefully thought-out protocols for dealing with the common ward-based emergencies, clear routes for accessing help, and excellent day-time management ensuring that each night the team has the full set of skills required to do its job. A scheme of this sort will improve training by stretching the length of the normal, consultant-supervised working day, and minimise the number of trainees on night shift. It will provide the basis for important learning about team- work and leadership. And most of all, it will improve patient care by reducing the interventions carried out during error-prone hours by over-tired junior doctors. The evaluation of the first four hospitals to pilot this approach suggest that patient safety improved.

AND SO TO THE FUTURE...

The NHS has never been better placed to develop a medical workforce that will be fit for delivery of patient care which is safe, accessible and effective; a workforce that is valued and developed at work, and whose life outside work is also respected; a workforce with the physical and emotional resilience to respond to disaster when it strikes, and the energy to drive change in a constant search for improvement. The policy developed through Modernising Medical Careers recognises that medical education and training are central to creating a medical workforce in which individual practitioners are committed to patient-centred and effective care delivered through quality assured and safe practice. Our vision for the future is for well-trained doctors who put patients and their safety and well-being at the centre of care, who can exhibit the professional skills which enable them to work effectively in teams, across a range of clinical settings and with a flexibility and adaptability that scientific, technological and demographic changes will require.

CHAPTER 24

PROPOSALS TO IMPROVE CLINICAL ACADEMIC TRAINING

Professor David E Neal and
Professor Mark Walport

INTRODUCTION

It is clear, and well-accepted, that the curricula for the training of all doctors should include modules which lead to basic competencies in research awareness and teaching skills. This chapter aims to address the career requirements of doctors who pursue a full time academic career as researchers and educators by considering the following issues:

1. Despite the enormous potential within the NHS research, academic medicine as a career has been under threat.
2. Increasing the strength of academic medicine to improve expertise in clinical research and education is of great benefit to the NHS and the wider academic and business community in the UK.
3. Overall, the prospects for academic medicine are improving, and depend upon working with the Colleges, Faculties and Specialties to ensure that new academic programmes are coherent with the changes in training.

CURRENT POSITION

Evolution in medicine depends upon new discoveries about the nature of disease and its prevention, new means of clinical investigation and the development of new treatments. The spirit of enquiry and research that generates these new discoveries is an essential part of the culture of a healthy National Health Service (NHS) and is for the benefit of all patients and the future of health care.

Recent years have seen major cultural changes within the NHS, with clinicians finding themselves under greater pressure to accomplish set targets and figures, which has tended to be at the expense of education, training and research goals. But clinical academics who undertake these activities form a crucial part of the workforce that will shape the future of the NHS. Warning bells have been ringing for some time over the perilous state of academic medicine in the UK. The deterrents for a clinical academic career have been well documented over the years but can largely be summarised as:

i.   A lack of a clear entry route and career structure;
ii. A lack of flexibility to create balance between clinical and academic training;
iii. A lack of options for geographical mobility;
iv. A shortage of properly structured and supported posts upon completion of training.

Several reports have highlighted difficulties facing potential clinical academics, as they attempt to negotiate the hurdles of dual training in clinical and academic skills. Various efforts have been made to resolve these difficulties, but these have had limited success, demonstrated by large reductions in the numbers of academic staff. For example, between 2000 and 2003 in many medical disciplines; particularly in the surgical specialties, pathology, radiology, public health and in psychiatry there was a significant reduction: a 12.5% overall reduction and a 30% reduction in the numbers of Clinical Lecturers, who provide the seed-corn for the future. Yet there has been no shortage of activity amongst the academic medical community to try to develop solutions to the problems of training clinical academic staff[1-4], however, there are serious workforce issues[5-7].

Reports from the Academy of Medical Sciences[1-4] and the Biosciences Innovation and Growth Team[8] have highlighted the importance of clinical academic medicine to the UK economy, and the numerous issues confronting clinical research in the UK. The reasons for the decline in UK Academic Medicine are complex, but include the point that for an academic in a craft specialty a critical amount of practical work is required each week to maintain clinical skills at a high level. Also, many of the recent NHS targets have disproportionately affected surgeons, anaesthetists, pathologists and radiologists because they have focused on cancer diagnosis and management, and in reduction of long waiting times for practical procedures.

In March 2004, the Chancellor of the Exchequer and the Secretary of State for Health announced an increase to NHS Research and Development funding (£100 million per annum by 2008) and the promotion of a partnership approach to strengthen clinical research through the creation of the UK Clinical Research Collaboration (UKCRC). This coincided with a major review of medical careers started by the Chief Medical Officer in 2002 with the publication of "Unfinished Business"[9] and continued by Modernising Medical Careers (MMC)[10–11].

PROPOSALS FOR CLINICAL ACADEMIC TRAINING

A recent report from UKCRC has identified the following key points as being crucial to the revitalisation of UK Academic Medicine.

MEDICAL SCHOOLS

Careers in academic medicine should be promoted at medical schools and students should be counselled in how to pursue their aims.

FOUNDATION PROGRAMMES

The establishment of Foundation Programmes provides the opening to set up an integrated academic programme.

SPECIALIST TRAINING

Specialist academic training should provide the opportunity to set up dedicated academic training programmes in strong host environments, in partnerships between Universities and local NHS Trusts and Deaneries – this was the core proposal of this report. Additional recommendations were made for academic GPs, many of whom enter academia once they have completed their clinical training.

WHAT DO THESE PROPOSALS MEAN?

The proposals mean that, for the first time, a well defined pathway for the clinical academic medicine could develop. The new Foundation Programmes are yet to bed down but several deaneries have established some pilot schemes for academic foundation programmes that include attachments to high quality academic units. All of this will provide a taster for the would-be academic. These proposals mean that there should eventually be about 750 new Academic Clinical Fellows, 250 new Clinical Lectureships and 100 new Senior Lectureships funded largely by the Department of Health. However, this remains a critical unknown whilst the transition is taking place.

THE ROLE OF THE COLLEGES, THE FACULTIES AND SPECIALIST SOCIETIES

The Specialist Advisory Committees (SACs) have traditionally held the view that the clinical academic should do precisely the same curriculum as the regular NHS trainee. Hence, the academic will take longer to train. Given the changes in the NHS whereby there is much greater team working and where consultants carry out rather specialised activities this may change. One possibility is that the SACs could look at the possibility of producing curricula that contain core, generic components that every trainee should know, and additional components. The danger for British Medicine in our view is that bright young doctors are "tested to death" throughout their training and have no space for creativity, original thought and research.

CONCLUSIONS

If there continues to be real commitment to improve careers in Clinical Academic Medicine from most of the organisations concerned with training, then prospects are good and the declining number of academics could be reversed.

REFERENCES

1. *Clinical Academic Medicine in Jeopardy: recommendations for change*. The Academy of Medical Sciences. (June 2002) http://www.acmedsci.ac.uk/images/publication/pclinaca.pdf.

2. The tenure-track clinician scientist: A new career pathway to promote recruitment into clinical academic medicine (The Savill Report). The Academy of Medical Sciences. (March 2000): http://www.acmedsci.ac.uk/p99puid29.html.

3. *Implementing the Clinician Scientist Scheme*. The Academy of Medical Sciences. (April 2002). http://www.acmedsci.ac.uk/images/publication/nimpleme.pdf.

4. Strengthening Clinical Research – report of an Academy working group. The Academy of Medical Sciences. (October 2003) http://www.acmedsci.ac.uk/images/publication/pscr.pdf.

5. Clinical Academic Medicine: The Way Forward. A report from the Forum on Academic Medicine. (November 2004) http://www.rcplondon.ac.uk/pubs/brochures/pub_print_clinacmed.htm.

6. StLaR HR plan project: Phase I consultation report. The Strategic Learning and Research Advisory Group. (January 2004) http://www.stlarhr.org.uk/phase-i-project-report.

7. Developing and sustaining a world class workforce of educators and researchers in health and social care: StLaR HR Plan Project Phase II Strategic Report. The Strategic Learning and Research Advisory Group. (August 2004) http://www.stlarhr.org.uk/phase-2-strategic-report.

8. Bioscience 2015: Improving national health, increasing national wealth. Department of Trade & Industry. (November 2003) http://www.bioindustry.org/bigtreport/.

9. Unfinished business: proposals for reform of the senior house officer grade – a paper for consultation. Department of Health, London. (August 2002) http://www.dh.gov.uk/assetRoot/04/07/18/35/04071835.pdf.

10. *The next steps: The future shape of Foundation, Specialist and General Practice Training Programmes*. The four UK Health Departments. (April 2004) http://www.dh.gov.uk/assetRoot/04/07/95/32/04079532.pdf.

11. *MMC Career Framework* http://www.mmc.nhs.uk/pages/specialities/specialityframework.

CHAPTER 25

THE FUTURE FOR HEALTH CARE MANAGEMENT: AN ANALYSIS AND SOME PROPOSALS

Professor Ewan Ferlie

INTRODUCTION AND BACKGROUND

The NHS is a vast, complex, knowledge based organisation with a high political and media profile, requiring first class management. This chapter discusses how the management function in the NHS and the wider health care sector could develop over the next five to ten years. It takes a clear managerial perspective arguing that good management will translate into better health care services and then better health care outcomes: our slogan should be 'better management; better health'.

In order to focus a vast brief, we argue that a fundamental managerial task is to contribute to 'better health care' through service improvement and redesign, the management of service change and quality assurance. This is a broader definition than a narrow focus on financial control, although this is also important. The chapter will take mini examples from the important area of cancer services to make the analysis more vivid. 'Better health care' means not only ensuring better final clinical outcomes (e.g. increase in the number of people who survive a diagnosis of cancer for more than five years), but also better intermediate service processes (e.g. lower waiting times; an enhanced organisational ability to improve cancer services delivery) and cultural change towards a more user focussed orientation (e.g. taking cancer patient's as well as provider's definitions of quality seriously). There is major potential for health gain in cancer services by the transfer of evidence based 'best' practices from leading edge sites across the NHS (if only we knew how to do it – the National

Service Framework is a start but much depends on local implementation), as well as the invention of new clinical drugs and treatments.

At its best, senior clinical and general management across the NHS is first class (contrary to popular perceptions), although the excellence is patchy and there are more weaknesses at the middle management level. Unfortunately, the conventional political and media debate – admittedly fed by public opinion – is misleading: headlines concentrate on 'too many bureaucrats' rather than the need for effective organisational and management development. We must of course ensure value for money in spending on management, but at the same time such a demanding organisation as the NHS needs high calibre managers. Each opposition party pledges to reduce 'waste' on NHS management; only to expand management when in office as the most reliable conduit for implementing ministerial policies against a backcloth of clinical scepticism and organisational inertia. The Department of Health argues[1] that managers account for less than 3 per cent of total NHS staff and that management costs have been falling and not rising: in 2003/4 less than 4 pence in every NHS pound was spent of managers, compared to 5 per cent in 1998/9. Any move to insurance rather than taxation based systems of health care could well entail higher management costs than at present.

However, there are some major management problems to address. Unlike many contemporary organisations, the NHS has continued to grow rather than 'downsize,' following the recommendation of the Wanless Report[2] to remedy decades of under investment in health care. Wanless called for substantially more NHS resources, but also reform to ensure that extra resources delivered productivity and quality gains. There is currently a dispute about the extent to which these policy goals have been achieved, although much depends on how health care productivity is measured. Has the new money been matched by reform? Controversial and stretching reforms to work practices will not occur by themselves and have to be actively managed: for example, the current two week wait target for referral from GP to consultant in urgent cancer cases marks a huge decrease in waiting times from the 140 days for urgent referrals achieved in 2000.[3]

There are managerial problems associated with such vast scope and scale. The nature of the NHS as a national and vertically integrated organisation makes achieving change across the whole system difficult. There are political concerns about increased decentralisation and greater local variation in health services ('postcode lottery' provision), but in managerial terms greater decentralisation to well defined sub units would be likely to speed up service improvements, at least in the 'better' sites. The introduction of Foundation Hospitals is to be supported on this argument.

Public expenditure figures[4] show NHS expenditure increasing from a £56B outturn in 2001/2 to a planned £84B in 2007/8. With new money, the traditional preoccupation of NHS management on financial control helpfully broadened to a wider agenda of service improvement and quality assurance. This post Wanless financial up-lift has now ended, as some NHS Trusts and PCTs (and whole health economies, such as Surrey and Sussex) are reporting deficits. Financial control has re-emerged as a central policy and management objective and the next five years is likely to be a difficult period managerially.

PART A: KEY ROLES AND RELATIONSHIPS IN HEALTH CARE MANAGEMENT

We now briefly consider the some key roles and relationships in health care management.

NHS GENERAL MANAGEMENT

Between 1948 and 1985, the NHS employed lay 'administrators' in a low key facilitative and coordinating role. Much decision making power in practice lay with the clinicians who formed a second and parallel power block. After the important 1983 Griffiths Report,[5] general management was introduced to take a more assertive role and provide a clear leadership focus. Griffith's other long term recommendations included getting more doctors into management and increasing market research and a greater user orientation.

Griffith's original plan for importing more private sector managers was not successful: they may have been deterred by a combination of tight political control, dominant clinicians and strong public sector unions. There was however a generational shift in NHS managers with many younger managers appointed which led to an increase in managerial energy levels in the late 1980s and 1990s. So there was an expansion of the management role, particularly at the strategic level with some powerful CEOs emerging in NHS Trusts. Top NHS management salaries increased substantially, but along with risk and turnover levels. Whereas in the 1970s the danger was one that NHS Administrators stayed too long in post, with consequent stultification; the danger now is one of excessive top management turnover so that stable leadership is absent. General management survived the change of political control in 1997, despite the previous opposition of the Labour Party. The system is currently over dependent on a small number of experienced and senior individuals who manage to 'keep things together' despite all the pressures and tensions, but now represent a limited and ageing talent tool.

A PROFESSIONALISED ORGANISATION AND GETTING DOCTORS INTO MANAGEMENT

Management in the NHS is too important to be left solely to general managers. The NHS is formally 'managed' by general managers, but the 'real work' undertaken by health care professionals. The NHS is distinctive in the large number of different professional groups it employs so that the changing relationship between different professional groups (e.g. the division of labour between junior doctors and senior nurses) is important. Often this is under the control of professional 'jurisdictions' (such as the Royal Colleges) which general managers can influence only indirectly. The Human Resource reforms associated with the 'Agenda for Change' programme have tackled some issues associated with parallel professional jurisdictions and this simplifying work needs to continue.

So the NHS is a highly professionalized organization. Managing professionals poses special challenges and calls for a sophisticated and subtle style of management. The development of a 'linking' cadre of effective clinical leaders is critical in bridging the gap between managerial and clinical worlds. The best health care organisations are those where managers and clinicians form partnerships and work together, although in practice wide local variation is evident. At the very least, health care managers need to be aware of the urgent need for foster the development of a cadre of effective clinical managerial hybrids.

Griffiths shrewdly argued that health care management would be better if clinicians were actively engaged. In the late 1980s, there were experiments in acute sector hospitals (for example Guy's) encouraging clinicians to undertake part time managerial roles. They were made responsible for running substantial blocks of services within so called clinical directorates (e.g. a Oncology Directorate), usually supported by a senior nurse and finance manager and normally working on a part time basis. By retaining some clinical work, they hoped to maintain peer group credibility with other clinicians. A dilemma for clinical directors is how close they can get to general management without losing credibility with their professional peers: they are at risk of being perceived as 'going over to the enemy'. On the other hand, they need to provide active leadership, taking unpopular decisions and dealing with 'difficult colleagues', where there may be some long term nettles which have been left ungrasped.

In the 1990s, the clinical directorate model rolled out across the acute sector, and clinical managerial 'hybrid' roles were later developed in primary care (such as the GPs who chair Primary Care Trusts). In the early 1990s, the Department of Health funded personal and management development programmes to support newly appointed Clinical Directors (and there is constant turnover of role holders), but these programmes are now less visible. So support for newly appointed Clinical Directors may be weaker than ten years ago.

QUALITY ASSURANCE SYSTEMS AND USER VOICE

Griffiths (highlighted the need for market research in the NHS.[5] To retain the confidence of affluent and informed users, the NHS must offer a high quality service as well one which simply manages waiting lists better. But who decides what a quality service is? The NHS has undergone 'provider capture' so that too much decision making is in the hands of health professionals rather than users and their carers. Providers' definition of quality may be very different from those of users: the former focus on clinical outcomes; while the latter also include the experience of care (e.g. access; continuity of care; organisational climate and the quality of interpersonal interaction).

There is a need for policy instruments which increase user 'voice'. The use of choice and of the market is popular with policy makers at present, but this is based on a narrow elective surgery model which fits complex and enduring conditions (elderly care; mental health; cancer; paediatrics; primary care) less well. The market is more viable in metropolitan than rural areas.

A non market alternative is to make greater use of market research such as the national patient's survey, patient focus groups, patient involvement fora and also to link these mechanisms more firmly to service redesign. We need to devise more 'downwards' facing accountability mechanisms which strengthen patient and carer 'voice' in collective service planning and redesign.

NHS BOARDS, NON EXECUTIVES, CORPORATE AND CLINICAL GOVERNANCE

Local NHS organisations are accountable to NHS Boards, whose members are appointed rather than locally elected. These Boards play an important role in ensuring effective corporate governance and accountability. An important aspect of the 1990 NHS reforms was the replacement of the old large and unwieldy Health Authorities with smaller and more focussed Boards, with equal numbers of Executives and Non Executives. Critics focussed on the removal or erosion of representatives from medical staff, local councillors or trade unions. However the better functioning post 1990 Boards managed to perform at a strategic level, going beyond their previous role as 'rubber stamps'. Non Executives with experience of running large organisations were able to challenge Executive Directors in Board meetings,[6] which can be seen as an important form of accountability. The question of membership mix can be addressed by appointing strong community based directors. Downwards facing accountability mechanisms (as in the Foundation Trusts) are also needed to balance current strong top down forms of accountability.

More recent reforms to make the appointment process of NHS non executives more transparent are welcome. The question is: who gets appointed to these important posts, why and how? There is a debate between those who argue that non executives should be drawn from the majority political party to ensure broad political oversight by the elected government and the more managerially minded (such as the author) who stress the need for NHS non executives to have relevant expertise and experience in running large organisations if they are to make any impact in the Boardroom.

The Board needs to have the collective capacity to keep financial control but also agree and monitor the implementation of strategies for service improvement and change; develop quality assurance systems and agree and monitor a local clinical governance framework.

There is a danger with the proliferation of private public sector partnerships (e.g. PFI) that accountability becomes more opaque. NHS Boards are likely to be seen as the 'default mode' of accountability by local publics. Board members need to monitor these new public/private forms carefully to ensure that the public interest is protected.

PART B: SOME PROPOSALS FOR THE FUTURE

Here is a personal agenda flowing from the above analysis to add to the capability of health care management in the medium to long term.

(I) STABILISING THE SYSTEM: LESS HASTE; MORE SPEED.

A major weakness of NHS management is the succession of mini crises which provoke poorly thought out 'knee jerk responses': the urgent drives out the important. Crisis management flows from the politicisation of the service, the centralisation of key institutions and a sensationalist media. Crisis management and short term initiative-itis have been institutionalised as a steady state, with later rounds of 'reforming' sometimes merely reversing previous reforms (e.g. the role of the private sector).

Short termism has been made worse by the growth of targets and performance management systems. Some of the key targets are valued by patients and can lead to service improvements (e.g. the two week target for referral from GP to consultant in urgent cancer diagnoses). But there has been target proliferation and an overconcentration by the service on appearing to meet targets on time. The superficial appearance of compliance is more important than substantive progress. There is a premium on speedy top down interventions which promise to remedy failing organisations, for example, the prospectus of the new NHS Institute of Improvement and Innovation[7] promises 'high impact solutions for the NHS in unbeatable cycle times'.

This short term perspective is surely counter productive, producing little lasting value. What is needed instead is a long term strategy to build up organisational capacity in *local* health care systems. This underlying capacity[8] shapes the quality of the relationships between manages and clinicians and determines organisational core competences such as the ability to learn, change, cooperate and also compete. Policy and managerial attention needs to switch from the short term to the long term; from the national to the local; from the prescribed to the customised; and from highly visible to more sustainable forms of service change.

A second key weakness is the frequency of politically directed structural reorganisations. Currently the NHS introducing Foundation Hospitals and reorganising Strategic Health Authorities and Primary Care Trusts concurrently. On average, there appears to be a major structural reorganisation every three years. Structural 'churning' poses a major danger to managerial capability: managers apply for their own jobs and teams are broken up, endangering their ability to progress strategic change.[8] Structural reform should be a policy of last rather than first resort, recalling the old adage: 'don't just do something; sit there.'

One suggestion is that Parliament could pass a self limiting ordinance restricting the maximum number of NHS reorganisations to one in each Parliament (four to five years).

(II) GETTING DOCTORS INTO MANAGEMENT AND DEVELOPING MEDICAL LEADERSHIP

Griffith's recommendation to get doctors into NHS management remains sound. We now have considerable experience in the development of clinical managerial hybrid roles locally. It appears that support programmes for new role holders have been eroded and may not be adequate. Against this, the development of the British Association of Medical Managers (BAMM) (www.bamm.co.uk) is an encouraging long term development and may encourage the creation of a new professional 'identity' for this group. The NHS III will now take this work forward.

We know that 'hybrids' have to be selected with care and that they have major development and support needs. They need to have credibility with their clinical colleagues and also leadership capacity (broader than just managerial competence). The experience of doctors who move into this group is variable and we need to understand more about why some flourish and others struggle. We also know that NHS general managers need to work hard to foster good relations with this critical linking group.

We need the NHS III to produce or commission a broad overview of the experience in the development of clinical managers and leaders and the development of a longer term and properly resourced strategy on the basis of this overview.

(III) OD/MD STRATEGIES AND PRIVATE SECTOR PROVIDERS

This chapter so far has been NHS centric, yet we are now moving to a mixed economy of health care. On what basis will these providers be offered NHS contracts? Clearly the cost and quality of the health care services offered will be prime considerations, but private provider's Organisational Development and Management Development (OD/MD) strategies are important. Intriguingly, there may be different approaches within these private providers from which we can identify promising new managerial practices not so far apparent in the NHS. Can they innovate and change more rapidly than the vast NHS (Ferlie et al, 2006)? How do these private providers spot and develop potential leaders? How do they get doctors and managers to work together? How do they diffuse best practice out from their leading edge sites and intervene in the tail of poorly performing sites?

We need to use the opportunity of greater pluralism on the provider side to maximise the learning about promising new managerial practices in health care organisations. This may include the franchising out of the management function to increase managerial contestability, as already seen in the introduction of 'turnaround teams' in failing organisations.

(IV) DEVELOPING AND 'ENACTING' EVIDENCE FOR HEALTH CARE MANAGEMENT

Finally, we should continue to work on developing a better evidence base for health care management. This is an old theme from the 1990s but it remains important. What do we know about 'what works' in health care management? Better evidence and also theory could be an effective lever to stop the continuing cycle of faddish restructuring and reduce the adoption of non evidence based managerial innovations in the health care sector. We have a growing number of good quality studies in health care management which are potentially available to policy makers and managers.

The current NHS Service Delivery and Organisation R and D programme will help develop and consolidate this evidence base. It is encouraging that the new Department of Health research strategy[9] contains a commitment to expand the SDO programme. There have been important SDO publications (e.g. Iles and Sutherland, 2001's overview of the change management literature in health care[10]). While there has been solid progress, some of the evidence base remains equivocal and contested and there are secure findings available only in some areas. We should identify those areas where there is now a solid evidence base (e.g. service redesign) and produce short and accessible overviews which can inform policy and practice.

We need a greater focus on Development as well as Research to get health care management research into practice. Reaching health care managers is not easy as there is not a well developed research culture and often they are often too busy to read primary research. There needs to be more work on 'translational strategies' to present health management research in an accessible and useful format. Researchers need to engage managers more with the research process, perhaps by using non traditional methods which increase feedback available to managers so that they can benefit directly and quickly. Again, the underlying history and role configuration locally[8] affects a health care organisation's ability to find and enact evidence in practice.

CONCLUSION

This chapter argues that better management can lead to better health services and better health outcomes. It sees a core management task as lying in the service and quality improvement agenda. This involves active leadership from both general and clinical managers to inspire and sustain collective service improvement activity rather than 'form filling' management for proliferating audit systems. We need more local and long term capacity building and fewer top down quick fixes. Health care management should be based on a secure evidence base as well as clinical practice.

However, this agenda will be difficult to sustain as the old financial control agenda reasserts itself. This could polarise relations between the managerial and clinical blocks, eroding joint working and leading to destructive short term measures to rein in overspends. The wise NHS manager will protect service improvement locally by avoiding crisis based financial management and by developing deep alliances with clinical managerial hybrids which can sustain the organisation in difficult times. More positively, the increase in non NHS health care providers represents an opportunity to experiment with different and contrasting managerial styles and approaches.

REFERENCES

1. Department of Health (2006a) *'NHS Management Numbers and Costs'* London: Department of Health, http://www.dh.gov.uk.
2. Wanless, D. (2002) *'Securing our Future Health – Taking a Long Term View'* London: HM Treasury.
3. Spurgeon, P., Barwell, F. and Kerr, D. (2000) 'Waiting times for cancer patients in England after General Practitioner's referrals: Retrospective National Survey', *British Medical Journal*, 320: 838–839.
4. HM Treasury (2005) *'Public Expenditure: Statistical Analysis'* London: HM Treasury.
5. Griffiths, R. (1983) *'NHS Management Enquiry'* London: Department of Health.
6. Ferlie, E., Ashburner, L., FitzGerald, L. and Pettigrew, A. (1996) *'The New Public Management in Action'* Oxford: Oxford University Press. Ferlie, E., Freeman, G., McDonnell, J., Petsoulas, C. and Rundle-Smith, S. 'Introducing Choice in the Public Services: Some Supply Side Issues', (2006) *Public Money and Management*, 26(1): 63–72.
7. NHS Institute for Improvement and Innovation (NHS III) (2005) *'Prospectus'* University of Warwick: NHS III.
8. Dopson, S. and FitzGerald, L. (eds) (2005) *'Knowledge to Action?* Oxford: Oxford University Press; Pettigrew, A., Ferlie, E and McKee, L. (1992) *'Shaping Strategic Change'*, London: Sage.
9. Department of Health (2006b) *'Best Research for Best Health'* London: Department of Health, http://www.dh.gov.uk.
10. Iles, V. and Sutherland, K. (2001) *'Organisational Change in Health Care: A Review'* London: London School of Hygiene and Tropical Medicine.

CHAPTER 26
NHS STAFF HEALTH

Dr Chess Denman, Dr Colin Payton
and Mr Daniel Barnett, barrister

INTRODUCTION

Much has been achieved by NHS occupational health services to
reduce the risks for health care workers. For example, there is
comprehensive vaccination against Hepatitis B. HIV post exposure
prophylaxis is widely available, although the risks of acquiring HIV
infection from needle stick injuries are very low (overall estimated to
be around 0.3%). It is important that health care workers who sustain
needle stick injuries report them as quickly as possible. Prevention is
obviously better than cure, and there is now an increasing emphasis
on prevention through bodies such as the Safer Needles Network
(http://www.needlestickforum.net).

Changes in policies with regard manual handling mean safer working
practices. Treatment services for staff who develop back pain or other
musculo-skeletal injuries vary, but some trusts have informal and
occasionally formal 'fast-track' treatment facilities.

Unfortunately, even with the advances in occupational health
services, problems with alcohol and other substance abuse continue
to rise – although it is unclear whether this is an increase in actual
numbers or simply the consequences of educational programmes
encouraging staff to recognise and deal with such problems. NHS
employers should provide support for staff who are prepared to
co-operate with occupational health and seek appropriate treatment,
and services such as random 'without warning' testing for both
alcohol and other substances are developing, permitting staff to return
to work when abstinent and to have their compliance monitored. In
house counselling services will offer expertise in the management of

alcohol and substance misuse problems. Sadly, despite this supportive and enlightened approach, the prognosis for rehabilitation and a sustained return to work remains poor.

According to the NHS Staff Survey for 2003–2004, 36% of staff reported work-related stress. Figures from the UK Workplace Bullying Advice Line suggest that around 2/3rds of stress absence cases involve public sector employees. Other surveys, using a standard psychiatric measure, found that 26.8% of health service workers reported significant levels of minor psychiatric disorders (as compared with 17.8% for the general population). This is not evenly distributed across disciplines, and some studies have shown doctors reporting higher levels of stress but greater job satisfaction than nursing auxiliaries. Doctors take the fewest days off sick but have high rates of suicide.

Psychological ill health remains therefore potentially the most serious problem for the health and well-being of NHS staff. This may be related to difficulties in achieving a good work-life balance, since although work pressure is rated as neutral or only mildly stressful by most staff, many (43%) are working between one and five extra unpaid hours over their contracted time.

Another cause of psychological ill health are experiences of violence, harassment and bullying. 15% of staff reported an experience of physical violence at the hands of patients or their relatives in the last year and 43% had experienced bullying or harassment, 27% from relatives and 16% from other NHS staff (Commission for Healthcare Audit and Inspection 2005).

An experience of workplace violence or bullying is associated with a range of ill effects including potential for developing post traumatic stress disorder (PTSD) and high reported levels of fatigue. Substantial rates of absenteeism among staff other than doctors (as much as 16 days a year for ward staff as compared with a national average of 11) are probably partly a consequence of staff psychological ill health. Lost working days represent a substantial cost to the NHS which could be spent on patient care. Staff must be replaced by agency workers who will not be immediately familiar with either the ward or the tasks in hand on the ward and therefore generate the potential for confusion and errors. Furthermore stressed and mentally debilitated staff are doubtless more likely to make errors of judgement or deliver poor standards of care.

For these reasons the mental health of health staff not only affects their own wellbeing but is also very likely to impact on the standard of care received by patients. Recognising this, the government has launched campaigns to help staff manage stress but it remains to be seen whether these will be effective (see www.nhsemployers.org "The stress campaign").

Many stressed employees enter into a cycle of decline. Their perception that they are not taken seriously exacerbates their underlying difficulties. Eventually they qualify as long-term sick, and attempts to dismiss (or failures to make reasonable adjustments to assist them in returning to work) can result in claims for unfair dismissal and for disability discrimination. These usually result in negotiated settlements, costing the Trust tens of thousands of pounds in settlement monies and often as much in management time, in-house and external legal fees.

What does not emerge from the statistical and survey data are the human stories which surround psychological ill health in hospital staff and the complex interaction of interpersonal and bureaucratic processes which mark each staff member's trajectory through the current systems in place in the NHS for caring for staff and protecting patients.

With this in mind, the following provides some positive suggestions for change in relation to improving the psychological care of the nation's carers. They fall into two categories. First, improved access to psychological care and second, more employee focused employment procedures.

ACCESS TO PSYCHIATRIC CARE

WALK-IN CENTRES

The first issue which needs to be improved is health worker's access to psychiatric or psychological care. This may be in the form of on-site or nearby walk-in centres which are specifically dedicated to NHS employees. The emphasis should be on prevention and avoidance of long term problems and this can best be achieved by early assessment.

REMOVING THE STIGMA OF PSYCHIATRIC TREATMENT

As well as improving access, workers also need to be educated about the benefits of psychiatric assessment and treatment. In particular, campaigns should emphasise the importance of monitoring one's mental health and attempt to remove the stigma that seeking psychiatric care sometimes carries with it.

CONFIDENTIALITY

One of the biggest organisation issues in increasing the help provided to staff is the maintenance of a strict regime of confidentiality. The system as it currently stands leaves open the possibility that fellow members of staff may accidentally stumble upon a colleague's records. It should not be difficult to eradicate this problem with records being held in a separate database or in a different (or locked) location – the issue becoming an explicit factor to be considered any proposed structure.

EMPLOYEE-FOCUSED EMPLOYMENT PROCEDURES

RISK ASSESSMENTS

The trust should carry out regular risk assessments to identify possible causes of stress and levels of risk to individuals fulfilling particular jobs. If a high risk is identified, something should be done about it. The assessments can be carried out by HR (often simply by asking the employee to complete a form) or by an external auditor (which is recommended as best practice by the HSE)

STRESS MANAGEMENT TRAINING

External consultants can be engaged to help employees recognise, and deal with, symptoms of stress. These consultants can be relatively inexpensive.

STRESS POLICIES

These should be clearly communicated to staff, and should encourage employees to come forward and tell the employer about stress rather than hiding the existence of stress through fear or embarrassment.

Procedures can often be defensive, rigid and legalistic when in fact a more conciliatory approach and attitude needs to be inherent to these procedures. Also informal procedures should be initiated much earlier rather than waiting for the problem to have become entrenched and then only having access to formal proceedings.

GRIEVANCE FORUMS

Feelings of stress are frequently caused by a subjective belief in one's lack of influence or control. Either open or confidential forums where employees are encouraged to raise issues of concern about working practices can help people discharge their frustrations, particularly if it can be seen that action is taken on well-founded complaints.

MONITORING

The HR department should monitor employees who have been off sick – particularly where the employee's GP has certified a stress-related illness – to see whether they are exhibiting symptoms of stress.

ADJUSTMENTS TO WORK

If any employee complains of stress, consider reducing the workload, reallocating work or rotating responsibilities

KEEPING WORKERS IN THE SYSTEM

Grievance procedures can often result in the victim being marginalised. This sometimes leads them to leave the NHS either for private practice or even for a complete career change. More emphasis is needed on valuing the human capital which the NHS possesses and making efforts to keep workers within the system. This means approaching problems with flexibility and understanding and the provision of more help in re-locating if necessary.

COLLEGIATE APPROACH

One of the difficulties in managing teams is ensuring that all points of view are integrated into the decision-making process rather than dissenter's view being dismissed. Dissenting views often offer useful constructive criticism. Further, valuing dissenters and bringing them into the mainstream helps to maintain morale. This avoids the growth of pockets of discontent and again helps to keep valuable workers within the system.

CHANGING THE CULTURE

Just as attitudes to psychiatric treatment needs changing, so too, in relation to the approach towards staff behaviour. Whatever, has been worked on in the past, there is a need for a constantly evolving approach to education in relation to staff behaviour and in particular to staff bullying and harassment. It is not enough to have done one round of training on a particular issue and then to think that it has been solved. Without the setting and enforcing of clear boundaries at a very low and informal level (well before the threshold of complaints procedures), there is always the possibility that new cultures of bullying or harassment in one form or another can take hold, very often without the perpetrators being aware of the harm they are causing.

CONCLUSION

Any chapter designed to explore difficulties in NHS staff risks presenting an over gloomy view of health services. It should not blind us to the fact that frequently NHS structures do manage to deal compassionately and effectively with sick staff. However few staff or patients would argue that there does not remain room for improvement in this area as in many others in the NHS.

An emphasis on improved access to psychiatric care and more employee-focused employment procedures will hopefully help to address some of the more common problems.

CHAPTER 27

FROM SELF-REGULATION TO PROFESSIONALLY-LED REGULATION IN PARTNERSHIP WITH THE PUBLIC

Dr Joan Trowell and Mr Paul Buckley

The professional regulatory bodies in Great Britain, of which the General Medical Council (GMC) founded by the Medical Act in 1858 is the oldest, are established by statute. The GMC's statutory and charitable purposes are "to protect promote and maintain the health and safety of the public by ensuring proper standards in the practice of medicine."

They have the powers required to oversee a register of properly trained practitioners. The statutory functions of the GMC are to:

a. Set the standards of good medical practice which society and the profession expect of doctors throughout their working lives.
b. Assure the quality of undergraduate medical education in the United Kingdom and co-ordinate all stages of medical education. This includes the supervision of undergraduate education and general clinical training. The GMC publishes guidance on undergraduate medical education and also, for all doctors, on their continuing professional development. The qualifying degrees given by the universities allows entry to the register, but only if the knowledge, skills and standards leading to those degrees are those determined by the GMC. It works with the Postgraduate Medical Education and Training Board, the medical Royal Colleges and Faculties, and others to co-ordinate higher and specialist medical training.
c. Administer systems of registration and licensing of doctors to control their entry to, and continuation in, medical practice in the UK.

d. Deal firmly and fairly with doctors whose fitness to practise is questioned.

The fourth of these functions is, inevitably, the most visible because of the intense media focus on particular, sometimes salacious, hearings.

This chapter examines the changing face of professional regulation and considers how it may develop in the future. While the focus is largely on the GMC, the trends identify conclusions which are intended to apply to the regulation of healthcare professionals more broadly.

REGULATION IN THE LATE 20TH CENTURY

During the second half of the twentieth century, following the establishment of the NHS, and the resulting far-reaching changes in the practice of medicine and the medical profession, turbulence gradually grew around professional regulation. These changes were also the result of the growth in scientific knowledge and the consequent development of the scientific and technical possibilities available to medicine, increasing both the good and the harm that could result from the intervention of doctors.

Society was changing with a growth in the voice of the consumer and the public began to demand a change in the behaviour of healthcare professionals with a voice for the public in the governance of the professions and a more pro-active, interventionist approach from the regulatory bodies. The GMC, no doubt sensing the changing mood, introduced some important changes to its governance and its fitness to practise procedures. The governance changes saw the size of Council increase to over a hundred members, mainly as a result of the addition of elected medical members to those medical members appointed by the universities and royal colleges, but significantly the numbers and proportion of appointed lay members also grew until, by the mid 1990s, 25% of Council members were lay. The impact of the lay members was felt both on the Council, the governing and policy making body of the GMC, and also the fitness to practise committees, at that time populated by council members, which were required to decide the sanctions appropriate for the concerns that had been raised about individual doctors.

These fitness to practise procedures had otherwise seen little change in almost a century. The GMC's powers to curb, or remove altogether, a doctor's right to practise were restricted to matters involving misconduct or criminal behaviour. These powers were widened through successive amendments to the Medical Act in 1978 and 1995. As a result, the GMC was now able to deal with problems with both a doctor's health and professional performance and, where necessary, impose restrictions on the doctor's registration although all this still depended on concerns being brought to the attention of the GMC, normally by the public, the doctor's colleagues, the doctor's employer or contracting authority, or the police or the courts.

1995 also saw the replacement of the 'Blue Book' (which attempted to outline those activities which were deemed to be unbefitting in a medical practitioner) with *Good Medical Practice*, which for the first time set out, in simple and accessible language, the principles of good practice expected of every doctor.

THE GMC'S REFORM PROGRAMME

Important though all these changes were, however, they fell short of addressing the increasing public and political concern about the effectiveness of regulation. This reached a peak in the late 1990s following a succession of high-profile hearings at which it was established that patients had been severely harmed by the actions (or the inaction) of dysfunctional doctors. A consistently striking feature was a failure within the relevant local organisation, mainly within the NHS, to detect, or take effective action on, actual or emerging impairment, but it became clear that professional regulation needed a new mandate, new governance with greater accessibility and increased transparency of procedures and decisions. The GMC brought forward a programme of far-reaching reforms of its governance and functions, intended fundamentally to transform medical regulation.

In 1999, the Council set up a review of the governance of medical regulation. The recommendations from the review included a reduction in the size of the Council to 35 and an increase in the proportion of lay members to 40% of the total. These recommended reforms were the result of the view that professional regulation should still be professionally lead but that this must be in a firm partnership with the public; that patients interests are best served by professionals who have ownership of the principles of good practice.

In 1998, the GMC launched its proposals for revalidation, which involved a departure from its traditional role of *management by exception*. With this established form of regulation, a professional remains registered provided they paid the relevant fees, maintained an effective registered address and were not found guilty of serious professional misconduct. The regulatory body acted only if concerns were reported. Revalidation turns this on its head by establishing a new model where an active process seeks positive affirmation that every individual registered doctor is up to date and fit-to-practise.

1998 also saw the GMC become concerned that it required greatly enhanced powers to impose interim sanctions pending the outcome of a full investigation and hearing of the evidence, for use in those situations where to allow the doctor to continue with unfettered registration could undermine the protection of members of the public or was otherwise in the public interest. This may occur, for example, when the GMC fitness to practise procedures are put on hold pending the outcome of police investigation and possible prosecution for a serious criminal offence. The new powers were put in place by the Government in 2000.

And in 2001, the GMC consulted on proposals to reform its fitness to practise procedures, and replace the separate conduct, health and performance procedures with a single, integrated, set of procedures that could consider fitness to practise in the round.

The GMC's recommendations for reform were accepted by the Government and after the passage of the necessary legislation, the Council first met in its new form in 2003. The new fitness to practise procedures were introduced in 2004, and revalidation will be implemented following a review by the Chief Medical Officer for England.

During the time of these changes in the GMC, similar changes have occurred in the regulatory bodies of the other healthcare professions.

THE CHANGING ROLE OF COUNCIL AND ITS MEMBERS

In parallel with this there have been wide reforms in the way the GMC delivers its statutory functions, as Council members no longer participate in the operational work. This is manifest by the appointment of both medical and lay visitors to participate in the planned scheme of quality assurance visits to medical schools and also medical and lay individuals to make decisions at all stages of the fitness to practise procedures. This separation of function between Council members and the casework within the Fitness to Practise procedures has been achieved in parallel with a complete separation of those individuals involved in the investigation and the adjudication stages of the procedures. At the adjudication stage, the panels are composed of a diverse group of panellists, all non-Council members, both medical and lay and either may be appointed to chair the hearing. The Council sets the standards and indicates, through general guidance, the sanctions on registration required to protect the public interest, but Council members have no part at any stage in the decisions required during the fitness to practise procedures.

As a part of the commitment to transparency in the development in these reformed procedures there has been the development of published criteria and thresholds to guide the decision makers and to improve the consistency of decisions between the different individuals involved. This has also allowed for the development of greatly strengthened quality assurance arrangements and improved training of those involved in making the decisions. The overall aim has been to produce simpler procedures, that aim to focus resources where they can do most good, and this has been achieved.

THE FUTURE DEVELOPMENT OF PROFESSIONAL REGULATION

These changes in professional regulation are just one part of profound developments that have taken place, including the NHS initiatives to assure quality and improve patient safety. These include clinical governance, the national quality assurance bodies and initiatives to detect and remedy poor practice before patients are harmed, together with a culture in which all could admit to errors and enable the organisations to learn from these. These are also intended to avoid lengthy and costly suspensions of medical staff.

These NHS initiatives have made all professionals who work within it more aware of their colleagues and this may have had a side effect in increasing both the numbers of doctors reported nationally and to the GMC and the level of evidence submitted in support of these concerns.

All healthcare regulators have become increasingly forward-looking, with an emphasis on managing and mitigating risk. This has lead to increasing emphasis on undertaking research to help to understand impairment, especially at an early stage when interventions may be deemed to have a greater possible effect. The GMC has insisted that within all medical schools there are robust procedures that focus on student fitness to practise issues and a greater emphasis on preventing the initial registration of inappropriate practitioners.

Professional regulation has ceased to be a discrete activity and is now more integrated into the overall framework that delivers healthcare.

Investment in IT programmes enables the integration of information about practitioners and makes it available to both regulator and employer. When concerns are to be investigated within the fitness to practise procedures, information about those concerns is shared with the doctor's employers at an early stage. This allows the regulator to include in its investigation any information about that doctor, both positive and negative, which is available through local clinical governance.

This link is strengthened by the concept of the 'approved environment', which enables the regulator, when satisfied in relation to clinical governance, performance management and appraisal processes, to rely upon the employer's or contracting authorities local procedures. This links professional regulation with workplace regulation, two of the four-layer model of medical regulation that the GMC believes provides a helpful framework.

These are:

Personal regulation: which reflects the way in which individual doctors regulate themselves, based upon their commitment to a common set of ethics.

Team-based regulation: which reflects the increasing importance of team working and requires health professionals to take responsibility for the performance of the team.

Workplace regulation: which reflects the responsibility that the NHS and other healthcare providers have for ensuring that their employees are fit for their roles. Workplace regulation is expressed through clinical governance and performance management systems.

Professional regulation: which is undertaken by the GMC and other statutory health regulators. Professional regulation is expressed through work on standards, education, registration and licensing, including revalidation, and fitness to practise procedures.

To these four national levels should be added *the international level*.

Building on this framework, and using a risk-based approach to regulation, the professional regulator will be able to ensure that its resources are used most effectively. A challenge for regulators is to remain independent, not independent from the rest of the framework, but independent within it.

Regulators must be able to regulate a mobile workforce and this requires better information sharing across national boundaries. This is especially necessary in the European Union (EU) where the political priority attached to freedom of movement has attenuated, or removed, the regulator's ability to control who is entitled to be registered.

In the United Kingdom, the healthcare regulators have combined to form the Alliance of United Kingdom Health Regulators on Europe (AURE) to lobby on regulatory issues at the European level. A notable success has been the inclusion in the Directive on professional qualifications of a requirement on regulators to exchange information about professionals who may be unfit to practise, and the exclusion from the final form of the Directive of a provision that would have entitled professionals to practise in another member state for 16 weeks without being registered in that state.

In the wider international context the GMC has been active in this drive to co-ordinate regulation across international borders, working with organisations such as the International Association of Medical

Regulatory Authorities (IAMRA), of which it was a founding member, and the Conférence Européene Des Ordres de Medicins (CEOM).

FUTURE TRENDS

The current reforms have seen a trend towards greater harmonisation between regulators. In 2003, the Government set up the Council for Health Care Regulatory Excellence (CHRE), which has an overarching role and powers that include the power to refer to the courts specific fitness to practise decisions if, in their view, the decisions are unduly lenient and the referral is necessary for the protection of the public. (There is nowadays less deference shown by courts to regulatory decisions than in the past.)

CHRE has an important co-ordinating role in identifying and promoting best practice among the regulatory bodies. This greater harmonisation of the regulators could be seen by some to mirror attempts to make the healthcare workforce more flexible by developing advanced practitioner roles, enabling other professionals to undertake tasks traditionally carried out only by doctors.

Alongside this, there is a changing profile of the professions, especially medicine, which in the United Kingdom is now qualifying more women students than men, and an increasing number of ethnic minority entrants to the profession, both those with training in a United Kingdom university and those who have been trained outside the United Kingdom. With the increasing number of graduate entrants to medical school, more people are now entering medicine as a second career.

All these trends may have profound implications for the profession and the requirements of the professional regulators in the future, but it is too early to assess fully what these will be.

The direction of inter-professional training might lead to the assumption that inter professional mobility will continue to increase, but the training period for a NHS hospital consultant, even under the new accelerated training programmes, is many years longer than that for most other healthcare roles. Some have argued that facts like these will place severe limits on how far harmonisation, whether of training or of regulation, can go.

CONCLUSION

Professional regulation is now unrecognisable from what it was even ten years ago. Many of the changes were long overdue, but the healthcare regulators, with the support of the Government, have responded decisively.

The recent reforms have lead to increasing similarities between the regulatory bodies but some would advocate yet further change. Given the clear willingness of the regulatory bodies to reform radically, further imposed structural change for its own sake or for the sake of continuing the momentum of change cannot be the answer. The effect of the recent reforms requires adequate evaluation.

The interests of patients are best served by professionals who have ownership of the principles of good practice. Public confidence in professional regulation will require active lay involvement in all the roles required and a clear framework linking the levels of professional regulation. Mere assertions of professionalism have been shown to be insufficient. Doctors must demonstrate to the public that they are fit to practise.

The new model of regulation, which is emerging, retains the strengths of professional ownership, but balanced by full public involvement. This is the true meaning of professionally led regulation in partnership with the public.

CHAPTER 28
MAKING AMENDS IN CLINICAL NEGLIGENCE

Dr Gerard Panting

With the cost of clinical negligence cases on the rise the government commissioned a review of this area of law in 2001. This ultimately led to Professor Donaldson's broad-ranging report in 2003 entitled *Making Amends*. It aimed to look at seeking to help victims in more ways than merely financial compensation that was often viewed as inadequate. In all, it made 19 recommendations for reform but the real meat lay in recommendations 1 and 2.

The first recommendation was that an NHS Redress Scheme should be introduced to provide investigations when things go wrong; remedial treatment, rehabilitation and care where needed; explanations and apologies; and financial compensation in certain circumstances. This scheme was aimed at the so-called smaller claims with a suggested ceiling on financial compensation at £30,000.

Recommendation two was, in effect, for a second redress scheme dealing with claims at the other end of the scale. As *Making Amends* put it *'the NHS Redress Scheme should encompass care and compensation for severely neurologically impaired babies, including those with severe cerebral palsy.'*

The rationale for picking out lower value claims was that in these cases legal costs frequently outweighed the compensation available to patients and often discouraged layers for taking on these cases under conditional fee arrangements.

Claims at the top end of the scale were singled out on the basis that they accounted for approximately 80% of the cost to the NHS and by providing compensation in cash and kind, the overall figure might be reduced. At the same time compensation packages could be made available to a wider range of children born under NHS care and suffering neurological impairment relating to or resulting from the birth. Compensation would include a managed care package (essentially NHS based care) plus a monthly payment for the costs of care which could not be provided through the care package up to a limit of £100,000 per annum and in addition lump sum payments for home adaptations and equipment at intervals through the child's life and an initial payment in compensation for pain, suffering and loss of amenity capped at £50,000.

In effect two schemes were suggested. The first for small claims with an alternative to court-based negligence claims but still reliant upon the claimant being able to demonstrate that their injury was due to a shortfall in care. The second scheme involved a no fault compensation scheme for birth injury resulting in severe neurological impairment.

This has been followed with the NHS Redress Bill currently going through Parliament. Published in October 2005 as enabling legislation, it contained very little detail. The nuts and bolts of the scheme will be set out in secondary legislation (Statutory Instruments) which will themselves be the subject of consultation, probably over the summer 2006 with establishment of the scheme in April 2007 and review of how things are going in 2010.

The published bill in effect reduced the proposals to establishing a redress scheme for claims up to £20,000 arising from acute NHS trusts in England, the intention being to provide a fast track alternative to court proceedings for less severe cases. The no fault compensation scheme for severely neurologically impaired babies was excluded from the bill. In some ways this did not come as a surprise. First, it could prove very costly. Second, confining available benefits to birth injury cases could result in accusations of arbitrary injustice. Third, running such a scheme in parallel with the existing court-based tort system is fraught with practical difficulties. Following on the theme of *Making Amends* the emphasis of the scheme is on apologies, explanations and remedial treatment as well as financial compensation.

Ultimately, the success of the Redress Scheme will depend on how individual trusts manage process at local level and a counter shift away from attributing blame towards preventing harm reducing risks and learning from mistakes.

In practice, the revised Redress Scheme is intended to work in the following way. First, so-called adverse events will be recognised by the trust as and when they occur. Whether or not the patient has noticed anything, the trust will explain what has happened and why, and apologise where appropriate. If the patient has come to harm as a result, the trust will also put the wheels in motion to offer a care package compensating for the harm suffered in cash and kind. If, however, both the trust and patient fail to notice anything is awry and start the ball rolling, the scheme may be initiated as a result of the Healthcare Commission or Ombudsman involvement.

Each incident will then be investigated by the responsible trust and compensation packages compiled under guidance from the National Health Service Litigation Authority (NHSLA) on eligibility and levels of compensation. The NHSLA currently manages the NHS indemnity scheme. Once an offer of redress has been made it remains on the table for a fixed time, likely to be three months but conceivably as short as four weeks or as long as six months, following which withdrawal is automatic.

Patients who decline an offer of redress may sue through the courts as normal but entitlement to Legal Aid for the few who now benefit from this may be affected as the Legal Services Commission can take refusal of the offer into account when deciding whether legal aid should be granted. It is also possible that the courts will take any refusal into account when considering costs.

The scheme envisaged is a major change of style and large organisations, and analogous to large tankers, they take time to turn around. In addition, there is the difficulty of maintaining trust and credibility whilst at the same time admitting fault.

Then you are offered a package in cash and kind. Do you want your remedial care in the hospital that harmed you? Do you believe that a physio unit already hard pressed can treat you as a priority? Does your conscience prick slightly as you think of the patients you are gently nudging back on the waiting list? When it comes to compensation, how do you know how much is enough? The scheme does allow for some legal advice but a question mark hangs over whether the available funds will stretch to definitive advice on how good a deal it is.

The scheme is to be overseen by the National Health Service Litigation Authority but does a second NHS body provide you with the impartiality and assurance the reasonable claimant requires?

From the clinician's standpoint, there are questions too. The key point is the standard of care that is to be applied. Since 1957, the courts have relied on the *Bolam* Test expostulated by Mr Justice McNair:

> *"a doctor is not guilty of negligence if acting in accordance with a practice accepted as proper by a responsible body of medical men skilled in that particular art even though a body of adverse opinion also exists amongst medical men."*

The language may sound clumsy to modern ears and although often criticised by claimants it does address all the key issues. Medical management can only be judged by individuals expert in the field – amateur second guessing leads only to injustice. Second, it applies to the state of the art at the time of the adverse incident not the expected level of expertise when the case is being reviewed. Finally, it recognises that alternative approaches may be valid.

But as medical care becomes increasingly specialised, who in the trust will have the expertise to determine whether the orthopaedic surgeon specialising in small joint replacement has done a good job or not? In many instances the trust will not have the necessary expertise to provide an expert opinion on whether something has gone wrong or not.

The government are admirably optimistic about their plans with answers to all the sceptic's questions. For a start, they say that the Department of Health has canvassed opinion from a wide variety of stakeholders and that in the light of those discussions, their proposals have been refined.

The trust's responsibility for carrying out an investigation is seen as an important component of the Redress Scheme, providing an opportunity to learn from mistakes and creating a local learning culture. Further, there is a genuine expectation in government that, over time, there will be a culture shift with mistakes being identified locally and taking remedial action.

By way of reassurance, checks will be incorporated into the scheme monitoring trusts to ensure consistency in the scheme's application.

The concept of inviting an independent body to investigate all potential claims for redress is rejected on the grounds that this would lead to a major increase in bureaucracy and lengthen the time taken for cases to be resolved. The bill, as government is keen to point out, seeks to speed up the process of providing redress to patients whether or not financial compensation is an integral part of the overall package.

On the question of the NHS Litigation Authority, there is the potential for change as the bill itself does not specify that the special health authority in charge of the kitty and responsible for overseeing the scheme will necessarily be the NHSLA. But having just undertaken a review of all the organisations with statutory functions in relation to the NHS and succeeded in reducing them significantly in number, it is unlikely the government will wish to set up another body when all the signals to date are that they believe the NHSLA can do the job.

Their rationale is that the NHSLA has the resources, expertise, experience and skill mix to deal with the Redress Scheme and already has a relationship with every trust in England through its work on the Clinical Negligence Scheme for Trusts so the position of the NHSLA, as the supervisory body, is vehemently defended.

So what are the implications of the new Redress Scheme? Would it, for example, be easier for patients to get compensation? At present, this is an impossible question to answer. However, the scheme is designed to provide accessible redress so it is likely to result in more patients with low value claims coming forward to use the scheme. Only time will tell whether the increased compensation costs are offset in whole, or in part by the saving in legal fees.

As to whether it will encourage a culture of complaining, the government may point out that in fact the scheme merely encourages the righting of wrongs and since it will continue to apply the same test (the *Bolam* Test) applied by the courts in clinical negligence cases, it should not open the floodgates to claims that would not otherwise have succeeded.

REFERENCES

Making Amends. A consultation paper setting out proposals for reforming the approach to clinical negligence in the NHS. London: Department of Health. June 2003.

Bolam v Friern Hospital Management Committee [1957] 2 All ER 118, [1957] 1 WLR 582.

CHAPTER 29
REDRESSING THE COMPENSATION CULTURE

Mr Tim Kevan

"Discourage litigation. Persuade your neighbours to compromise when-ever you can. Point out to them how the nominal winner is often a real loser – in fees, expenses, and waste of time. As a peacemaker the lawyer has a superior opportunity of being a good man. There will still be business enough."

Abraham Lincoln, Notes for a Law Lecture, 1 July 1850

INTRODUCTION

FIGURES

Arguments go both ways as to whether this country is in the grip of a co-called 'compensation culture' or not. What is clear is that the costs of litigation have risen enormously in recent years. For example, in 1974 the cost of NHS clinical negligence claims was only £1million. By 2003, this had risen to £477 million, an amount equal to the cost of 22,700 extra nurses. However, the cost is nothing like the scale of that in the United States that is almost always the source of reference when raising the issue. In that country, medical litigation costs are estimated to cost £13 billion a year or 0.2% of GDP as opposed to 0.04% of GDP in this country.

TENSIONS

Whatever the truth of it, no-one likes to see the NHS losing money and resources on legal claims. However, there are not many victims of clinical negligence or malpractice who do not feel the right to be compensated in one form or another. So, too, no-one wants doctors to be free of any accountability whatsoever. On the other hand, nobody wants doctors to feel so threatened by litigation and professional sanction that they will not act if there is the slightest risk.

These are some of the tensions inherent in the system which allows for both compensation for accidents and some degree of risk in medical treatment. Ultimately, it boils down to a balancing act of two issues in particular. First, allowing risk but maintaining safety and second, reducing cost whilst avoiding injustice.

RISK

COMPENSATION CULTURE

A large part of the bemoaning of a compensation culture involves not the overall figures that do not appear to bear out the accusation but instead the extreme cases. Often apocryphal, they range from being burnt by coffee in a restaurant to being injured due to failing to apply the brakes on a toboggan run in an amusement park. Whilst the public rarely get to hear the full stories of such cases they become part of the collective unconscious, something to rail down the pub or in the canteen.

As with many myths, however, there is often a degree of truth and certainly this is borne out by the facts in personal injury generally. In the past thirty years personal injury law has been extended into all sorts of realms never before expected. Part of this has been down to judicial activism and partly due to both national and European legislation. A classic example of how the courts have extended liabilities comes in the area of sport in which we have seen liabilities established in recent years not only against players on the field but even as far as referees and governing bodies. As for legislation, this is most frequently seen in the health and safety at work regulations which were introduced in the 1990s and which place onerous duties on employers in relation to health and safety. This change towards a culture of blame and arguably away from personal responsibility was reflected in the increasing costs of litigation for the NHS.

LEGAL RETREAT

The high water mark of such a culture was reached in the courts in the case of *Tomlinson v Congleton Borough Council* in 2003 in which the House of Lords dismissed a claim for injury caused by diving into a shallow lake on the basis that the risk was obvious. Lord Hutton, for example, stated "it is not, and should never be, the policy of the law to require the protection of the foolhardy or reckless few to deprive, or interfere with, the enjoyment by the remainder of society of the liberties and amenities to which they are rightly entitled." This was very much seen as a retreat from previous decisions and as sending a message for all litigants in personal injury, which would equally include those claiming for clinical negligence.

The spirit of the judgment in *Tomlinson* is now being enacted into law in the Compensation Bill currently before Parliament. In particular, it will allow a court to be able to consider the wider social value of the activity in the context of which the injury or damage occurred. Clearly, this is aimed at everyday activities such as adventure holidays rather than clinical negligence cases. However, it will be interesting to see whether it might also be employed in this context in further trying to limit scope for liability in this area.

CHESTER V AFSHAR

However, despite the moves in *Tomlinson* and the Compensation Bill to redress the balance back in favour of personal responsibility, the House of Lords in fact moved the other way in the field of clinical negligence on the issue of causation in 2004 in the case of *Chester v Afshar*. In that case they held that where a surgeon had failed to warn of a particular adverse outcome and that outcome in fact occurred, a Claimant did not need to then go on and prove that had she been so warned she would have in fact acted differently. This case in effect turned the law of causation on its head for cases of failure to warn and has made it much easier to prove liability than might otherwise have been the case. Whilst the effects of this judgment will continue to be worked out for years to come in the courts, the important thing to note is that once again it was the courts exhibiting their own form of law-making in order to ensure that a claim did not fail.

RISK-AVERSE

The real difficulty with these extensions to the law of negligence and the inevitable increase in claims which follow is that professionals and in this context doctors become more risk-averse. Not only may it discourage the little kindnesses which doctors may have offered more readily in the past but it also potentially has an adverse effect on clinical judgments. As the Prime Minister Tony Blair warned more generally on 26 May 2005, "A risk-averse public sector will stifle creativity and deny to many the opportunities to be creative while supplying a few with compensation payments."

This is a significant concern for health care professionals and above all risks undermining the spirit of public service and clinical excellence which has always been associated with the NHS. In order to combat these effects, it can be looked at from three angles.

I. LEGAL BASIS

The first is to review the law of liability for clinical negligence generally and to assess whether it may need narrowing. Until recently, when the rule was overturned, barristers were immune from being sued for any advocacy they undertook in court. This was on the basis that the fear of litigation may make barristers more wary of being forthright in their submissions and may instead start over-qualifying anything they had to say. Such a principle may be analogous to the position of a surgeon in the operating theatre or to a psychiatrist dealing with an unstable patient. The addition of the risk of litigation to an already stressful situation is unlikely to help a surgeon or psychiatrists' concentration, particularly when things start going wrong and need remedying quickly. Outright immunity from litigation in certain circumstances or for certain practitioners may therefore be considered. Other issues which could be reviewed include the issue of causation outlined above.

II. ALTERNATIVE BASIS FOR COMPENSATION

This is not to say that litigants need not be compensated when doctors are given a status immunity. Instead, alternative systems may be considered. In Sweden, for example, a no-fault system of compensation operates for clinical negligence cases. This was considered in 2003 in the Chief Medical Officer, Sir Liam Donaldson's report

'*Making Amends*' and ultimately dismissed on the basis that it would probably increase the overall costs due to an increased number of claims. However, it might still be considered appropriate in areas where it was deemed that the public interest is better served by doctors being immune from litigation, such as the examples of surgery and psychiatry mentioned above.

III. PROFESSIONAL RAMIFICATIONS

Another way of enabling doctors to make their judgments independently and without being affected by concerns over litigation would be to ensure that doctors are immune from being disciplined either by their professional body or their employer for mistakes that may have been made. This would be on the strict condition that they provide full and frank disclosure as to their mistake and how it might have been avoided. This would also help to encourage a culture of openness in which doctors not only own up to their mistakes, but are then able to assist in ensuring that lessons are learnt so that they can be avoided in the future. Clearly, this could not be done without any caveats and potential exceptions that might be considered include where the professional action has resulted in the commission of a crime or where the doctor's continued service might be a danger to his or her patients. This would cover not only the very high stress situations encountered by surgeons and psychiatrists but also the more general concerns of, for example, general medical practitioners.

In order to make this work in practice, a rule would also have to be introduced which disallowed such disclosures being able to be used against doctors in subsequent litigation. This would mean that any evidence would have to be gathered independently of these disclosure statements.

COST

REFORMS

Much less needs to be said about reducing the actual cost of litigation as there have already been many excellent reforms in this regard. First among these were the so-called Woolf Reforms which aimed to speed up the civil litigation system and to reduce its overall cost. In addition, the Compensation Bill currently before Parliament aims to provide better regulation of claims managers and will hopefully forestall abuses such as the encouragement of frivolous or hopeless claims.

CAUSATION

The real difficulty with clinical negligence cases is that by their nature they tend to be complicated, particularly on the issue of causation since they involved litigants who were already ill before the harmful event. Therefore, the separating out of the pre-existing illness from the event itself can end up in numerous experts arguing over minute pieces of evidence.

NHS REDRESS BILL

In order to try and tackle this, the government has put forward the NHS Redress Bill which is currently before Parliament. This provides for the establishment of a scheme to enable the settlement, without the need to commence court proceedings, of certain claims that arise in connection with hospital services provided to patients as part of the health service.

Currently, this scheme will only apply to claims under £20,000 and it is to be hoped that this will be extended to all claims in the future as it promises significantly to reduce costs if implemented effectively.

COST OF CARE

One of the most significant parts of the legislation is that it allows part of the settlement to include contracts for future remedial care that is needed, alongside financial compensation. This is highly important since at the moment, litigants are entitled as of right to claim for the cost of private provision of care (under section 2(4) of the Law Reform (Personal Injury) Act 1948). It is to be hoped that in the future, consideration is given to repealing this section in relation to claims against the NHS and instead enabling the NHS to offer their own care packages for the future. This, in the long term, will hopefully bring down costs with the NHS providing those services it can cope with, and contracting the others in from the private sector.

MEDIATION

The other issue that really hasn't yet taken root within litigation, despite its encouragement in the Woolf Reforms, is that of mediation. One of the difficulties is that parties often pay lip service to considering mediation and then simply get on with the business of time-consuming and expensive litigation. Whilst is very difficult to do much more than encourage it, there are measures which might be used to facilitate this process.

The first is a more thorough investigation by the courts into what efforts were in fact made to try and mediate the case. Judges could be specifically trained to be aware of ways that parties in effect avoid mediation. Further, amendments could be made to the costs rules to ensure that more detailed investigations are undertaken into this area. For example, a condition of seeking costs might be for a party to make a detailed statement setting out the efforts which were made which could then be challenged by the other side.

In addition to this, stricter guidelines for the granting and continuance of Legal Aid could be made with particular reference to the positive and realistic efforts that have been made towards mediation. It appears that in relation to the Redress Scheme the Legal Services Commission will be able to take the refusal of an offer into account when decided whether legal aid will be granted.

CONCLUSION

Tacitus wrote "The desire for safety stands against every great and noble enterprise". It is to be hoped that this will not be the case with the NHS and that the need for safety can be balanced against the need for a culture where freedom and creativity are not stifled by rules and regulations. It is therefore suggested in relation to risk that:

1. The law of liability for clinical negligence is reviewed and that certain areas such as surgery and psychiatry should be immune from litigation.
2. Alternative forms of non-fault compensation should apply to these areas.
3. Medical practitioners should generally be immune from discipline subject to certain basic exceptions on condition that they

provide full and frank disclosure of their mistakes which would not be able to be used in litigation.

In addition, there are limited areas which still need to be addressed in reducing the legal costs associated with litigation in this area:

1. An extension of the Redress Scheme to cases over £20,000.
2. Consideration of repealing the provision which allows litigants to claim for the cost of private care as of right.
3. Stronger forms of encouragement towards mediation such as greater costs sanctions and stricter Legal Aid Guidelines.

SECTION IV
FUNDING SECTION

CHAPTER 30

FINANCING THE NHS: THE CURRENT SYSTEM

Mr Tony Harrison

THE SYSTEM IN OUTLINE

The NHS is almost entirely financed from general taxation[1] as it has been ever since its foundation. The proportion financed in this way has varied slightly over the years but has never been less than 95 per cent of total expenditure.

In principle NHS services are 'free at the point of delivery'. This principle was breached, from the 1950s onwards, for prescription drugs and also some other services. The present Government reasserted in the NHS Plan (Department of Health 2000) that charges were neither efficient nor equitable, but did not draw the obvious inference that existing charges should be abolished.

Despite rapid increases since the 1960s, in the real i.e. inflation adjusted cost of prescriptions, the contribution of charges to the cost of the NHS has never exceeded 5 per cent of the total budget. Because of the rapid increase in the total budget in recent years, its share is now only 2 percent.[2]

While the overall financing system has remained more or less the same for five decades, the way that the funds are allocated *within* the NHS has been significantly changed.

The mechanisms have changed considerably at a detailed level over the years, but essentially two main changes have been made from the way the NHS was financed at its outset.

- From the mid-1970s onwards an explicit policy was developed towards the distribution of NHS funding between different geographical areas
- From the 1990s onwards funds have been allocated to purchasers i.e. the agencies financing NHS services at a local level rather than directly to providers – i.e. hospitals and community services such as district nursing. Finance and provision of GP services had always been divided as GPs are generally self-employed.

We consider these two changes in turn.

DISTRIBUTION

Until the 1970s the distribution of NHS resources between different parts of England reflected the level of provision on the ground that in turn largely reflected historical factors – where hospitals had been established by charitable trusts or where local authorities had been active in promoting health facilities. Some parts of the country e.g. London were well endowed: others much less so.

In 1975 the Resource Allocation Working Party was established with a remit to design a means of distributing finance, which would produce a fairer allocation of resources between different parts of England (DHSS 1976).[3] The general principle they worked on was that the NHS should be able to offer equal opportunity of access to healthcare for people at equal risk of needing it- which the existing distribution of resources clearly did not do.

The word 'opportunity' reflects the fact that a funding formula in itself can only create the *potential* for equal access. It cannot guarantee that services will in fact respond to need in exactly the same way in all parts of the country, nor that individuals would necessarily present themselves to the system for treatment in an equal way. Postcode rationing[4] remains but its extent would probably be vastly greater in the absence of a resource allocation formula of the kind currently in use.

Such an objective – the equity objective of resource allocation – has to be based on a measurement of need for care on the one hand and the cost of care on the other, neither of which have proved straight-forward. During the 1990s the formulae were reassessed on the basis of extensive research and analysis commissioned by the Department of Health and in 1998 a further objective was set for it: that it should contribute to the reduction in avoidable health inequalities.

As a result of these and other changes such as the availability of new data sources, the way the formula is calculated has been modified a number of times. For example, the formula now includes a separate element for mental health and for acute and maternity services, which did not appear in the original version. In addition, changes were made to offset the effect of differences in the supply of services on the levels of observed utilisation. The main element remains population, weighted to allow for the higher costs of the very young and the old.

In addition the range of expenditure included in the formula, has been extended from hospital and community health services, to include expenditure on general practice and prescribing. As a result, it now covers the great majority of NHS spending. However, although the formula consists of estimates of need for different services or categories of spending, the allocation themselves are not tied to particular forms of expenditure.

While further adjustments can be expected in the light of new data and analysis, the prospect is that the broad approach will remain broadly the same, as long as the current structure of funding of the NHS remains in place.

ALLOCATION TO SERVICES

The flow of NHS funds from the centre – currently the Department of Health has always been 'cascaded' through one or more administrative levels until it reached services on the ground. However the precise route taken by the cascade – and how many distinct cascades – have changed over the years.

The single most important change occurred in the early 1990s when a key distinction was introduced between purchasing and providing. Prior to that regional health authorities had exercised some discretion over where funds went, eg where new specialised services should be provided but by and large existing providers could be assured of continuing financial support. In principle, the creation of fee-standing purchasers meant that funds were allocated only in return for the supply of specific services and might be switched to providers who could offer a better deal.

In principle district health authorities could purchase services from any trust, not solely those for which they formerly had administrative responsibility: so too could GP fundholders. In this way the then Government hoped that a market in health care services would develop.

Provision of hospital and some community services became the responsibility of hospital, community or mental health trusts: the district health authorities became responsible for contracting for services from the trusts as well as financing general practice. In addition the opportunity was offered to GPs to become responsible for purchasing some services themselves – typically elective care but in some cases a wider range of services.

Since that time the structure of health care purchasing has changed more than once and it is currently in the process of being restructured once again. In its first white paper (Department of Health 1997) the Labour Government indicated that it intended to abolish fund holding but that it would preserve the purchaser provider split for hospital and mental health services. District health authorities would be abolished and replaced by primary care trusts, which would purchase these services, and both purchase and provide GP and other community based services. This structure is now being revised – essentially however it seems set to revert to the structure introduced in the 1990s. At the very local level purchasing will be carried out by GP practices or groups of practices in what is now termed practice based commissioning. According to the Government this will allow GPs to commission services – under the general aegis of the relevant (Primary Care Trusts) PCT – which align more closely with the needs of their patients.

The reversion to fund holding version 2, or practice based commissioning reflects a fundamental U turn in Labour's approach to running the NHS in response to widespread criticism that the NHS had become over centralised.

In 2002 Alan Milburn then Secretary of State for Health, announced that the role of the centre would be reduced, and as part of that reform 75 per cent of NHS funds would be allocated directly to primary care trusts i.e. without cascading through other hierarchical levels. In 2004 his successor proposed practice based commissioning as a further step in the direction of decentralisation.

At the next level primary care trusts will have overall responsibility for purchasing in their area and at the level above them with a small number of strategic health authorities exercising general oversight. However, in 2005 the Government came to the view that the purchasing structure as it then was, needed to be changed again. Accordingly it set in train a process for amalgamation, which is still underway.

This latest reform reducing the number of purchasers is driven by two main factors – the Government's desire to reduce administrative costs, and to strengthen the purchasing function, so as increase purchaser's influence over the way services were provided.

In a white paper issued in 2006, the Government made clear its view that more services should be transferred to community settings (Department of Health 2006). In this the Government is once again reverting to a policy espoused by its predecessor but which failed to reduce the role of the hospital in the 1990s. The Government believes that it requires larger purchasers with greater expertise and market power at their disposal to impose changes in the way that services are delivered.

The changes in purchasing structure being introduced as another financial reform being implemented. Whereas in the 1990s, purchasers in general used block contracts to pay for services, the new regime, known as payment by results, is based on the cost of individual procedures and contrast to the earlier regime the tariff is set at national level. Furthermore, the Government is also giving patients the right to choose their place of treatment. At least in respect of elective care (for emergencies most patients have little effective choice), purchasing will, in effect, be carried out by patients and/or the GPs who advise them. In these ways the Government is creating the potential for a market in health care services.

These changes, the Government hopes, will bring genuine pressure on providers to reduce costs. Furthermore, that pressure is being intensified through the deliberate expansion of the role of private providers, initially of elective care but – although no targets have been set – of other services as well.

COMMENTARY

As this brief account has shown, the decision to finance services almost entirely out of taxation still leaves a large number of issues to be resolved within the NHS itself.

As long as the NHS persists, it is highly unlikely that the *principle* of equalising resources between different parts of England relative to need will be abandoned. But the elements of the distribution formula will continue to be modified in the light of new data and analysis.

It seems more likely, that the design of the 'cascade' from the centre to the frontline will continue to change in the light of changing circumstances and changing views as to what is required. Although the present Government decided to retain the purchaser provider split and to reform purchasing structure for the reasons set out above, there is remarkably little evidence of what the impact of purchasing has been.[5] There is a good chance therefore that the structure which the Government is currently creating will be revised yet again.

At one end of the scale, for example, the idea has been floated that individuals – or groups of individuals with specific conditions – should be allocated a sum of money-or equivalent voucher – giving them complete freedom to buy the package of care they want. At the other, it has been proposed that a major service such as cancer, where a national improvement plan exists should have its own ring-fenced funding, determined at national level, to protect it from the pressure to improve other services. A recent report from the National Audit Office (2005) revealed that there remained significant differences in the availability of service as between different parts of the country. A future government may decide that the current system of allocation which generally leaves local purchasers free to buy what they wish – within a broad guiding framework of what services they should make available to their local populations – will have to be modified in areas where there is a strong national interest.

It also seems likely that the financial framework created by payment by results and patient choice will have to be progressively modified, in the light of its actual impact on providers. It remains to be determined, for example, what the response should be if a provider consistently cannot meet the cost levels set in the national tariff. Changes may also have to be made in response to new medical innovations and the way that healthcare is provided.

One question remains to be considered here: whether it is appropriate to continue to rely on tax finance. The Government is committed to it: so is the Conservative Opposition. Nevertheless it may come into question in the very near future.

The traditional complaint has been that the NHS would never attract sufficient funding if it remained almost entirely reliant on the Treasury. The position of the NHS in 1997 relative to other countries appeared to confirm this. In comparison to countries with similar per capita income health spending in England was low (the same was not true of other parts of the UK).

In defence of this low level, the argument was usually put that the NHS by virtue of the simplicity of its funding structure and the central control over key costs such as pay which it offered, was uniquely able to provide cost effectiveness. That argument began to fall apart when it became apparent that, not only did the NHS have long waiting lists, but also service quality in other areas was below that available in other countries. It has lost further force in the last year or so when it has also become apparent that the Department of Health has not been successful in containing the costs of running the service particularly the pay of GPs and hospital consultants, despite the fact that their contracts were centrally determined.

The Government's response, set out in the NHS Plan, was to argue that tax finance remained the best option but that substantially more resources would be needed if the NHS was to provide standards of service comparable to those available in countries with similar gross domestic product per capita. The result was the largest sustained increase in NHS spending ever experienced.

The rapid rate of increase will continue until 2007. But there is no reason to believe that the level achieved then will be regarded as 'good enough': the pressure to spend more will continue from new technology, the need to continue to raise clinical quality and from the Government's own desire to respond to what it perceives as rising public expectations for a more convenient and responsiveness service.

REFERENCES

1. We include in the health element in national insurance payments. Although part of these is nominally designed to pay for the NHS, in practice it is just another tax.
2. In Wales, prescription charges are being abolished, so that share is set to decline further: Scotland too is considering their abolition. There is no sign that the Department of Health is considering such a change for England.
3. Allocation between the different countries comprising the Uk is achieved by quite different mechanisms and is not considered further here.
4. That is, the situation where some treatment such as a drug is available in one part of the country and not in another.
5. One exception is GP fundholding: see for example Glennerster *et al*).

FURTHER READING

Department of Health, *The NHS Plan: a plan for investment: a plan for reform* London Department of Health 2000.

DHSS *Sharing Resources for Health in England*, London HMSO 1976.

H Glennerster *et al Implementing GP Fundholding*, Buckingham, Open University Press, 1994.

Department of Health *The New NHS: modern: dependable*, London TSO 1997.

National Audit Office, *The NHS Cancer Plan: a progress report*, London TSO 2005.

Department of Health *Our Health, Our Care, Our Say*, London TSO 2006.

CHAPTER 31
TAXATION AND INSURANCE

Professor Alan Maynard

INTRODUCTION

The focus of public and policy debate on the financing of health care is often on "crises" about "under-funding" and deficits. Such debates usually ignore the central issues of policy, in particular the cost effectiveness of health care delivery, the production of health, and equity in the distribution of health. The objective of the NHS and all other health care systems is to improve population health at least cost. However, instead of focusing on the clinical and cost effectiveness of competing interventions and measuring clinical success in improving the length and quality of consumer's lives to ensure "value for money" in the use of society's scarce resources, [1] the media and competing politicians debate alternative funding methods and propagate the illusion that more and/or different funding will "cure" the system's often ill-defined problems.

The purpose of this chapter is to clarify the costs and benefits of competing funding methods in the context of the competing ideological debates that permeate health care policy and to demonstrate that arguments about funding are often ideologically driven and reflect the different and often implicit preferences about who should bear the burden of financing health care.

COMPETING IDEOLOGIES

The Concise Oxford Dictionary defines ideology as "a manner of thinking characteristic of a class or individual; ideas at the basis of some economic or political theory or system". In the health care policy debate two ideologies compete, which following Williams, [2] will be labelled the egalitarian and the libertarian.

The influence of these ideologies wax and wane, as epitomised by the resurgence of the latter during the governments of Reagan and Thatcher. Worldwide the libertarian ideology is in the ascendant, and its influence is epitomised in "Communist" China where "laissez faire" dominates economic life. The egalitarian ideology is in retreat as individualism and "choice" dominate political intercourse and universality is questioned.

The libertarian ideology puts freedom of choice as the primary social goal. The achievement of freedom requires that individuals are free to make their own choices, constrained by Government only to the minimal necessary extent to provide security and legal systems that protect private property rights and ensure contracts are enforced. In such a system individuals will pursue their own interests and those unable to make their way will be cared for by charity, funded by voluntary donations from the well endowed. These inequalities produce economic growth and ensure the freedom valued so highly by libertarians.

The egalitarian perspective puts equality of opportunity forward as the primary social goal. In such a society all individuals have the right to basic goods and it is for society to define what these basic goods should be. In this world lack of achievement must not be punished and collective mechanisms are needed to ensure all receive care. For egalitarians equalising opportunity may necessarily involve restricting the freedoms of others through taxation and the law. Such restrictions on freedom are an anathema to libertarians.

FINANCING HEALTH CARE

All methods of funding health care, whether they are publicly or privately organised, involve depriving households of resources. All resources are owned and generated by households. Thus wages are a return to households for labour, rent income accrues from the ownership of real estate, profits arise from shares owned by household or the pension funds in which they have rights, and interest accrues to households who lend their assets. These income-yielding assets are owned directly by household or indirectly through banks and in shares and other ownership rights.

Government typically spends over 40 per cent of Gross Domestic Product and its assets are in principle owned by the households that make up the electorate. Government funding is drawn either from taxing households or borrowing from them through intermediaries such as banks.

Taxation may be direct (e.g. income tax) or indirect (e.g. value added and corporation taxes, and excise duties). National (or what continentals call "social") insurance is a tax on labour, paid by employees and employers, on behalf of their staff. This form of "insurance" is controlled by the State although the power to determine rates and collect the revenues may be shared with quasi-independent entities such as the social insurance funds in the Netherlands, Germany and France. Such schemes involve disguised taxation as they are managed on a "pay as you go" annual basis and do not involve the investment of funds to create future benefits as may happen in private insurance.

Private insurance companies fund their expenditures from premiums levied on their members or paid on their behalf by their employers. These premiums may be risk or community rated. If in private health insurance (PHI) they are risk related, the premium will reflect both individual and group illness characteristics and age. Thus typically in an individual or group scheme those with poor health records and/or more elderly and consequently more likely to be ill on an actuarial basis will face higher premiums. Some countries, for instance Australia, oblige PHI to be sold on a community basis in which case young, good risks subsidise older poor risks as happens in the tax financed NHS. [3]

Thus both Government expenditure and PHI expenditure is derived from the same source: households. The former involves compulsion, which the libertarians regard as an unacceptable infringement of freedom, in particular freedom of choice in how to spend household resources.

PHI usually involves freedom of choice: in Britain you are free to buy BUPA or PPP PHI and receive it from your employer. This is consistent with the libertarian ideology's goal of the individual being free to determine how their resources are allocated. However in some societies that freedom may or may not be constrained. In

Chile employees are obliged to elect for the State system or private insurance. There are few constraints on PHI and individual and group risk and household's willingness and ability to pay determine purchase. In Australia PHI is not only community rated but also the industry's freedom to set premia is regulated by the Commonwealth Government.

Freedom is never absolute and in the health care market, ideological influences wax and wane. The new Conservative leader has surprised traditional libertarians in his party by arguing that a tax based NHS will dominate health care financing in the UK, a position identical to his Labour opponent. However this will not prevent libertarian ideologues and their commercial supporters from continuing to launch proposals that "rediscover" health care funding problems and advocate private funding initiatives such as user payments and private insurance. Why, apart from ideology, will they do this?

FINANCING HEALTH CARE AND THE DISTRIBUTION OF FUNDING BURDENS

The libertarian ideology is a convenient vehicle for those wishing to increase health care spending. As witnessed during the Blair Government's spending bonanza of recent years, public funding of health care provides good income and profit streams for providers Typically those health care systems that use private funding exhibit poorer cost control and thus greater scope for profit making for both labour groups (e.g. doctors) and other powerful marketing lobbies (e.g. the pharmaceutical industry).

PHI in general [4] and the US health care system in particular usually exhibit premia inflation two to three times the rate of general inflation. The expenditure inflation rates of publicly funded health care systems rarely reach such levels because Governments have the necessary means of controlling spending i.e. controlling public expenditure. The control capacity in the NHS and other public health care systems occasionally exhibits some volatility, particularly in run-ups to elections as politicians purchase political support. But public growth rates such as those recently in the UK-NHS are the exception that proves the rule.

These relationships are illustrated in figure one, where all funding for health care comes from households on the left of the diagram. The household can pay for health care with user charges, explicit taxation, implicit taxation (national or social insurance) and private insurance. Expenditure control can be exercised to varying degrees by restricting these funding "pipes".

The easiest expenditure pipe to control is direct taxation: Government manages this directly. Indirect taxation or national insurance may be less easy for Government to control if social insurance funds have some degree of delegated discretion in setting contribution rates. The control of PHI premia is fragmented between provider companies that typically tend to act more like bank clerks than efficient purchasers of health care who protect their members financial interests. Providers typically drive their expenditure with considerable discretion in setting fees and determining utilisation and the level of service delivered.

This is also the problem for user charges. Such a method of finance is difficult to control because although the charge is fixed, the provider determines the volume. Thus expenditure control with user charges may fail as providers can induce demand for services for consumers. Although charging may initially deflate demand for care, physicians by altering their treatment thresholds, can increase the intensity of care and the size of the population they serve to maintain their income streams.

Canadian researchers reviewed the literature on user charges and concluded:

> "Most proposals for 'patient participation in health care financing' reduce to misguided or cynical attempts to tax the ill and/or drive up the total cost of health care while shifting some of the burden out of government *and insurer* budgets".

In the USA the policy "fashion" is to deploy user charges to control patient demand even though the evidence shows they have not been efficient instruments of expenditure control in the past. This preference is basically ideological, reflecting the libertarian, Bush focus of avoiding "big government" and leaving markets as free as possible, thereby protecting the inefficiencies of the US system and its inequities, where 45 million citizens have no health insurance cover. Unsurprisingly US health expenditure is 16 per cent of Gross National

Product and premium inflation is two to three times as fast as general inflation.

Thus providers interested in the expansion of their markets and profits typically like unregulated markets, such as those offered by PHI, particularly as this is consistent with the ideology of business, which generally favours small Government except when it's regulation, as in the pharmaceutical market for instance, reduces competition and increases profits. Another reason for the congruence of interests of libertarians and some industrial interests may be that "free market" policy solutions affect not only the level of funding but also the distribution of the burden of funding across income groups.

The concern about the distribution of the funding burdens across income, affects policy preferences. Thus egalitarians prefer the use of taxation, particularly direct taxation such as that on personal incomes, as this facilitates the redistribution to the poor and away from the rich.

Libertarians confronted by universal National Health Services often tend to advocate increases in user charges. Such levies, unlike direct taxation, may not relate to ability to pay but are funded by users, many of who are elderly, ill and relatively poor.

The impact of such charges on different social groups is often disguised by their advocates arguing that they are "necessary" to curb inefficiency or inappropriate use of health services. This argument is flawed in several respects. Firstly the evidence shows that most patients present to a doctor when they believe they are ill. Dealing with the "worried well" absorbs scarce resources but may identify illness earlier than would occur if price barriers reduced utilisation.

Further if expenditure on treatment is wasteful, this is the responsibility of the primary demander of health care, the doctor. The patient usually makes the initial decision to consult, but after that primarily the doctor determines the use of NHS resources. Thus if there is an inefficient use of resources, this is the responsibility of the doctor and not the patient. To penalise the patient with user charges for the inefficiency of the doctor seems perverse.

Egalitarian advocacy of taxation as the means by which health care should be funded ensures that the richer pay for care consumed often by poor, elderly patients. This is consistent with their redistributional goals. During discussions about the funding of the NHS Modernisation there was a debate about how to finance it. The "old Labour" egalitarians wanted to raise income tax, but the "new Labour" Prime Minister had pledged no income tax rises for political reasons. As a consequence the funding of the "modernisation" of the NHS has been funded by social or national insurance contributions that are less redistributive than income taxes. Spreading the cost burden under the fiscal illusion of "insurance" preserved new Labour's desire for the votes of middle England, which is sensitive to income tax increases.

Public debate about financing health care and the distribution of the burden of funding amongst income groups is often disguised beneath some convenient rhetoric that is ideologically based. Egalitarians do not always wish to be direct in redistributing tax burdens from the rich to the poor. This is epitomised by the Blair administration's use of "stealth" taxes and its reluctance, for instance, to use a fifty per cent tax rate on those earning over £100,000 to fund NHS improvements. Libertarians are similarly evasive advocating greater emphasis on private insurance and user charges, as seen in the current US policy debates, as means of shifting funding burdens on to users. Such policies are particularly difficult when the major users of health care, the elderly can be very effective lobbyists e.g. obliging Bush to introduce a chaotic and expensive Federal system prescription benefits before the last Presidential election.

CONCLUSIONS

The principle conclusions to be derived from this discussion of funding mechanisms in health care are that reasons for advocating change may be disguised by ideological and political agenda and all proponents of change have to be challenged to be explicit about how their proposals affect not just funding streams but efficiency and equity. All health care systems, public and private, exhibit gross inefficiencies in terms of variations in practice and failure to deliver what the evidence base shows to be cost effective. Policy makers universally spout the equity argument but pursue policies in a lazy manner that favours health care investments rather than redistribution of income and education opportunities. Often the debate around funding provides a means by which policy makers from the competing ideological persuasions can maintain the status quo. This can often be attractive as it preserves the incomes of powerful provider groups

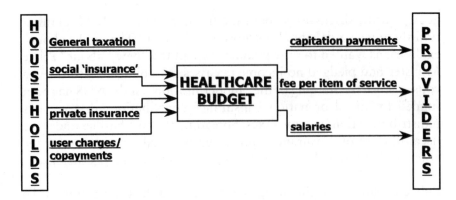

Figure 1:   The expenditure-income identity (Reinhardt 1984)

such as the pharmaceutical industry and the medical profession and ensures their political support. As ever, as in figure one, one household's expenditure is the income of some provider!

The challenge for all who enter the debate about funding is to be transparent about their ideological concerns. Also they must recognise that pouring more money into a health care system may not improve the level or distribution of population health. [5]

REFERENCES

1. Kind P and Williams A, Measuring Success in Health Care: the time has come to do it properly, *Health Policy Matters*, 9, University of York, March 2004 (accessible at www.york.ac.uk/healthsciences/pubs/hpmindex.htm.
2. Maynard A and Williams A, Privatisation and the National Health Service, in J Le Grand and R Robinson (eds), *Privatisation and the Welfare State*, George Allen & Unwin, London 1984. Williams A, The pervasive role of ideology in the optimisation of the public-private mix in public healthcare systems, in A Maynard (ed), *The Public-Private Mix for Health: plus ça change, plus c'est la même chose?* Radcliffe, Oxford 2005.
3. Hall J and Maynard A. Healthcare lessons from Australia: what can Michael Howard learn from John Howard. *British Medical Journal*, 2005, 330, 357–9.

4. Columbo F. *Private Health insurance in OECD countries organisation for Economic Cooperation and Development,* OECD Health Working Paper 15, Paris, 2004.
5. Maynard A (ed) *The Public-Private Mix for Health: plus ça change, plus c'est la même chose?* Radcliffe, Oxford 2005 Maynard A and Sheldon T, *Funding for the National Health Service,* Lancet, 360, 576, 2002.

CHAPTER 32
ALTERNATIVE FUNDING MODELS

Dr Eamonn Butler

By world standards, the UK's state health system is an oddity. Firstly, it is huge. With a workforce of over a million, the NHS is one of the world's very largest employers. Its budget is now larger than the Gross Domestic Product of 155 members of the United Nations.

Second, the UK is also unusual in that the overwhelming bulk of healthcare spending comes through the public sector. In 2003, some 83.4% of healthcare spending in the UK came through the state. Of the Organisation of European Cooperation and Development OECD countries, the public-sector share was higher only in Luxembourg, some Nordic countries (Sweden, Norway, Iceland) and some former Communist countries (Slovakia, Czech Republic). By contrast, government accounts for less than two-thirds of all health spending in Switzerland and the Netherlands, and less than half of all health spending in Korea, Mexico and the United States (44.4%).

Thirdly, this public-sector spending is highly centralised. Virtually the entire NHS budget originates from central government. In most other countries, including some of those which do spend more, public-sector health services are organized and funded much more locally, at the municipal or regional level.

FAIRNESS AND EFFICIENCY

One argument for having healthcare funded mainly (or even wholly) through the state is fairness. If people were paying for all healthcare themselves, some might be unable to afford the expensive or long-term treatment that they needed, while those at most risk might be unable to secure insurance at almost any price. But if the state is paying, these access problems might be averted.

A second argument for state finance is efficiency. It should theoretically be possible to make savings if things are done on a larger scale; and until recently, the NHS did seem to be holding down the cost of healthcare, which in other countries was escalating.

The fairness argument of course has merit. But it does not require the state to pay for and provide for all medical care, as it – almost – does in the UK. It suggests no more than that the state should fund those who cannot fund themselves. That is, of course, what happens with other necessities of life. The state does not run and finance grocery or clothes shops; rather, it supports the incomes of those who cannot otherwise afford food and clothing, so that they are empowered as customers in those markets. It does not fund people who can fund themselves.

The efficiency argument is looking even more ragged. Until recently, the NHS really did look like a cheap healthcare system. But the Blair administration decided that a massive rise in NHS spending was justified, and now the UK's spending exceeds the European average. People have also come to see the limitations of large, centralized state monopolies. They are hard to run, and even harder to reform. If their funding comes from the government rather than from users, they are slow to change in response to changing user demands. Since they are not facing competition, they have little incentive to innovate, or raise quality, or keep their costs under control.

Even after record budget increases, the NHS's finances are still in a rough state, with many trusts reporting deficits and some being plainly unable to bring their budgets under control. Some of this may be down to demographics, such as the baby-boom generation now reaching an age where they need more healthcare; and the longer length of time that people now spend in old age, where they are likely to make a larger demand on the NHS.

It is also due to the fact that healthcare is a moving target. The founders of the NHS assumed that once the infectious diseases of the day had been overcome, costs would fall. We now know that all that happens is that people live long enough to contract other diseases that are just as costly to treat, and often much more costly because they require expensive medicines or technology.

Lastly, a generally richer and more demanding population expect the NHS to intervene on health problems that years ago they would have borne quietly as being not worth the doctor's time. And if they are not paying directly, the bill being picked up by taxpayers, why indeed should they hold back?

RESPONSIBILITY AND ACCESS

There is therefore a strong case for looking at alternatives for how the UK healthcare system should be funded, and by implication, provided. A key element in such debates has been patient responsibility – the realization that if care is apparently free, people will demand more and more of it, presenting with more and more trivial conditions. Only if the patient sees or suffers at least some of the cost can such over-demand be avoided. The question is how to restore that link while at the same time ensuring that it does not deter people from seeking and getting the medical care that they truly need.

Politicians are reluctant to meddle with NHS funding, and one can see why. The NHS is built on the principle of service being free at the point of use; any suggestion that some form of payment should be made breeches this founding principle. Indeed, any proposals to change the basis of funding, however fair and rational they might be, are too easy for critics to misrepresent, leaving the suggestion in people's minds that reform would favour only the rich – not an outcome that anyone would actually want. NHS funding reform is therefore effectively off the political agenda for the time being. Nevertheless, reform on the provision side, bringing in diversity among the producers and choice for users, may strengthen people's trust in non-centralized and non-state approaches, which could in time bring funding reform back into play. So it is instructive to look at some of the alternatives.

A HEALTH TAX

One idea that has been mooted is a 'hypothecated tax'. When NHS spending comes out of general taxation, as it does today, few people understand how much it costs. So the idea is to have a dedicated health tax which is much more visible. This would have the benefit of making people aware that healthcare is far from free. This might prompt people, to avoid making excess demands on the system.

However, the Treasury has deep-seated objections to hypothecated taxes; they feel that if they conceded the principle, then motorists would expect the whole of the taxes they pay to be spent on the roads, not a quarter of it; while drinkers might object that very little of the excise duty they part with goes to deal with problems of alcoholism or drunkenness, and that the duty should be reduced; while peace campaigners may demand to be excused their contribution to the defence budget. And in any case, it is questionable whether the mere knowledge of how much is spent on the NHS would actually of itself curb over-demand. It might indeed have the opposite effect. The hypothecated tax idea was considered briefly by the Thatcher administration in the 1990s, but soon discarded.

CONTRACTING OUT OF A HEALTH TAX

If there is a dedicated tax for health, then it becomes possible to stimulate competition by allowing people to contract out of it. The contracting out principle has been used for the upper-tier of state pensions, where people who could demonstrate that they had equivalent or better private provision could choose to pay lower state contributions and divert the money into their own private-sector pension plan. In principle this could be done with a health tax too.

The idea would be to stimulate the growth of private provision and private finance by allowing people to leave the state system and purchase their own medical insurance. And it gets round the argument that you have to pay twice to go private – once through taxation for the state system you do not use, and once again in fees for the private system that you do. Instead, people would be getting back at least some of their contributions to the state service. The same sort of effect could be achieved through a tax concession, such as the rebate offered by the Major administration to pensioners who maintained private medical insurance.

However, such ideas have not found much favour with the public. If the tax rebate is less than average health spending, then the system favours wealthier people who can afford to pay the difference. If it is higher, then people argue that health spending on those who choose to remain in the state system will be sorely reduced. Many people who take the rebate would be insuring privately anyway – the so-called deadweight cost. The Major administration's plan was to reduce the age threshold so that more and more people would be subsidized to leave the NHS and make private provision; but in fact the Blair government simply abolished the concession.

LOCAL FUNDING AND PROVISION

Another idea is to make the tax funding of healthcare, and the management of its provision, much more local. In Denmark, for example, around 80% of public healthcare finance is raised locally by 14 county councils. Since this is around three-quarters of the councils' total spend, healthcare is always a big issue in elections. Commentators argue that this system encourages people to look more critically at the value for money being delivered, and enables them to focus on healthcare spending without the distractions of too many other spending programmes – as would be the case in the UK, for example.

In principle it would be possible to go even further than Denmark goes, and set up dedicated local bodies to raise money for healthcare and to manage its application, so that the focus on value for money was complete.

Nevertheless, this system is built on local monopoly (or monopsony). While there is some opportunity for comparing the efficiency of the local system with those of neighbouring areas, such comparisons are much more limited than they would be in a completely free private market.

CHARGES

Charges are a further way of raising money for healthcare. Within a few years of the NHS's creation, charges were introduced for medicines and some medical equipment, in response to the huge demand that had been unleashed by free provision. But the scope for charging is limited. Prescription charges bring in less than one per cent of what the NHS costs. Furthermore, most patients could not be expected to pay for very large or lengthy medical interventions – only state funding or private insurance could deal with these. So charging becomes limited to smaller items. And charging can be seen as regressive, absorbing a larger part of the budget of poorer families.

Even so, it has occasionally been suggested that NHS in-patients should pay for food, and make a contribution to laundry costs, all of which they would have to bear if they were at home anyway. Mrs Thatcher rejected such proposals on the grounds of their probable political unpopularity. If charges were introduced, election debate would no doubt focus around which party could abolish or reduce them. And given that the scope for charges to cover much of the total cost is small anyway, this does not seem a very promising way forward.

France, though, has an intriguing system of reimbursements. There are user fees for various medical services, which the patient has to pay. However, patients can apply for reimbursements from the government that can repay up to 75% or 80% of the cost, depending on their income and on the nature of the service. The poorest six million or so people in France pay nothing. This has the merit that people realize that healthcare has a cost, and it helps develop a user-led market in healthcare services. On the other hand, there is widespread agreement that the system is very bureaucratic and expensive to run. It would be interesting to speculate, however, whether new technology could shave the operational costs.

SOCIAL INSURANCE

More radical, at least for the UK, would be various forms of social insurance. These are quite common in other EU countries, and there is a wide variety of structures to choose from. Private medical insurers say such systems are certainly practicable in the UK; but politicians have always found them too hard to explain, and too easy to misrepresent, so it seems unlikely that any progress will be made in this direction soon.

SOCIAL INSURANCE WITHOUT COMPETITION

Again, France – which in many years has topped the WHO charts for the popularity of its health system – provides the first example of this. It has a social insurance system where employers and employees both pay towards a basic healthcare package. The basic compulsory insurance is about 20% of payroll in total, with employers picking up roughly two-thirds of it. There are eighteen different insurance funds managing this revenue, although they are regional funds and do not compete. The system allows people a good choice of family doctor, and they can go directly to specialists with no need to approach a gatekeeper (like a GP in the United Kingdom). Nevertheless, most people (about 85% choose to buy private top-up insurance, which guarantees them benefits such as better comfort and privacy while in hospital.

This part of the funding system is not so different from that of the UK, although here the supposed national insurance system has failed to preserve its identity, and has really become merely an adjunct of the income tax system. And the revenue in the UK goes to central government, rather than direct to regional agencies. So in France there is some prospect at least of comparing the efficiency of the different insurance funds, and they are depoliticized in the sense that their funding is not mixed up with the funding for other social issues. But otherwise, there is not a great deal of competition in the funding system.

SOCIAL INSURANCE WITH LIMITED COMPETITION

The German social insurance system is again funded by contributions from employers and employees, but it works through multiple insurance funds which actually do compete with each other. About three-quarters of the population, all except the richest and the self-employed, are obliged to contribute, the cost being split equally between employers and employees. A government agency pays the contributions of unemployed people who cannot pay for themselves. The money is collected and managed by 450 separate sickness funds, although there is in reality very little real competition between them. It is the sickness funds who pay the doctors and contract with other providers to deliver healthcare services to their members. Once again, the system allows completely free choice of family doctor, and it has produced 50% more specialists in the UK. But about 16% of the population supplement the system with their own voluntary insurance.

The limitations are much the same as in the French system. Despite there being large numbers of insurance funds, they are heavily constrained by regulation to deliver a standard product, with very little competition emerging between them. The system is also bureaucratic and costly to manage.

INDIVIDUAL-BASED SOCIAL INSURANCE

The next most radical step in this progression is Switzerland, which has a compulsory social insurance system that is paid by individuals, not employers, and where the insurance funds actually compete – albeit that they compete in delivering a standard insurance model approved by the government.

Within that, however, there are various choices, the patient being able to choose a comprehensive service package, or a managed-care type of service, or one where a general practitioner acts as a gatekeeper to secondary provision. There are in fact 26 different systems in Switzerland, based around cantons; making it fairly easy to compare the performance of each. In general, though, there are few waits and little rationing, and the system is very popular. Three-quarters of hospital provision is still subsidized by the government, and around a third of the population buy voluntary top-up insurance, which gives them better access to dentistry and to senior physicians along with better comfort and privacy in hospital.

SOCIAL INSURANCE WITH TAX-FUNDED CATASTROPHIC COVER

The Netherlands maintains an interesting system that is part tax-funded and part social insurance. Tax funding covers the big-ticket items such as long-term or uninsurable or catastrophic conditions, just as the NHS does, although it is managed by twelve regions rather than by central government. But for acute care, there is compulsory social insurance. Higher earners do not have to become members of this, although most of them, nearly a third of the population, buy private insurance cover for their acute care needs. In line with the fairness principle, contributions are income-related, and contributors have an annual choice between thirty, non-profit, funds. Access to secondary care is through GP gatekeepers, where again choice is available, and there are no charges. In addition, nearly everyone buys supplementary insurance for items such as dentistry, elective care, medical aids, and alternative medicine.

Arguably the Netherlands has found a good way of mixing tax funding for the unaffordable items with a fair, income-related social insurance plan for acute care, while leaving wealthier people to their own devices. The mixture does, however, lead to almost constant debate, and political pressure to include more and more items in the free, tax-funded part of the system.

TAX-SUBSIDIZED PRIVATE INSURANCE

Australia too has a universal public Medicare system, funded by a hypothecated tax. Nevertheless, nearly half of Australians buy private insurance from one of around 40 competing providers, giving them more choice in their doctor, shorter waiting times, and access to things such as dental and optical services that are not covered under the standard package. The government promotes the take-up of private insurance by subsidizing it with a large tax rebate, and ensuring that premiums do not vary according to health risk.

EMPLOYER-BASED PRIVATE INSURANCE

The American system is based largely around private insurance, even though their government-financed systems for poorer families and the elderly, Medicaid and Medicare, are in absolute terms even larger than the NHS. The remarkable thing about US health insurance, though, is that it is bought almost entirely by employers and provided as part of the employee's remuneration package. This leads to significant problems, such as people being temporarily uninsured when they switch jobs.

American healthcare is far from being the private-sector extreme that it is often caricatured as being, and perhaps as a result, has many of the deficiencies for which it is often criticized. Regulation is oppressive, for example. Some states legislate in minute detail what services must be included in an employer's healthcare package, and the political pressure is always to expand that list, making insurance increasingly expensive and unaffordable.

HEALTH MANAGEMENT ORGANIZATIONS

One response to this rising cost in the United States was health management organizations (HMOs), where members contribute lower premiums but access to service is restricted through an actively-managed gatekeeper function. The oldest of these, Kaiser Permanente, has many millions of members, mostly in blue-collar jobs; its premiums are little different from the average per capita

spending that the UK makes on the NHS, but the service levels it provides are much superior, with very little waiting to see a GP or for
hospital treatment thereafter. Nevertheless, many Americans resent
the rationing implicit in the HMO model, contrasting it with the free
access afforded by the comprehensive insurance system.

In principle it is possible to graft the HMO idea onto a state insurance
system like ours in the UK. Instead of contributions going to the
government, they would go to an HMO – which could be a local
monopoly or one of a number of competing bodies between which
patients could choose. The HMO would buy in healthcare on behalf
of its members, acting as gatekeeper but seeking out better value for
money than is likely to be achieved in a monopoly system like the
NHS. This idea was mooted in the 1990s and has been revived since,
but there still seems to be little enthusiasm for it among politicians.

MEDICAL SAVINGS ACCOUNTS

Another solution that has grown up in the United States as a response
to the high cost of comprehensive insurance is the idea of medical
savings accounts. When insurers agree to cover every dollar of
every insurance claim, their service becomes very expensive. The
administration cost of small claims can easily outstrip the cost of the
medical treatment itself. And yet, trade union pressure has made this
comprehensive or first-dollar insurance the norm in US workers'
remuneration packages. So some employers have instead offered their
workforce a much cheaper policy covering only catastrophic or long-
term conditions, while passing on some of the savings to their
employees for them to invest in dedicated savings accounts for healthcare, now helped by tax concessions. Employees like this arrangement
because they are in control of their own medical savings, which they
can use more freely on the services they believe they need, instead of
having to take the standard care package offered by the old insurance
system.

COMPULSORY MEDICAL SAVINGS

The idea of providing catastrophic insurance and combining it with
a medical savings account to pay acute and minor healthcare costs is
in fact much older, having grown up in Singapore in the 1950s.
Workers in Singapore are required to contribute a small proportion
of their earnings into a saving account that can be used to purchase

hospital care when they need it. Employers match their contributions. These accounts grow tax-free and over a lifetime can provide a large reserve that can subsequently be used to fund retirement. A state-funded system remains for those who are unemployed and cannot fund themselves, though families are expected to support each other and this is a system of last resort only.

COMMUNITY-RATED PRIVATE INSURANCE

It is feasible, of course, to have a system based wholly on competitive private insurance, with some state backing to ensure that the poorest have access, say through a form of voucher. That would still leave the problem of people who may not be poor but who are at high risk of expensive medical conditions and therefore uninsurable. This can to some extent be solved by community rating, as in Ireland, where the state legislates that premiums will reflect only broad risk categories (such as age) rather than individual risks, or where insurers have to take on all-comers without pre-examination. But insurers are accomplished in pitching their advertising to the kinds of people they want to attract. "And in addition," there are benefits in making people pay for at least some of the risks that their lifestyle choices – such as smoking – impose on their health.

POLITICAL INSTABILITY OF HYBRID SYSTEMS

A businesslike division of responsibility might be for patients (except the very poorest) to bear the cost of very small medical expenses, which would be costly to insure, either in a state or private insurance system; for private or social insurance to cover the burden of acute care; and for taxation to cover long-term or expensive treatments that are not easily insurable. Many of the world's health systems do in fact have this kind of division: the UK is unusual in trying to cover everything through taxation. But such division is inherently unstable. There is constant political pressure to expand the supposedly free service by expanding the range of treatments or the number of people who qualify to receive the state-funded package.

Many, perhaps most, of the systems funded by a mixture of tax and insurance or social insurance deliver a better service than the NHS, valuing their users more (because patients and not politicians are their immediate paymasters), and achieving superior medical outcomes. But in hybrid systems, politicization remains, and regulation serves to increase uniformity at the expense of competition. In any event, whatever the advantages of a pluralist system, UK politicians on all sides have made it clear that they are not up for reforming the funding basis of the NHS.

However, there remains much scope for reform on the provision side, perhaps opening up the supply of healthcare to more and more independent providers, with the government contracting out what it presently pays its own NHS workforce to deliver. If such contractors were remunerated on the basis of what they actually do – how many patients in the different diagnostically related groups they successfully treat, for example – that might well stimulate enough transparency, patient-focus, and value for money awareness to achieve all the benefits that funding reform is intended to achieve; but without the political angst.

CHAPTER 33
THE CASE FOR PLURALISM

Nick Bosanquet and Andrew Haldenby

NHS performance has been constrained by the iron triangle of triple nationalization – it was nationalized in funding, in resource allocation and in provision. The government is seeking to move towards pluralism in provision but there is very little support for such a move locally. In this chapter we make the case for a full move towards pluralism not just as a threat but as a major contribution to supply.[1]

In the private sector, companies, whether they are airlines, mobile phone companies or hotel chains often have more capacity than they need – but they are rewarded for finding ways of using this capacity; markets grow and consumers and there is a virtuous circle of market expansion, rising productivity and falling prices. The public sector lacks this dynamic. In the NHS, capacity is used to limit demand, rather than "excess" capacity being used to meet demand and provide more. Waiting lists are the consequence.

Effectively liberalising the supply side will both cause more capacity to be made available to consumers and improve efficiency. Private sector involvement in the delivery of services varies. It is used, often expensively, as the means of funding the construction of buildings. It is contracted to provide services on behalf of the public sector, often to expand capacity. But most effective use of the private sector will be made when it is free to supply in a competitive environment, so that it invests, innovates and responds to consumers.

There has been limited progress in some areas towards supply reform – the development of supply with a greater variety of providers and patient choice – but the change is limited and fragile. Giving customers a choice of providers can only be a reality if the alternative providers have a substantial share of total capacity and if they have the security and reputation for stability which will assure customer confidence. Choice cannot be a reality without confidence in the integrity of the alternatives and this can only be secured with time and the opportunity to earn funding through quality service.

The advantages of pluralism are also sought in terms of greater innovation, new thinking on how services are provided and access to capital and skills. Again these advantages are not going to be achieved except through real commitment. The longer gains from competition are not going to be attainable where there continues one overwhelming and dominant provider with complete power over the market.

There are four key conditions for effective pluralism:

- Increasing information about choice. If the client is to have power there must be a first priority to increasing access to information. For example, the NHS current IT programme appears to be mainly about improving transmission of information between professionals. It needs to be adapted to serve patient power.
- Developing the market for alternative supply. For the longer term it is unlikely that the full gains in choice and flexibility in public services will be realised unless alternative providers can win 30 per cent of the market. Anything less creates a mixture of short-term tension with the existing public sector providers – without the longer term gains from innovation.
- Recognising that reform through supply pluralism will take substantial launch costs. It will be difficult to fund these and to continue with rapid rates of increase of spending in the existing system. Without concentration on the funding of alternatives, both the traditional system the new providers are likely to face problems of deficits and unfunded cost increases. Reform supports the aims of an NHS which is patient led and with a variety of providers. To work, however, such a system has to have scope for local initiative and flexibility
- Supply pluralism would be greatly assisted by wider use of advertising. The OFT report on opticians services set out the benefits which would be likely to follow from deregulation. "The variation of prices between opticians could be expected to be narrowed; the average level of prices to be reduced; the efficiency and innovativeness of opticians to be increased. There would be increased competition between existing opticians and an enhanced threat of competition from new entrants."[2] Marketing expands the

size of the market and thus permits lower prices to be associated with greater economic viability.

GAINS TO REFORM

The pilots of private and voluntary sector delivery since 2002 have demonstrated the gains to efficiency and capacity.

The Department of Health has piloted choice after six months of waiting for patients in London (between 2002 and 2004) in certain specialties and across the country for heart disease patients (July 2002–November 2003). In both cases, patients were able to choose another NHS provider or an independent sector provider. In London, 12,500 patients were offered a choice of where their treatment takes place and 7,480 accepted it. For heart patients, 3,034 were offered choice and 1,550 opted for treatment elsewhere.

The result has been that services for heart patients have been transformed and the waiting list almost eliminated. The National Heart Hospital, bought to increase NHS capacity in cardiac surgery, found that it was short of patients because waiting lists had been reduced by the choice programme and had to convert to non-surgical uses.

In addition, South East London treatment centres in Orpington and Bromley now have spare capacity and began advertising for patients from February 2004. Private hospitals in the area have become concerned about declining patient numbers.

The Independent Sector Treatment Centres are already showing a great improvement in productivity compared to other NHS providers. In 2002–03, the NHS in England carried out more than 270,000 cataract providers in 141 different providers. This equates to about five cataract removals per provider per day. The mobile Independent Sector Treatment Centres have achieved 39 cataract removals per day, an increase in output of 700 per cent.[3]

These reforms are already putting pressure on traditional large hospitals, including foundation hospitals. Despite resistance from within parts of the NHS, with complaints that some units face lower demand, the Government is rightly pledging to press on with reform.[4]

THE NEED FOR GREATER COMPETITION

Reform has argued that the very tight financial environment of the NHS after 2008 demands greater pluralism in order to achieve stronger competition and so higher productivity.

NHS spending will continue to increase at around 4.5 per cent per year in real terms until 2007–08, after which it will increase at 2.0 per cent per year. Over the five years 2006–11, the NHS is likely to have total growth in real revenue spending of 15 per cent, amounting to £11.4 billion.

Looking forward, the cost of spending commitments – PFI schemes, Agenda for Change, consultant and GP contracts, NHS Connect and the likely increase in staffing from the expansion of training programmes and of services – will roll on into the period when the rate of increase of funding declines. The Reform report The NHS in 2010: reform or bust estimated that the cost of these spending commitments will be £13.2 billion.

It is also necessary to estimate the cost of additional activity. The current Department of Health view is that once the current period of heavy expenditure on building capacity is over, spending pressures will reduce or even disappear. Much of the capacity, however, requires additional staffing and revenue spending. A reasonable estimate of the costs of additional activity would be £5 billion in 2010. Efficiency savings cannot be relied upon to fund this increase in the longer term.

As a result there will be a resource gap in 2010 of nearly £7 billion, equivalent to the gap between the real terms funding increase of £11.4 billion and the total cost pressure of £18.2 billion. Given that the increase in real spending over the period is likely to be £11.4 billion, there is a clear resource gap of nearly £7 billion. We are left with the hope of a productivity miracle to bridge the gap.

The resource gap by 2010

	£ billion
Additional recurrent expenditure	18.2
Real terms funding increase	11.4
Resource gap	6.8

MAKING PLURALISM WORK

The NHS faces alternative futures – it can either make a difficult adjustment to a mixed economy with greater pluralism or it can face a series of local deficits which will undo many of the gains of the last few years. New forms of postcode rationing will emerge, waiting lists will increase once again and staff morale will fall with rising turnover.

Simply put, the solution to the resource gap identified above, is productivity improvement. NHS productivity, as measured by straight forward inputs and outputs, has been clearly falling, as both the Office for National Statistics and the OECD have shown. The Department's recent arguments that productivity statistics should be uprated in line with improvements in "quality" do not reflect the true picture of recent years which is that improvements have been achieved at unnecessary cost, and often due to reform rather than extra funding.

Achieving real gains in productivity will require competition. What is needed is not so much "re-engineering" of services as redeployment of resources which will inevitably involve some redundancies.

The key policy themes needed in this new environment are as follows:

- Strengthen patient priority in commissioning. Even with a lower rate of growth in spending the resources available to the NHS are massive – amounting from 2008 onwards to some £500 billion (or 50 per cent of one year's national income) over a five year period. If we were starting from scratch with freedom to develop services and to contract with providers there would be little difficulty in turning this amount of funding into a great service. Commissioners have to have a much stronger drive to secure value even where this conflicts with the interests of established providers. Is the last two years of 10 per cent funding increases going to be used to prop up existing providers or to develop a new system? PCTs should be renamed Health Care Trusts and should be given an HMO role in managing care. They would contract with outside providers and develop new linkages between primary and secondary care.

- Invest in greater pluralism. At least £1 billion a year should be spent to develop new providers. It will be much more difficult to do this with more limited funding growth. Unless the NHS makes the transition to a mixed economy of care there will be no chance of securing the major productivity gains that are essential to bridge the gap between expectations and funding.

- Accelerate the move towards Foundation Trusts, practice based commissioning and payment by results. The NHS priority has to be much better financial discipline – in the past managers and clinicians have not had proper information on their costs or on whether funding covers costs, nor have they information on how costs vary with activity. Value for money starts at a very local level with direct managerial responsibility for budgets.

- Move from Private Finance Initiative (PFI) to Local Improvement Finance Trust (LIFT) that allows much more choice locally. It is essential to allow much greater local flexibility so that new types of ambulatory treatment and diagnostic centres can develop. This requires a much greater role for local initiative and local decision-making on affordability. The LIFT project has much clearer local responsibility for design and funding.

- Reconsider the role of the private sector. A shift of work into the NHS does not add to the total of services available in the UK and it also removes an important source of competition. Some policy-makers seem very keen to see a time when shorter waiting times will lead to a reinforcement of the NHS monopoly but such a move will reverse the reform.

We would recommend a six-point action plan to ensure that the NHS can adjust to greater competition, payment by results and patient choice.

- The key priority has to be better financial management so that managers come to regard getting value for money as a key part of their job. At present outside Foundation Trusts many managers do not have timely information on their costs. Improved local budgeting and a drive to get better value for money is key to improved local services.

- Trusts should be empowered to hold reserves against the great uncertainties created from payment by results. By 2008 Trusts should have reserves equal to 5 per cent of annual budget.
- Review costs of the 18 week target and proceed with it (a) only if it is affordable with the limited growth of spending and (b) if it is approved by NICE as evidence based.
- Stop the current PFI programme for all schemes which have not reached financial close and move over to the LIFT model for locally determined investment on a coherent and balanced basis so that there is the same process and standards across primary and secondary care.
- Review medical training plans in the light of the likely shortage of funded posts and the greater than expected recruitment of doctors from outside the UK on a career basis. There is little point in pulling more able young people into training with heavy costs when their employment chances are poor.
- Use direct payments in long running areas of poor care and poor access such as stroke care and audiology.

REFORMING FUNDING

Real reform must extend to demand as well as supply. A more dynamic NHS requires a national environment where there are independent sources of funding. Without change in funding, any supply side only reform is likely to run into new problems of rationing as improvements increases the demand for services. The belief that it will be possible both to have reform and continue with taxation as the sole source of funding is unrealistic. Supply pluralism will bring forward demand pluralism:

There is a powerful case for co-payment:

- Fiscal constraint will increase the role of co-payment for improved services. Many health services will remain entirely tax funded where there are some objective standards for clinical need: but for many services there are different levels of intensity which are subject to individual choice. Although core services will be tax funded there will be many supplementary services at differing levels where there will be an element of co-payment. This is already happening in services such as those for infertility and for services such as physiotherapy.

- Co-payment adds to tax funding: it also acts as a brake in moderating demand. Equity concerns can be met through subsidies and exemptions. The alternative to increased co-payment is a new form of rationing as demand rises to meet the increased and more attractive supply from supply side reform. Co-payment is also more equitable in a situation where younger taxpayers are paying for today's services for the older generation yet cannot expect to enjoy such a level of services themselves.

There will still be key government roles in public health and in regulation across public and private providers: but rising expectations for better health services can only be met by releasing UK health services (and not just the NHS) from the iron triangle of triple nationalization.

REFERENCES

1. Bosanquet. N. (2001) A fair innings for efficiency in health services? Journal of medical ethics. 27 228–233.
2. OFT (1982) Opticians and Competition. London HMSO.
3. *Treatment Centres: Delivering Faster, Quality Care and Choice to NHS Patients*, Department of Health, 2005.
4. *Reform* bulletin, 28 January 2005.

CHAPTER 34

LOCALISM IN THE NHS: REDUCING THE DEMOCRATIC DEFICIT

Daniel Hannan MEP and Mr Tim Kevan

"Election is a better principle than selection. No Minister can feel satisfied that he is making the right selection over so wide a field."

Aneurin Bevan

INTRODUCTION

When the people of Kidderminster objected to the closure of facilities at their local hospital they started a campaign. Such was the strength of feeling that not only did they gather together supporters but they transformed themselves into a political fighting force. Eventually this led them to winning a majority of their local council seats and even the local parliamentary constituency of Wyre Forest. However, despite all of these efforts, they remained disenfranchised. They were unable to exert any direct control over the decision-making process which remained entirely in the hands of the Secretary of State for Health.

This illustrates one of the major challenges for the NHS in the years to come: reducing what has become known as the democratic deficit. It is perhaps ironic given the noble and seemingly democratic ideals upon which it was founded: fair access to health care for all, regardless of wealth.

However, it is also perhaps representative of a deeper malaise in the provision of public services which has become increasingly centralised. Politicians and mandarins in Whitehall issue directives to teachers setting out every detail from the curriculum to class sizes. So, too, with the NHS which is driven by the need to meet a limited number of targets set by central government rather than a goal of fulfilling the disparate health requirements of local communities. Whilst well-intentioned, such centralised decision-making over such an enormous organisation often leads to unintended consequences. A good example of this occurred in the last general election when it transpired that a government directive that all patients must see their GP within 48 hours hadn't resulted in the desired effect of having appointment times being pushed forward. Instead, patients wanting to book more in advance were told that they would have to call back nearer the time.

The centralisation of decision-making in government has also been accompanied by a rise in two particular entities in the bureaucratic structure: that of the expert and the manager. Increasingly, when there is a difficult decision to be made, government ministers will side-step the issue and set up a commission to look into the matter or a quango to actually make the decision. This is well-intentioned but takes important decisions even further away from the people who they affect. It also often shrouds what are in fact political decisions under the veil of expertise. In effect, it simply abrogates responsibility to others who are less accountable.

So, too, with the rise of the manager. The professionals who deliver public services have been separated from its organisation even at some of the lowest levels. This function has been taken instead by managers. Few would suggest that there is no need for managers or that they do not have the best interests of the various public services at heart. However, again it has led to decision-making being taken away from the local level and moved more to the centre.

These developments have led people to become disillusioned both with politicians and very often with the provision of the services they control. We suggest that those who run the NHS return to first principles and aim to reform it with two particular principles in mind:

1. decisions should be made as closely as possible to the people they affect; and
2. those people should have as much say in those decisions as possible.

In effect: localism.

The following merely provides a number of suggestions and illustrations as to how this may better be achieved and is not in any way meant as a comprehensive review of all the possibilities.

PATIENT CHOICE

One of the biggest problems facing the NHS is that despite the undeniable good intentions behind it, it has produced what the Prime Minister has called a "deeply unequal" system where the rich opt out and the least well-off sometimes receive the worst health care. One way of tackling this issue is to try and give patients as much choice as possible in the services available to them, the ultimate devolution of power.

This is now being provided in a limited form with every patient needing a hospital referral being given the right to a choice of at least four. The target for elective treatments is that by 2008 the patient will be able to choose from any hospital in England that can provide care to NHS quality and price.

However, it is to be hoped that this does not end up becoming a choice in name only, with no diversity in the services which are offered. In particular, it is hoped that private provision of state care will be allowed to flourish. Private companies should be allowed to bid to provide patients with the care they need and ultimately the funding to provide that care.

Further, whilst it is recognised that informed choices will be difficult for those without capacity, it is hoped that the general principle of giving patients the power to choose the service provider is extended to as many services as is practicable to do.

In answer to the argument that such measures may ultimately result in unfairness with some patients being giving more choice than others, the answer is simple. The unfairness currently exists due to the one-size-fits-all system. For example, figures show that patients are twice as likely to die in the worst performing hospital in England as they are in the best. Increased choice will reduce unfairness by catering to the particular needs of particular communities, recognising that inner city populations have very different health care needs to rural areas. By embracing pluralism, standards will be driven up for all.

DIVERSITY OF PROVISION

Inextricably linked to providing patients with as much choice as possible is the need to liberate the NHS from the top-down approach of a state monopoly obtaining services only from itself. This can be replaced by a flourishing market, attuned to local conditions and needs. If private and not-for-profit organisations can provide the same or a better service for less cost, there is no reason why they should be restricted in doing so. This currently accounts for only about 10% of electives and overall around 1% of the total NHS budget.

Private providers should be encouraged to bid for as many services as possible and there should be little or no limit on the amount of services they provide. The move from a command to a mixed economy will help to stimulate competition and vitality within the health sector. This in turn will produce innovation and improvements in productivity which will be essential in the years to come in helping to meet ever-increasing health expectations.

ELECTED BODIES

In addition to the democratic effect of increased patient choice, the structure of the NHS itself should also be democratised. The most significant body within the present structure is the primary care trust (PCT) which commissions the majority of NHS services. They make the decisions as to what resources are given, in what form and also what resources are allocated to secondary care such as hospitals.

The major difficulty with these bodies is that they contain no directly elected representatives. Further, there is nothing to stop its current membership, simply allocating resources in a way that suits themselves without sufficient reference to the local needs of patients and of hospitals and other services.

One possible route is simply to make PCTs more representative with hospital and community doctors being added along with private providers and also members of the community. However, other than the public representatives, all the other groups would have a potential vested interest to simply argue for more resources to be allocated their own way.

Given the significance of the decisions which the trusts make in terms of resource allocation, the authors advocate that PCTs should be abolished in their present form and replaced by an independent Commissioning Body. This could take one of two forms. One might be a panel of experts or managers who could listen to all the arguments and then make the decisions. However, not only is this wholly undemocratic, it also falls foul of the difficulties set out above which occur when panels of experts start making political decisions.

The preferred option is that the commissioning body should consist of directly elected representatives. These would be under a duty to consult all stakeholders as to how resources should be allocated. These would include GPs, hospital and community doctors, private sector providers of health care and patients. Local people should then be trusted to make the decisions that most suit their own communities having been provided with the best possible advice from the professionals, thus invigorating community involvement in health care.

Unfortunately, the only elected representatives so far introduced into the NHS have been to foundation hospitals which would seem to be a case of putting the cart before the horse. It is the commissioners rather than the providers of health care that most need accountability if local people are to be truly empowered.

TRANSPARENCY

The means of providing the elected representatives is connected to another reform necessary for making people feel closer to the decision-making process. At present the structure of the NHS is so complicated that even those who work within it hardly understand how all the funding streams tie together. A big reason for this is the *ad hoc* nature in which the NHS has developed, often rolling from one crisis or reform to another without any principle underlying it.

The whole structure needs to be revisited and simplified down to as few layers as possible. It would be hoped that primary care trusts and other health organisations could be given geographical boundaries that coincide not only with each other but also with local authorities. This would facilitate the provision of directly elected representatives so that the new commissioning bodies could consist of locally elected councillors. This would tap into the already vibrant local party politics and help further to politicise the electorate over deciding the future of their own health care services.

It should be noted that ironically this would truly be bringing the NHS back to its roots since the original plans contemplated much local government involvement. However, in order to appease the medical profession, when the NHS was finally introduced the primary care administration of the NHS had the least amount of local democratic accountability.

INCREASED LOCAL POWERS

One issue which the introduction of elected representatives to Foundation Hospitals has highlighted is the need clearly to define the powers and responsibilities of those who are elected. Commissioning bodies should have their functions clearly delineated from the start.

The introduction of directly elected representatives not only invigorates an organisation but it also empowers it through the extra legitimacy. With this democratic safeguard, there is no reason why decisions which are currently made centrally should not be made at the more local level of the new commissioning body. It is therefore hoped that their responsibilities would be wide.

A good example of a power that could be devolved is in relation to the guidelines issued by the National Institute of Clinical Excellence (NICE). These were introduced to try and end the so-called postcode lottery in NHS prescribing and enforce the same rules across the board. However, this suffers from a number of problems. First, it fails to respond to local needs. Second, it again disguises what is a political decision (cost/benefit analysis) as something solely for the realm of experts. This false distinction was highlighted recently over the use of Herceptin for early breast cancer which led to legal action and the Health Minister taking the unusual step of in effect overruling NICE arguably for political expediency.

If NICE was transformed into a Parliamentary Select Committee, it could deal properly with recommendations for drugs and conduct detailed consultation. The experts involved with the Institute (who themselves are to be applauded) would be able to give their advice and opinions and then the politicians could produce a report spelling out all the costs and the benefits, making the recommendations. The newly formed Commissioning Bodies could make their own decisions in the light of this advice in consultation once again with all their local stakeholders. The irony is that many experts might welcome being able to return to their traditional role of providing medical guidance and opinions without being forced to make what are in effect political decisions.

An example of a policy which could be abolished following the introduction of the Commissioning Bodies would be the use of national targets. The priorities for each particular area could be decided in advance by the locally elected body following full consultation. In fact, this is the sort of issue which the local representatives would probably have addressed in their manifestos.

EMPOWERING PROFESSIONALS

The other way of ensuring decisions are made as closely as possible to the people they affect is by bringing doctors and other health care professionals back into the decision-making process.

The first way to do this is through a formal role in the consultation with the Commissioning Bodies. Doctors have been subjected to growing numbers of national standards frameworks. These hinder their clinical autonomy and their ability to provide for the needs of specific patients. It is hoped that decisions on issues such as this can now be made at a local level initially by the Commissioning Bodies and then implemented by the doctors.

In addition to the limitations which have come from centralised planning, doctors and others have also had many of their policy and operational powers given to managers. Whilst the policy-making decisions which managers currently take should be devolved to the Commissioning Bodies, other more day to day decisions on resource allocation should be returned to the doctors and others who previously made the decisions. Those managers who remain should be left with at most truly administrative responsibilities.

CONCLUSION

Almost sixty years after its foundation, the NHS is in need of invigorating and entrusting back to the people it serves. Through a mixture of patient choice, diverse providers, democratic accountability and re-empowering of the professions, it is hoped that a new flame of civic pride will be lit which will guide the institution through its next sixty years.

The authors express their gratitude for the inspiration for much of the thinking in this article to the authors of the publication 'Direct Democracy: An Agenda for a New Model Party', by Daniel Hannan MEP and 22 others and published by direct-democracy.co.uk, 2005.

CHAPTER 35
FUNDING EXPECTATIONS

Jennifer Rankin & Jessica Allen

"What might have been held to be adequate twenty years ago would no longer be so regarded today, while today's standards will in turn become out of date in the future. The advance of medical knowledge continually places new demands on the Service, and the standards expected by the public will continue to rise."

This extract reads as if it might be from the latest Department of Health White Paper or a memo written by the Treasury, thinking ahead to the Government's next Comprehensive Spending Review. It is actually the conclusion of the Guillebaud Committee, published in 1956 less than a decade after the NHS was founded. In the decade when the British people where told "you've never had it so good", policymakers were discovering that what was good enough yesterday feels like second best tomorrow.

It has long been understood that rising public expectations are one of the main cost pressures on the NHS. And since the NHS was founded in 1948 people's expectations have risen dramatically. Politician's promises, media reports of new and expensive medicines and technologies all help to fuel ever higher expectations about what health services can and should deliver. As the work of the Guillebaud Committee underlines, high and rising expectations have always been a feature of the NHS. But it appears that the pressure of public expectations has significantly intensified over the last two decades.

We are living in a time of unprecedented consumer abundance, where people have a far greater choice of goods and services. In an age of virtual banks and bespoke financial services, people expect that public services will also be characterised by fast access, high quality and responsiveness to individual needs. The explosion of different channels for communication, such as the internet, has heightened

people's expectations for improved cures and treatments. This is a
stark contrast to what people expected when the NHS was originally
set up. As John McTernan, a Number 10 special advisor, has written,
in 1945 the ethos was "be patient, join the queue, wait your turn, be
grateful it's free." Of course, despite, major social and political
changes, the founding principles and values of the NHS continue to
command the strong support of the British public. The general public
and politicians of all parties are generally united on the importance
of ensuring that the NHS remains free at the point of use according
to need.

In 2002, the Labour Government committed itself to unprecedented
increases in the level of NHS funding in order to support the original
model of the NHS *and* improve the service in line with people's
expectations. By 2007–8, the UK will be spending around 9.2% of
GDP on health compared to 7.3% in 2000, which brings the UK into
line with average spending in other European countries. This
unprecedented increase in spending is unlikely to be repeated. After
2008, the rate of growth in NHS spending is going to fall, but political
ambitions and public expectations will remain undiminished. This
underlines the need for an honest dialogue between people and their
elected representatives about how to safeguard the founding
principals of the NHS in a consumerist age.

Sceptics may be wondering if a concern with public expectations is
simply a distraction from the real business of delivering fair access to
high quality health care. Surely, if the NHS is delivering timely and
effective care, that will be enough to meet public expectations?

Unfortunately, this is not the case. There is often a gap between what
the public expects and what the NHS delivers. Politicians should be
concerned with closing this gap, so the NHS is not overwhelmed by
high expectations or undermined by low expectations. Furthermore,
as public expectations are a key driver in pushing up Government
spending on healthcare, there is a need to pay greater attention to this
phenomenon.

High expectations are not intrinsically a bad thing. Both as taxpayers
and service users, it is right and necessary that the public have high
expectations about what public services can deliver. But problems
arise when people's expectations are too high or too low. Excessively
high expectations about what the NHS can deliver can lead to
disappointment with services, which may ultimately undermine

support for the NHS from those who can afford to go elsewhere. Excessively low expectations are a problem for the NHS too, as low expectations may allow the NHS to stagnate and increase disaffection. Low expectations are often related to experiencing less care or worse care so can exacerbate existing inequalities in access to health services.

A related problem occurs when public views and perceptions are too far removed from the objective performance of the service. Most people who use the NHS report a positive experience. However, they often believe that their personal experience or the experience of a family member is a one-off and not in line with how the service works in the rest of the country. Pollsters have described this aptly as "the 'I've been lucky' syndrome". This perception gap means that people don't believe in improvements in the NHS even when they are experienced at first hand. For example, in 2004 Mori conducted research on public perceptions for the Cabinet Office. They asked people whether they believed that getting a GP appointment was faster, whether access to treatment in NHS hospitals had improved and if they agreed that there were thousands more doctors and nurses working in the NHS. Less than four in ten people believed these statements, even though they are all true, can be objectively measured and have been prominent in government announcements about the NHS. The problem of the perception gap is not unique to the NHS. The public doubt the validity of similar factual statements on smaller class sizes in schools and an increase in the number of bus passengers. These findings – and the erosion of trust that lies behind them – should cause profound concern to politicians of all parties. We might all be doing better, but feeling worse.

Having realistic expectations is also good for ensuring the long-term sustainability of NHS funding. Economists have long recognised that expectations are a key factor putting upward pressure on healthcare spending, alongside rising labour costs, demographic change and new drugs and technologies. In all developed countries, healthcare spending has risen over time. In 1970 countries in the OECD spent around 5% of GDP on healthcare, in 1980 this had risen to 7% and by 20000 was just over 8%. Of course, there is no economically optimal or ethically correct amount to spend on healthcare. Different countries will make different decisions about healthcare spending based on their policy priorities and history. All healthcare systems have to balance different functions: firstly they have to be affordable, secondly they have to maintain public support, thirdly they have to contribute towards public health and good health outcomes for all citizens. But, these objectives are in tension with each other.

All governments need to make tough choices and not every promise in a party manifesto can be the top priority. The eternal dilemma in spending on healthcare is how to balance spending on delivering a sustainable health service alongside spending to achieve better health outcomes. The NHS plays an important, but ultimately, a limited role in delivering good health. This has been the subject of some academic debate, but according to one analysis, just one sixth of the extension in life expectancy can be attributed to medicine. By and large, people are living longer because of improvements in public health. The major preventable risks to health are smoking, lack of exercise, poor diet and alcohol, which all relate to individual choices. As such they are often beyond the control (although not influence) of healthcare professionals. For example, almost all coronary heart disease in people aged under 65 is preventable through increasing exercise, improving diet and reducing smoking.

"Prevention is better than cure" is proverbial common-sense. However, it is only relatively recently that the UK government has attempted to make this the basis of healthcare policy, with efforts to move away from a national sickness service towards a genuine national health service. In 2001, HM Treasury commissioned Derek Wanless to review future funding of the NHS. Published in 2002, the Wanless Report concluded that the sure way to a financially stable NHS would be achieved by cutting off the causes of demand for the NHS. Wanless described a "fully engaged scenario", where patients are engaged in their health and use the health service appropriately, where the health service is responsive and makes better use of resources and technology. Wanless estimated that if the UK health system became fully engaged, this could reduce healthcare spending dramatically. Spending on health would be nearly 2% *less* of GDP by 2022, compared to the alternative scenario where public engagement in health remained unchanged.[1]

So how do we achieve this virtuous circle of good health, public engagement and reduced health spending? A big part of the answer must be a better collective understanding of what the NHS is for and greater personal responsibility from the public. This might be described as bringing our expectations into line with a fully engaged scenario. But we are still a long way from this point and our political culture presents a barrier to engaging people in difficult political decisions about health. The political process must bear considerable responsibility for creating excessive expectations and disillusionment. Politicians and the media have become so focused on the success and failings of the NHS as a service for individual patients, that we have lost sight of the NHS as a collective service that supports everybody's health.

Firstly, politicians ratchet up people's expectations. In 1997, Tony Blair came to power with the heady phrase that "we have twenty four hours to save the NHS". Under the first term of the Blair Labour Government (1997–2001), high flown rhetoric, combined with a bad habit of double and triple counting (modest) increases in resources over-inflated public hopes and expectations about how quickly the NHS could be improved. The Government subsequently adopted some more realistic language, talking about progress that would take years rather than months. But opposition parties are also guilty of using loose language around the NHS. Shortly after becoming leader of the opposition, David Cameron said that the "NHS could no longer ration treatments as it used to...[because] patients will demand them". He used the example of Herceptin for breast cancer. But, in a system where resources are limited and demands are infinite, rationing will remain a necessity. Clearly, the NHS has to ration treatments according to need. It has always done and will continue to do so. There are powerful arguments for making that rationing process more open, transparent and accessible, but it is counterproductive to underplay the importance of rationing.

The media also fuels unrealistic expectations. In 2003, the King's Fund tracked health stories covered by three core programmes on the BBC and three national daily newspapers. This study found there was an obsession with stories about NHS waiting times, but much less coverage of the underlying determinants of health. The researchers also found examples of coverage that was simply misleading with headlines creating the impression that the NHS was failing in areas, such as waiting times, where it was actually improving.

These problems go beyond the NHS and are part of a wider problem with our political culture. Politicians and the media are locked in a dialogue of mutual distrust and voters often feel disconnected and disengaged from politics. Meg Russell at the Constitution Unit has argued persuasively that we have not adapted to the culture of a mass politics characterised by mass democracy and a multitude of channels for communication. She writes: "politicians and the media fail to communicate the very essence of politics – that is about negotiation and compromise, difficult choices, and taking decisions together as a society". It goes without saying that this is a difficult and wide-ranging agenda. But politicians could start with the NHS, which is an iconic institution, where there are strong reserves of interest and support.

We need to fashion a new political dialogue about how we value the NHS. Firstly, policymakers need to communicate what people are entitled to and how these entitlements can be fairly distributed among the population. As a starting point, there needs to be agreed and acknowledged standards of what it is reasonable to expect. The Wanless Review proposed that these would include: safe, high quality treatment, fast access and "waiting within reason", integrated and joined-up services, a good standard of accommodation in a modern and comfortable setting. But setting the standards is not enough. Politicians need to lead an honest and realistic debate, where resource constraints are acknowledged and where different policy choices and options are presented and discussed. We need to shift our understanding of the NHS from a service based purely on meeting individual demands to a service based on collective good. This means a better understanding that the service is not "free", but paid for by taxpayers and that resources are rationed to distribute them fairly. It could entail making the case for shifting more resources to poorer areas, where access to health services is worse and need is greatest.

This new political dialogue also needs to articulate that much of the achievements of better health and more effective health services will come from changes in people's behaviour that go well beyond the remit of the NHS. Politicians and NHS staff need to foster a better understanding that the NHS is just one part of a wider health system that delivers population health. Good health is the responsibility of individuals, local government, business, schools, environmental protection agencies and many other players. As part of this wider health system, the NHS will play a more pro-active role in supporting people to lead healthy lives and look after their own physical and mental health. This culture of responsibility also extends to how we use the NHS. Part of this debate should help to ensure that people make responsible use of health services, for example finding new ways to stop people from missing GP or hospital appointments.

The Guillebaud Report came as a shock and a disappointment to the government of the day, with its recommendation that the NHS required more resources rather than less. Health spending tends to increase over time, but public expectations are frequently not well matched to what the spending can achieve. The public should have high expectations, but they should also be fair and realistic expectations. Ultimately, a better understanding of health and health services will enable the NHS to pull off the difficult balancing act of maintaining public support, doing more for health and remaining affordable.

REFERENCES

1. It is interesting to note that the Wanless Review also investigated alternative ways of financing the NHS. The Review concluded there is...*no evidence that any alternative financing method to that currently in place in the UK would deliver a given level and quality of health care at a lower cost to the economy as a whole. Indeed other systems seem likely to prove more costly.* A tax-funded system also scores highly on the basis of fairness and equal access. Ultimately, changing the model of the funding is a distraction to the critical task of reducing the demand for health services.

INDEX

Getting yourself known for medico-legal or pharmaceutical company work can be difficult. Equally, lawyers and pharmaceutical companies need assistance finding the right doctor. UK Expert List's team of practising lawyers and medics have teamed up to produce a new simple-to-use website designed to work as you work.

Experts – Do You Want to be Found? – *Introductory offer*

Experts – make sure you can be found with a few minutes spent registering.

- *FREE INTRODUCTORY OFFER: until 31 October 2006 full listing will be free of charge.*
- After this, basic listing will remain free
- be promoted heavily to the legal profession and other interested groups through publications such as *Personal Injury Brief Update,* the highest circulation in the PI industry

Full details are on our site at www.ukexpertlist.com – but if you would like to discuss any of the details you find there, we can be contacted on 0870 143 2569.

Looking for an Expert?

Rapidly find a selection of experts and then allowing you to filter them.

- No need to register
- No fees
- Filter by location and keywords.